THE BEST OF TUPELO QUARTERLY

The Best of Tupelo Quarterly

Introduction copyright © 2023 Kristina Marie Darling. All rights reserved.

ISBN: 978-1-946482-78-5

Design by Josef Beery.

Cover details: Photograph from the series "Julia" by Jenny Grassl, used with permission, with thanks to Julia Kanno Tlou, the Muse.

Copyright © 2023 Used with permission of the artist.

First paperback edition: January 2023

Library of Congress Control Number: 2022939062

Tupelo Press

P.O. Box 1767

North Adams, Massachusetts 01247

(413) 664-9611 / Fax: (413) 664-9711

editor@tupelopress.org / www.tupelopress.org

Tupelo Press is an award-winning independent literary press that publishes fine fiction, non-fiction, and poetry in books that are a joy to hold as well as read. Tupelo Press is a registered 501(c)(3) non-profit organization, and we rely on public support to carry out our mission of publishing extraordinary work that may be outside the realm of the large commercial publishers. Financial donations are welcome and are tax deductible.

THE BEST OF
Tupelo Quarterly

An Anthology of
Multi-Disciplinary
Texts in Conversation

Tupelo Press
North Adams, Massachusetts

EDITED BY
Kristina Marie Darling

CONTENTS

LITERARY CRITICISM

PROSE

COLLABORATIVE AND CROSS-DISCIPLINARY TEXTS

LITERATURE IN TRANSLATION

VISUAL ART

Kristina Marie Darling

An Introduction

Since its inception in 2011, *Tupelo Quarterly* has demonstrated a commitment to innovative work that questions the boundaries of genres and mediums, publishing new hybrid texts by Rachel Eliza Griffiths, Kate Greenstreet, Rachel Blau DuPlessis, Kristy Bowen, Nick Flynn, and other notable multimedia practitioners alongside that of emerging artists. In many ways, championing work in innovative, cross-disciplinary forms is essential to publishing writers—particularly those from historically underserved communities—who challenge the status quo. After all, a groundbreaking message often requires new forms of discourse.

With that in mind, most of my work as an editor attempts to expand what is possible within received forms of writing. For innumerable writers, the questions of genre and medium are inherently questions of power. These beliefs about what texts are legible, what texts are considered legitimate, reflect larger structures of authority in the literary community and in the academy. Poet and critic Sarah Vap writes, "I am extremely interested in what is often called hybrid or conceptual within the outstandingly elastic abilities of poetry—these efforts that pose a challenge to the . . . categories of writing (scholarship, journalism, coding, etc.), asking them to also expand their abilities and considerations and concerns and ways. To democratize." What Vap is suggesting is that dismantling the categories of writing is a larger ontological and metaphysical challenge to the social order—it calls into question the values and hierarchies that we impose upon language. So when she's saying that hybridity is a democratization, this is what she means. Hybridity—placing disparate forms and/or types of language in conversation—is a way of challenging rules but also the people and institutions in power who make those rules.

For me, the act of writing—and, importantly, the act of selecting writing or the act of championing another writer's work—has always been linked to social justice, and relatedly, the politics of language. Grammar, after all, is the very foundation of the social order. Even the most simple sentence contains within it a very particular kind of logic, as it implies hierarchies and a clearly delineated causal chain. By changing or expanding our sense of what is possible in language, one ultimately challenges the rules of society itself.

According to feminist scholar Helene Cixous, most of language privileges a definition of logic—a preconceived idea of what makes sense—that comes from a mostly masculine and mostly Western philosophical tradition. She calls this type of writing, which is inevitably linear and familiar in its structure, "marked writing." Yet this is the kind of work that many readers tend to value, usually at the expense of texts that experiment, that take risks and break new ground. Cixous rightly calls for alternative ways of inhabiting language, new ways of ordering and structuring our experience of the world around us, and for us as readers to understand and appreciate their value.

Part of this necessary work—the work of fostering social justice through innovation in language—consists of offering the tools needed to engage with innovative texts or unfamiliar forms. With that in mind, the editors of *Tupelo Quarterly* have been especially thrilled to curate a robust offering of literary criticism, which includes roundtables with leaders in feminist theory and cultural studies, as well as rigorous book reviews and literary criticism, a portion of which has been excerpted here. *Tupelo Quarterly* strives to widen not only the conversations in the arts and letters, but also the critical discourse around that work.

I hope you will join me in celebrating *Tupelo Quarterly* with the launch of this rich and rewarding anthology.

POETRY

G. C. Waldrep

OVATOR

I.

TWOMBLY

At length we rested where two seas met. A night bird unfurled itself like an ancient scroll shaken by gloved fists. We drew in chalk on the flat slates we'd carried in our packs, from the city of sorrows. Rather than build a wall. Rather than build a wall.

TWOMBLY

House sparrows in the crabbed ebb of the quince pecking at memories of one another. Wind stirs me like a gruel. Light frost. Vertigo has learned my secret name again.

TWOMBLY

From the deck of images, your card, a pilgrim's smear against glass. As if someone inside were looking out, or someone outside looking in. But you weren't, were you. You drew a circle around the name. And left it there, as if it could roll itself away.

TWOMBLY

Emigrants planting little pockets of ash in an otherwise barren plain. Are they following orders. What do they suspect. Are they in league with that traitor, the sun.

II.

TWOMBLY

Nobody cares about your sixteen shades of miracle. Photographs of
a draped cloth, a chair. Something hidden. Something to wake with,
something to soothe the bone.

TWOMBLY

Church of smoke mistaken for an alphabet. Now how do you pronounce
it, Senator.

TWOMBLY

Small house rubbed almost out. The hero, fresh from his bath, his war.
He sets the metronome, settles himself into a low chair. Listens to the
map behind the veil.

TWOMBLY

The light gathered in the little ship until it sank. Then the light built
another ship.

TWOMBLY

Each year, time set out a dish for him. He photographed not the workers
but their labor, the muscles they made in the gears' depths. Next to the
eclipse he placed another eclipse, then asked what "separate" meant. So
what does "separate" mean, he asked. The seasons leapt, surrogate sails.
LOOK this time we will teach the wind, we know what we are doing,

thickets. Autoclaves. A vast hand pointing. And then, at each year's end, another little dish, carved as if from some saint's wrack or braille.

III.

TWOMBLY

It is possible, via refraction, to display time's dreamwork inside-out, as if the seams were showing. But those aren't seams, what you see, then. Not seams at all.

TWOMBLY

i. Orchestral setting for architecture, trumpets, and unsuitable ghosts.

ii. A ship in a cage. Variations on the ship. Variations on the cage.

TWOMBLY

Some of us were blind & then some of us were not & what are you going to do about that, patrons of the axe.

(We are going to build a tower with it. We are going to call that tower The Sea.)

TWOMBLY

Pretty little map the mind left, first in the rain, then among soldiers at attention in ranks along the ancient, dusty avenue. Crutched orchards, almanacs. A lapsed mean.

Julie Carr

I pray, O

I was just learning how to see. And what I saw, as if through fog or smoke—surrogate mouths, belonging to no one, wet from a sadness that had no cause. In the west where women wear white, in the east where the sun is red, in the European gardens with their lines and lawns, the uncountable absences, the gaping holes: an archivist's assistant, a boy pouring mescal, a gathering of mothers holding vessels, and my own mother five years underground. I was just learning to see, having passed over a massive highway like a hawk. Like other women, I'd been raped, and like other children, I'd been hit. The air is always filling some other body, a body younger and drunker than mine, for the bellows, like a book, are never done.

My mother threw a pot of boiling water at my father's face. She grabbed hold of a cutting board and hurled it at his feet. I see these things though I never saw them. The best bookstores are the ones in which all of the books are written in languages you cannot read.

As Veronica and I walked through the woods, she told me of Guillermo's grief. Two months later, Guillermo corroborated the tale. He'd been left by a woman in Boston. Homesick and alone, he was too afraid to board a plane to return. When finally he managed it (with drugs), he wanted only to leave again. Now that he had written two books, he no longer wanted to be a writer. Instead he would re-issue the old humorous novels that had gone out of print. There are, he tells us, very few funny Mexican novelists; his mission is to keep those few from falling into oblivion.

It takes a very sad man to care so much for the jokes of the dead.

I was just learning how to see my life as if from a vantage point far off or above. There are too many books, Guillermo says, even as he labors to restore them. A woman in a zebra-striped jumpsuit fakes an animated conversation for a camera. The man who films her will soon be dead, just like me. With a popsicle stick in his back pocket, he hangs his head, resting his elbows on his knees.

Gillian Cummings

House of No Memory

When the house had eyes, it looked outside.
Looked over the black street in bewilderment.

It saw the yellow street sign, the hemlock
bowing under snow or in blue-green freedom

to a sky empty of the shut eyes of birds. If God
flew through windows with white curtains saying,

Only the holy will be admitted to this hospital.
Only the lightless will fail. The way sight failed me

in the house of lidless eyes. The way all I knew
was the blue dog. It was dead. It did not cry,

played a song if I cranked a hook in its side.
It sang, though dead, and I never pulled its tail,

never pulled close the curtains to shut out
the light. I wanted the hemlock to sing back

the forced cries of wind. *If the holy. If wind*
entered the house through holes. If the holes

equaled a hand. The touch of God is mighty,
mightier than a house with eyes or the prayers

of a girl with a blue dog pleading, No, no, no,
as the hemlock loosed blue needles.

And God replied,
Yes. Yes.

Julia B. Levine

God Speaks to Me from the Almond Orchard

You wanted me to say it through their flowering,
didn't you? To declare my love

with these ferocious prairies of snow?
I know what you desire.

Attached as you are to equity,
you too want a chance at resurrection.

And when one of you lies face up under a canopy,
wind flicking petals from a branch,

you like to think,
This must be God's fingers touching my cheek.

I advise you to stop imagining the aftermath
as something you can apprehend.

The singular could never withstand
what the whole must endure.

Not that it matters,
but beauty was a distraction I invented once

in a moment of boredom,
musing—

before possession, what can I crush?
Not the antidote you want to believe.

But beauty in all its cruelty
piercing one world with the next.

Brianna Noll

This Servant of God Does Not Have a Mind at Peace

Sometimes I wonder if the unquiet
mind is itself a miracle, a flintwheel
spinning an impending, abundant spark,
its fiery possibility a motivating terror.
When you are born wet, this fear
has little power. And then you dry.
Don't rehearse tragedy, the sisters
tell me, but it seems my thoughts
have too much power. I've set myself
on a path that ends either in glory
or in nothing, and nothing is worse
than damnation. Like a medieval
mystic I am campaigning for my own
sainthood, but I'm a millennial woman,
Lord, a perfectionist who cannot rise
to her own standard. When I close
my eyes I see women gifted impossible
feats, their corporeal bodies surpassing
the limits of the flesh to become something
like pure spirit, so no wonder their births
were announced by the chime of God's silver
rattle, and I see that, like so much else,
this is not a meritocracy. I've become
instead a skilled interpreter
of the ambient room, fashioning

a narrative of shame to people its spaces
and flood its corners with a revelatory
light, and I inhabit that imagined space,
alone and not alone. The sisters also tell me
to stop minimizing myself, so I'm trying
to see the good, the divinity, in overthinking
my flaws and my regrets, and perhaps
they have a point because I'm sure
if I worried just right I would become
immense, swelled by fear and flame, a force
self-fulfilled and staggering as if
I'd learned, at last, my own ineffable name.

Jeffrey Pethybridge
Force Drift

ALEPH

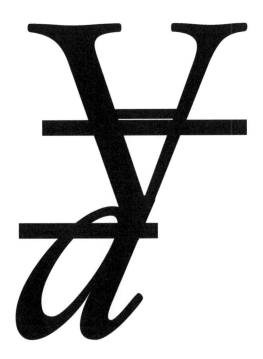

Abu Ghraib as the Aleph.
Abu Ghraib as the tragedians would write its sounds: aiai aiai aiai.

A document as irrefutable as the sun to the eye.

A layer of sound, a layer of silence,   sound silence sound inaudible
sound sound sound silence, a history of pain,
a lever——and spiraling down those vowels.

April now, and what does that mean—new earth is all, and nothing
      of world-building spring for Yasser Talal Al-Zahrani,
      for Thaar Salman Dawod, for Ameen Sa'eed Al-Sheikh,
      for Ali La Pointe, for Rachel, for Joan of Arc.

A prisoner, exhausted—fetal on the floor—in the hell-yellow glare
      and greasy light, after his own body was turned into a science
      of infliction.

"A 'soul' inhabits him and brings him into existence, which is itself
      a factor in the mastery that power exercises over the body.
      The soul is the effect and instrument of a political anatomy;
      the soul is the prison for the body."

Asymmetrical this warfare, as eyes to sun, as the will to state-power.

A version of the torture memos in which only aiai, and the words
      for the many violences remain unredacted.

A version with only the names of the detainees; and could it register
      as something other than a memorial—a demand on the future—
      or would you skim it like a catalogue of ships.
A version, as in conceptual art, you make yourself according to three
simple rules;

a whole library of them there in the (future) City of Otherwise & If—
      here, now in the small theater of your reading, a reckoning lyric.

Azaleas outside, April now, redstarts in the sun.

FORCE DRIFT

To wear a beautiful dress
is a human right

(and no less true in war);
to look up into a clear

day-sky, and not fear
a signature strike; to walk

through your city, no
curfew, no checkpoints;

to be utopian—even
if only for the duration

of the ~~poem~~ thought; to swim
in the sea (and in thought)—

all human rights,
o extraordinary flower

of the "I," to meet you
in that secrecy,

there in the folds
of that obsolete rose,

that universal
treaty of the person,

find me so that I might
exist—we might

exist in that human
right, the anti-epic

we're trying for—
blue-black, black water, sky-blue,

redquartz, background dark—
I'm always writing you.

FORCE DRIFT

—for Elle Longpre

> The city is strictly performative: you eat
> paper, it's ordeal & passage, a trance—*gold, red,*
> *chromium, weapon-grade bronze*—and the abolition
>
> of men, a password you made through obliteration
> & performance, a transmission of ardor,
> in memory now a reaction: parts per million of you
>
> and "privacy, quickening—*gold, red, chromium*—
> Strange flora wilding the aftermath city,
> martyr-crown, I heard you say of or through metastasis,
>
> there in the small arms survey, a book code,
> against the terror-logic of reversals & doubles:

FEAR UP HARSH   EGO DOWN   ISOLATION   FUTILITY

> bite on that, o men of Athens, the mouth to tear
> at swaths,   and carcinogens, it never leaves you
> does it, the long sentence of the traumaeffect,
>
> radicalized, transmogrified through the postures—
> *weapon-grade bronze*—your body took, oracular
> punk, Sibylline in faded black jeans, first poised—
>
> *chromium*—above the bowl of melted snow,

then the soaked swaths, impossible communion,
you gagging, arachnidian, on the vehement sun of it—

gold, red, fire-black—ritual against infliction, against
the body turned instrument of infliction—*gold, gold,*

weapon-grade bronze—ritual for the body alchemical,   and yet.

12. MOCK BURIAL

And then almost at will the sun disappeared
then almost at will the sun disappeared
almost at will the sun disappeared
at will the sun disappeared
will the sun disappeared
the sun disappeared
sun disappeared
disappeared
appeared
pear
red
ear

disappeared thru the will the sea the annul
then the sun all will stilled disappeared
pain the aleph wielded as sun as pain
under willed pain he disappeared
almost red almost ashed pear
as a deer will almost near
devasted in stilled pain
dead under the mare
white appeared red
heard the rape
bruise red
red tear

Kara Candito
Pendulum

I collided with a verb that burst
    into gild like a can of gold
spray paint. First in fear
       and then in recourse, I collided
with *ahorcarse* whose stem is
    an instrumental noun.
Horca: gallow.

In my twenties, I craved an expensive
    swing so that I might be
suspended and fucked over
       a common foam mattress. I made
a grave mistake. I let myself be fucked
    on the ground and am
ground down

now into catastrophe. I want to be
    more devout about positioning
the husband and the rope,
       the husband and the intricate
map of hat hooks he drilled
    into the door of the coat closet
the day

he drove somewhere, I know
    not where, to hang himself
I touched the back of the door
    where he spray-painted our son's

name and asked what
    it meant to wrestle an angel.
Giacomo, Jacobo.

There are two ways of committing
    suicide by hanging; suspension
hanging, the suspension of the body
       at the neck; and drop hanging,
a calculated drop designed to break
    the neck. When Virgil called
the noose

the coil of unbecoming death, he meant,
    I know not why, to disparage
hanging as an effeminate method
       of suicide. *Arrendar*: to use
reins to tie an animal. *Rienda*: rein.
    In June, the rain is a dead language.
It capitulates,

it consoles. In June, everything
    is as loud and desolate as a tuba.
I made a grave mistake.
       When my husband said help, I hid
the rope in a wheelbarrow. Who is not
    repositioned by language?
I sought

answers in the potting soil and have
    to bury myself now. A catastrophic
misconjugation.
       Two incipient people create a third

and the words that make them

    more and less coherent to themselves

are encoded

in the gild of repetition. A verb sets

    them in motion. It signifies no kind

of contract.

Raena Shirali
on projection

supposing i board
the plane, remain suspended
like some sort of cloud,
buoyant, detached

for one full day, followed by my arrival
in a place not of my mother's
dialect, not of my father's
kin, armed with language—[patrilineal],

[marang buru], [flower feast], [nage era].
how surely i'd arrive with detriments
to the likelihood of survival. consider the visible
tattoos, hair dyed lighter at the ends, english

like a target pinned to the chest, the west,
the inescapable truth of my birth.

+

to explain the distance
between self & subject is to admit
the unlikelihood of my self
understanding a given subject. i'm talking : theorizing

understanding. i'm talking :
my inevitable failure to embody.
reader, consider
the basic elements of this narrative—daayan, ojha : hunted,

godly. assume
telling any story fully
involves considering all sides.

+

men wield village secrets
like weapons, catapult accusations
through the fields. i've read so much

about legs & backs : ache-laden
& no choice but to eat [paje] daily
& yet—.

i'm just camera. i'm shutter, closed, i'm protected
from light, i'm just telling a story
to which i'll never know an end.

+

no boarding the plane

no bitter root

no lean season

no poem

+

the gun to my head is ownership.
the gun to my head is
i'm taking the word *empathy*
& hanging it as on a laundry line
& watching it waver in wind
& not believing in words & also
relying on them. reader, men & women alike
shutter themselves with superstition.

Yerra Sugarman

Aunt Bird, Conjured

—for Feiga Maler, 1919–1942,
who died in the Kraków Ghetto

i.

When I still spoke the language of falling snow bending in the wind, and believed the world could be a different way—that we could learn to dress ourselves in the life of another—my young aunt's soul slipped into my bedroom and bloomed like a pear tree.

My fingers were beating a keyboard, dust zigzagging in the woolen light of the winter afternoon. The river outside my window was taut along a horizon that clung to the fuzzy nap of sky. In that sky, the sun had begun to burn a hole, so that the atmosphere seemed to be fraying.

My aunt's sapling soul was nervous and mute, her mouth having been stopped up with earth for so long. Still, she grew—white flowers bursting from her chin—but remained silent.

ii.

Years later, haunted by my computer screen's membrane of light, I discovered what her fate had been, her brief story chronicled on the flare of the Internet's pages. But I couldn't stop seeing her beyond the monitor's plastic skin.

(Genocidal little earth,
I imagined you sniffing
the hem of her skirt,

letting death piss
against her moon ribs

and carve up her nights, erase her desire
to inhabit a whole life,
to tear away her scrim of sadness.)

iii.

What I found out: she had taught in a school for girls, and was killed in Kraków in 1942. She was just twenty-three. The Germans occupied the city, its vast squares stained by the dregs of each dawn's milk-tea light.

On the far side of the Vistula River, the enemy had created a Jewish ghetto in the area known as Podgórze. Gone were the buzzing lanterns on the garrulous streets of Kazimierz, the quarter that had housed the largest Jewish population. And vanished from the porches and balconies, leaning on the breeze, were the slumping succahs, the small shelters built in memory of the Jews who had lived in the desert, their roofs covered with fir tree branches.

No one could be seen praying on the riverbanks on the second day of the New Year anymore. No one could be seen tossing breadcrumbs into the water, the ritual for casting away sins. This was what the occupation authorities wanted. By March 20, 1941, the resettlement of the population was complete.

But after Passover, the ghetto began to look strange, carpenters and bricklayers building walls around it in the form of Jewish headstones. Large arches hunched along a crooked sky. Bars were fastened to windows, their boney shadows clutching the floors of crowded rooms.

iv.

(I share a skin with her now.

Her life unleashed
from time's body.

But how far can I picture
the edge of her breathing,

guess the shape of her collarbone
or grasp a God gone wild?

I, who am so unencumbered,
watching the snow of a new January swarm

and soften my world with its fat whiteness.)

v.

Her life was like a thick soup in my mouth. Her name the Yiddish word
for "bird": *Feiga*. She wiped a grain of soil from her lips, and I could
hear the meat of her voice speak. It climbed up and down my mind, so
that she inhabited the weave of each thing.

JinJin Xu
To Red Dust

Under the cover of night, I read about the Forbidden in a language my parents do not speak.

[   ]

My father is not looking at me because he is driving.

Our World Is Red Dust, he explains, preparing me for The Master.

The Master speaks slow, a mantra from the book with the lotus flower. Foreigners gather at his feet. My father says, Put Your English To Use. I make up a poem about rivers flowing into our lives, and then we all turn into bubbles. They clap and task me to do all future translations. I feel not too guilty because the Master only speaks in metaphors.

My mother hides in the bathroom and angry whispers: They Are Swindling You. But she can't say that out loud because what if his powers are real. A Master from her home province entrapped disbelievers in a roomful of snakes. It's true, all the newspapers said so.

Of Course, my mother says, You Are Taking His Side.

[STATIC]

In the dark of a theater:

The mother's body is too close—so close it vibrates, blurs into shapeless color. The filmmaker recites her mother's words.

[   ]

My father and I swallow Tibetan Red Flowers to keep us from getting sick as the train climbs up to Lhasa. The veins in my friend's nose popped when she took the plane straight up; the bleeding stopping only when she got on the plane home.

Over three days, the train rises, guiding with it our eardrums, lungs, stomachs. On the top bunk, I dream I am the lost reincarnation of Panchen Lama. On the plateau above the clouds, I am taken away by a hundred robed hands.

On day two, the air presses inward and the land outside looks violated, stripped bare. My father begins throwing up. He is ashamed. He stares into the small tin trashcan beside his bunk. I take out the trash, wipe his spit with a wet tissue. He says, It's Good You Are Strong.

[STATIC]

On screen, the naked body of her mother. Forbidden imagery. The filmmaker is too-close, unrelenting in her nearness.

[   ]

A lump hardens in my mother's breast. In the hospital bed, she sees a vision of Ye Su through the white screens, the singing white savior her grandmother talk-storied into streams that ran through my mother's childhood.

She blows dust off her grandmother's Bible and the three of us are baptized in the upstairs bathtub. I go first.

[   ]

This is not the first trip people have mistaken me as my father's lover. Two Beds, we stress, when they write down our shared name. The first time it happens, we are on a beach in Bali. I am fourteen and just beginning to feel okay in the bathing suit stretched tight across my chest. My father goes to the bathroom and leaves me haggling with the surf-shack men. Your Boyfriend? They wink.

I stutter, blood rushing upwards, pooling in my head.

[STATIC]

The filmmaker's father finds her filming her mother in the bathroom. A father's rage; a husband's envy.

Her mother: It's as if you have trespassed/ on his property.

[   ]

My mother wakes singing, her voice ringing clear as a girl. Six a.m., her singing wakes us to her schedule of walks and organic foods and the desire to live.

She is learning to live in a body less woman than mine—but my body is hers, her arm is my arm, her eyes are my eyes, and her new concave hardness my own.

You Are The Reason I Will Live, she says. I grip the showerhead and sponge her off carefully, rinsing away the streaks on her face.

[   ]

My father and I spin bells in the temples of Lhasa. Ready-made prayers lift from their golden bellies into the heavens.

The bells never end. One sends another into frenzy. We touch them, mouthing prayers because we want things too badly to speak them out loud. I watch my father's lips turn.

[   ]

On the first of each month, my father visits the Master in the mountains. He says food is forbidden there.

He donates money; our names are carved into the gilded temple gates, the stone railings, the orange shingles.

My father doesn't tell us until our names are forever engraved. He takes me to the temple, asks me to find our names, horizontal next to each other.

[   ]

The Man My Parents Don't Know I Sometimes Say The Forbidden Word To is driving. The road is icy. He is concentrating. He needs silence to keep us safe. Music? I ask. No response, he is keeping us safe.

[STATIC]

She pulls the viewer close/ too close to see properly/ this itself is erotic/ interacting up close/ close enough for the figure to be boundless.

[   ]

The second time it happens is also the third and the fourth. We are sitting in a restaurant, a table for two, the candle twitching between us. We are at a pool, we are checking in, we are at his college reunion.

My Daughter, he clarifies.

[   ]

My mother begs my father to throw out the Master's Idols. She points to the Master's calligraphy, the tapes, books, gold figurines tucked into corners. Her pleadings always turn my father mute.

One day, we wake to find it all gone. As if our past life never existed.

[STATIC]

Mother's words, read out by the daughter.

The words: I don't know what you mean/ when you talk about the gap between us

[   ]

My mother's friend injects sheep hormones to keep her estrogen flowing, keep her husband around, temper her hot flashes.

My mother isn't like that. Her body running dry relieves her the sin of sex.

Now, her only sin is wanting. He Only Speaks When She Is Home! She wails into the phone.

I know she wants me to overhear, wants my father to overhear.

[STATIC]

The viewer gives up her own sense of separateness.

[   ]

The Man I Sometimes Say The Forbidden Word To reminds me to say it out loud in daylight, as well.

[   ]

My father chases me up the stairs with the house key. I am seven. In our new apartment, my own room. We are racing. He presses the key into the back of my pants. I screech, laughing, breathing hard, taking the stairs two at a time.

This is our game. Then I get older and stronger and ashamed, I run faster so he can't reach me.

[STATIC]

The camera pulls back.

Now, the mother's nakedness in her entirety.

To the left of the frame: a window, new light.

Light traces her mother's body, illuminating it as the daughter finally pulls back.

Mystery light, light without source. Bubbling within the frame, beneath the cracking paint, between the film grain.

The flashlight inside my covers. Light tucked inside my palms, inside the membrane of a page. In clutched breath, I am mouthing The Forbidden.

[   ]

The Forbidden Word cries to her mother, who does not hear her, because she does not exist in the language of this household—she is stuck between the crevice of our teeth:

> is the meat dripping thick oil, is my mother
> moving between the pork and my half-
> nibbled bowl;
> filling me until my body knows she is seeing
> me;
> at times so sour I suck in my jaws, retreat inside
> myself;
> let the syrup roll off my tongue and down
> my throat like tapioca bubbles before I've
> had the chance to swallow.

I say The Forbidden to my parents in a different language, tracing its etymology back to the stories they were once told;

> where they came from, who they were, who
> they can be;
> my father as my father and my mother as my
> mother, before they were either those things,
> before him and her and boy and girl;
> before the wanting for an I.

Silence swells, splintering out from beneath the table legs, from beneath the paint and window ledges, blooming into the space between us until:

it is all there is, all there can be; we breathe in its
cotton body, catch figments of its hair with our own.

The Forbidden Word bows to her Master, who shaves all her hair, lights an
incense to blacken three dots on the top of her newly sleek head;
Chu Jia Le, the Master announced,
You Have Left Home/
You Have Joined Us

The Master strips The Word of her Name, tossing it behind his shoulder
into red dust;
mouth to mirror
carving name
to fog—

[   ]

The three of us in a hotel room. I am trying to change. I hook my bra
beneath my shirt. I do not change in the bathroom, I do not want to change
us, to offend my father my mother, to see my changing body in the mirror.

My mother says, Are You Not Ashamed In Front Of Your Father?
As if I am not of my father's body.

I do not want to change/ I do not want us to change.

[   ]

When I say words out loud they become real.

Under the rising cover of night, I lift the Forbidden from my mouth.

Cole Swensen
Elements of the Garden

Moon

Things grown in moonlight—metallic in sound—the moon sheds a wind—needle in kind. Any seed planted under a new moon will come up poisonous—any planted under the full will walk on its own. Will walk all night—casting a mineral light that will blind the moon.

Sun

Unlike the moon—there is no new sun—and the man walking with a blazing torch will disappear at noon.

Water

Who walked a lake—waking every small thing golden in its light—who walked on back—behind the sun—walking over water—farther goes the going over—to calm, now morning and all egret all around it, a pond.

Birds

Birds are small things—they are berries in the branches bending the branches—breaking the berries with their tendency toward bursting—staining—and instantly the stain of birdsong all over the otherwise pristine air—the air now beyond repair—and yet they continue to be small things—too small to be held accountable—stealing—or called feasting on seedlings—so that at times the berries never come up at all.

Night

Dim silence in stamen—in pistil drawn blind. Night is a fall of footsteps—a rhythm in the leaves—the bells come back alive. Night counts by them—or by the branch that scrapes—or the pear that drops and never lands. While land goes on—its singing own—inside each seed.

Weeds

There is no such thing as a weed.

The weed—essential in its station—without hesitation, crucial to the niche it causes—unfurled across the creases of a field across which cattle amble—seeds and burrs sauntering along in their fur—and birds, their pockets full of the most unexpected things.

Tools

The hand grows on, grows a steel edge, the hand conforms, the bones wrap around, some of the earliest tools were made of bone, the hand wraps around a year and makes it a stone, and the year rages on.

The hand is man's only real tool, basking in the sun throughout a busy afternoon.

Gardeners

Think gardener of every—think gardener of signs—let me hand you the hand of a man who gardens time. Birds, the gardeners of the sky. There's a person at the far end of the garden who seems not to be paying much attention to all of this—who seems to be leaning over and raking the dark earth with her hands—though, in fact, it's not the earth—and it's not so dark—but it is your heart.

Caroline Crew

Bucolic

I have grown long / leggy / a stringing vine
in my own hollow / ready for the tired bloom /
of green realism / in the domestic scene /
I am opened surgically / rebound in
artificial material / my red thread / frayed
from its fibers / but what of the ivy /
suckered in my pores / the small spikes
of pine / the trailing garden rose / beyond
the garden wall /back and back / the body /
the sideline of my own scene / quaint /
a question of focus / soft grasses / the soft
light hampered by the petals / of a cheap
IKEA shade / the foreground shapes / a cult
of nostalgia / or a horse / dark as memory /
galloping / what drags into view /
the synthetic scent of moss burning /
to scry in the mirror / a more convenient
lake / reflecting the already ruin /
the green arch of childhood

Sally Rosen Kindred
Self-Portrait at Twenty-One as Wish Without a Meadow

Sometimes, back then, I was a girl.
And I was roomdark: a candle and a spell.

In the mirror, a flicker brings blue horses.
Flare as the fearsong that calls to their hooves,
their lips closing on black apples,

bruised glass. *Let,* quivers
the wet wick. *Let.*

In the mirror a flare. Light's starved clatter and wrack.
Repetition transforms:
each day her legs thicken. Her black phone rings. As the

water boils, the cup fills, the hands
    I had back then
fetch the white bowl from the kitchen. Over the clavicle the skin

blooms. *Let me.* Her mouth remains still, a seam, a pearl, but the candle
tells with light, in the safe place—
syntax of tremble, withhold.

Belief tongues the grassy air.

A vision could shine manes in night silk.

A vision could be galloping at high speed
from the waiting room

where, on the other side of the wall,
    —I remember how it moaned a radio hum—
the doctor is also counting down.

In the white bowl, home, the movie starts again.
The horses growl like rainchoked violins. The bowl is afraid,
spinning vicious like a moon.

    When I burned the eggs I burned the whole pan.

Hooves slam sand, blue as a bruise.
Only safe when she's wax, slipping—*Let me,*
Let. The candle sings to the ends of her dress

and the dust is rising.

    When I burned the pan I ran
    out into the empty parking lot.
    Everyone else was at work.
    Everyone else had grown up.
    I hid it for good in the trash.

Repetition transforms.
There are whole rooms, she learns, made for waiting.
Chrome after chrome chair willing to hold her.

I hid it for good, for good.
Next I hid my shoes.

Tender as the dead, the mares dip their necks
to the longhaired stars. *Let me thirst and heat.* They huff
at her hunger: *let.*

In the sapphire dark and nicker of that year, I learned.

Let me bite. Let me cook the light.
Let—let—

Again how to meadow and mouth.
Again, soft manes, how to ask you
and burn: gutter, gutter and tell.

Vera Kroms
Alice in Darkness

This is the world I wanted,
        out of drowse and discontent,
midsummer loosening
the petals of my skirt, dusting
        the longitudinal.
All the whispers in my tumble
        couldn't turn me back.

I wear a smallness furnished me
        by carefully arranged
           disappointments.

Eight swipes of butter feed
        your pocket watch.
In a loose pluck of teacups, a black
        honey soothes the lizard mad.

The where of Queen. The whose of Queen.
        The she of Queen.
Gleamy-eyed, like a nanny who sat on a tack,
        she is spite and want, want, want.
Even the color of her roses struggles
        to obey.
Croquet is a mandatory circus, the outcomes
        mortal.
I am out of curtsies.
I stamp my foot, am done with it

Jennifer S. Cheng
A Biography of Women in the Sea

Nü Wā

To think of the world as a series of doors, to consider not walking through. Everything covered in a succulent mist, a cloud of droplets through which to peer and be. With a boat she could wait & watch some very big sky as if pouring over, observing the line between cloud & storm, a mercurial spreading of eventide. With a boat she could keep a surface, shifting or not; she could keep a world

under. Here is the part one always forgets to recall: it was her wayward cloud, her movement that made the storm gather; she buried a tooth under a mound & the largest mountain crumbled. To remain still: to be flanked by fear, absent of want, to hold out for something better. She will wait to want the sky settling down, she wants to watch the sky taking root.

Asa Drake

In the Tradition of Women Who've Blessed Me to Transfer Their Virtues

I give you what I don't have.
Strawberries in the mouths

of birds. Unopened pomegranate
blossoms devoured by ants. Fruit dropped

from unpollinated vines, all varieties.
Tell me the last time a flower wasn't

the shortcut to desire. One year
in the middle of my life

I asked *how full do I want to be.*
Like hunger in the years before,

I asked fullness to be endless.
Every noise, I gave cause to.

An excuse to find comfort
in the sounds of eating,

the small soul cutting a summer
lawn. I hear the thrum and wait

in my hothouse for my dinner
to line up petal to petal.

Plant fruit I've germinated
in my own mouth. Let

the animals in. I mean
to say I'm in love

with that small mouth.
But I can't call love out

without telling the difference
between one mouth in the grass

and another. Permission is a fruit
I've cut from the tree, meaning

I've taken human sacrifice.
When I say *be careful*

I want to use your hands
in place of my hands.

When I feed the animals
the rabbit stands up

so straight she falls over.
That's the part I want

you to know. We are
that kind of animal.

LITERARY CRITICISM

Feminist Poetics of the Archive: A Forum

*Edited by Karla Kelsey, with responses from Mary-Kim Arnold,
Rachel Blau DuPlessis, Danielle Dutton, Amy E. Elkins,
Camille Guthrie, Lucy Ives, Ashley Lamb, Poupeh Missaghi,
Lisa Pearson, Chet'la Sebree*

We might evoke the term "archive" to describe many different holdings—
for example, all that goes on record via the Net, an institution's offi-
cial repository of valuable texts, or a culture's canon. An archive might
also be personal, housed in alternative architecture: a shoebox of post-
cards, a bookcase constructed of planks and cinder blocks, a recipe box.
Regardless of application, all archives imply recordkeeping and an insis-
tence that *such-and-such a thing* is a document worth preserving.

While archives are historically aligned with gatekeeping, a feminist prac-
tice of archival work entails openness and an investment in valuing the
undervalued, of preserving the overlooked, of raising to the level of the
"archive" materials and architectures that have not previously qualified.
Implicitly or explicitly a feminist approach offers critique of past para-
digms' exclusion. This always has been, and continues to be, crucial work.

The ten participants in this forum, "Feminist Poetics of the Archive," ac-
tively engage in the transmission of fragile histories—through creative
and scholarly writing, art making, editing, publishing, translating, curat-
ing, teaching. I've invited them to wear any or all of their archival hats
and to respond creatively or critically, briefly or at length, to three dif-
ferent kinds of questions. First, I ask each participant a question tailored
to their individual practice. Second, each participant responds to the
"Collective Questions" that you can find below. Third, each participant
answers a question created by another writer featured in this forum. I
also include visual artwork by three participants: Rachel Blau DuPlessis,
Amy Elkins, and Ashley Lamb.

Working with these participants on "Feminist Poetics of the Archive" has
been markedly affirming during 2020's spring and summer months of

pandemic, police violence, and social unrest. By thoughtfully engaging the past, these responses suggest ways we can empower the future.

For the purpose of this print format I've included only the Individual and Exchange Questions and Answers. To give you a taste of what we discussed in the Collective Questions, which provided the backdrop for all of our discussions, I include my questions, below, and invite you to visit the online version of this forum for our participants' rich perspectives.

Collective Question: *The Call of the Object*

In *Spontaneous Particulars: The Telepathy of Archives*, Susan Howe writes: "Often by chance, via out-of-the-way card catalogues, or through previous web surfing, a particular 'deep' text or simple object (bobbin, sampler, scrap of lace) reveals itself *here* at the surface of the visible, by mystic documentary telepathy. Quickly—precariously—coming as it does from an opposite direction."[1]

With this idea the borders of what we might think archival material contains open to admit deep text and simple object, web work and library time. Also opened: the process of engaging archival material, allowing us to see the material itself as animated and willful, "revealing itself." It is as if material has a plan of its own. As such, Howe invites us to overturn a sense of orderly rule, orderly access, of patriarchal law that often dominates historical objects. The call of the archival object invites us to understand the power of texts and objects outside of ourselves to urgently speak.

Have you experienced such a "call" from an archival object or text that led you down the path of response? If so, please describe one such moment and how you responded to the call. Did this response result in a project? Do you now (or did you then) understand this call, or your response to the call, to challenge established systems of value and record?

If you never have received such a call, what is your process for engaging historical material like?

Collective Question: *The Ethics and Aesthetics of Archival Work*

A feminist approach to the greater cultural archive engages aspects of history that have been overlooked, under-told, misrepresented, silenced. Some of these stories, as M. NourbeSe Philip articulates, must be told but, like the stories of the drowned African slaves for whom she writes in *Zong!*, some "can only be told by not telling."[2] She elaborates on this tension, drawing attention to the importance of approach, the *how* of response:

> What I feel strongly is that we can't tell these stories in the tradi-
> tional way, or the Western way of narrative—in terms of a begin-
> ning, a middle, and end. I think part of the challenge, certainly for
> me, was to find a form that could bear this "not telling." I think
> this is what *Zong!* is attempting: to find a form to bear this story
> which can't be told, which must be told, but through not telling.[3]

Consideration of this *how* seems to me important not only to narratives silenced by violence, but also to other archival absences—for instance the overlooked lives of plants, animals, and other nonhuman organisms. Or the often underestimated affective, relational expression that is an address book, a family photo album. Aspects of a life, any life, that are not part of the usual record.

What is one of the most powerful experiences that you have had as you've engaged an overlooked or silenced element of the archive? How were the practical, ethical, and/or aesthetic aspects of your research and response informed by the ignored or silenced status of your sub-ject? What surprises does the underestimated hold? What techniques or advice do you have for culture workers interested in exploring the overlooked?

Collective Question: *Preservation and Access*

In the last chapter of *Deviations: A Gayle Rubin Reader*, Rubin recounts her quest for knowledge about lesbian history and culture during the 1970s. At that time even the search for a bibliography of lesbian texts proved extraordinarily difficult until she came upon the University of Michigan's Labadie Collection, an archive she calls one of the "most extensive repositories of homosexual publications in the country at a time when most university and public libraries dismissed them as pornographic trash."[4]

Rubin celebrates late twentieth-century formation of queer archives while highlighting the fragility of systems that make such collections possible. She urges us to care for and preserve the vulnerable, the marginal, locating in such material a resistance to institutionalization and to the gesture of conformity that lends itself to preservation. Nevertheless, "to paraphrase Marx and Marshall Berman, all that seems solid can vanish in a heartbeat, and to mangle Santayana, those who fail to secure the transmission of their histories are doomed to lose them."[5]

In the twenty-first century awareness of archival gaps has grown apace with user-friendly technology, giving rise to institutional collections development as well as online archives created by individuals. For example, Marysia Lewandowska's online Women's Audio Archive of interviews and public events features key female figures in the arts. Northeastern hosts Women Writers Online, a digital archive of pre-Victorian texts, and Brown University Library houses a Feminist Theory Archive Collection in their physical library. The National Museum of Women in the Arts is housed in a physical location; the National Women's History Museum is virtual.

If you could create any kind of archive you wanted, anywhere in the world, to house any kind of materials, what would you create? Would you consider this archive as part of a feminist practice? Alternatively, do you have a favorite archive of the overlooked that you'd like to share with readers? How does its form (virtual, physical, public, private, free, paid, etc.) amplify or trouble its contents? All of you are engaged in archive building through transmission of information in your own writing and creative work as well as through editing, publishing, translating, teaching, and curating: what models can we use to ensure both the security *and* freedom of materials?

And, now, on to the forum.

Mary-Kim Arnold

KARLA KELSEY

In both *Litany for the Long Moment* and your new book of poems *The Fish & The Dove* you work with archival sources to tell a story both personal and political, taking as catalyst your adoption to the United States from Korea at two and a half years of age. The linked essays of *Litany for the Long Moment* employ documents, photographs, school lessons, and letters, deftly revealing many ways in which visual material communicates. For example, the photographs you include document time and place while catching the fleeting thing we think of as personality: the figures in your photos are often caught mid-gesture as they exchange smiles, whispers, glances. Documents like the chart of the Korean alphabet remind us how much communication is evoked by the forms and shapes of letters—a fact that you echo in the rhythms you create with paragraphs of various sizes beautifully arranged on the page.

The Fish & The Dove continues many of the themes of *Litany,* delving into what it is like to grow up in America as a woman of color. The book's series of eight visual poems expands the personal into the larger historical field by overlaying rectangles of museum-styled wall text that describe quotidian objects (a tobacco pipe, a girl's locket) over a report issued by the Republic of Korea's Truth and Reconciliation Commission detailing the human rights violations of the Korean War.

Your work serves as a rich model for many techniques a writer might choose from in including historical and personal archives. A difficult thing to decide is the amount of mediation an archival document should go through: should it be scanned and printed? translated? woven into dialogue? rendered as story?

What kinds of things do you consider when deciding on the form archival incorporation will take? Do certain kinds of documents ask for particular modes of presentation?

MARY-KIM ARNOLD

Thank you for this question and for such attentive engagement with my work.

I think I am attempting to strike a balance between instinct and intention.

For the personal documents, I rely primarily on instinct, the way I respond to the documents themselves, what it feels like to look at them, to be with them. I try to be attentive to where the energy or heat of the object is for me, where it feels particularly significant.

I'll take, for example, the letter that became the cover of *Litany for the Long Moment*. It was one of a series of handwritten letters between On Soon Whang, the director of the Orphans' Home of Korea, and my adoptive mother. I was drawn to this letter because it documented one of the more transactional aspects of the adoption. There is money exchanged. My mother sends a few items—dress slip, vitamins, doll, socks—in preparation for my trip and a check for $25. In other letters, there are some references to small sums of money—sometimes referred to specifically to cover postage. These are beyond the official costs of the adoption—the administrative fees, travel expenses, cost of required home studies and necessary medical examinations, all of which together were likely to have been tens of thousands of dollars.

So here is a reminder of the transactional, rendered through the motion of the hand on the page. I was not able to reproduce the blue airmail page, but I found the small, cramped handwriting very moving, the fact of it, the trace of the hand, the hand addressing my mother. This seemed to me a close approximation of a core paradox of the adoption. Transactions represented and exacted through the physical body—of this woman's hand, but also, of course, in exchange for, in anticipation of, the actual body of the child, delivered.

I was also drawn to this particular penmanship, its smallness, its tightness. On Soon Whang's letters—and the couple photos included in the book—constitute the only evidence that I existed before my arrival here in the United States. So as evidence, as objects, I am looking for a lot from them. There is a way in which they carry all this information, but what I most want to glean from it remains enigmatic and resistant to my interpretation. For it to be reproduced, for it to be represented as itself—as much as itself as possible—and not through my interpretation of it—seemed important.

The photographs—most of which I took myself—are already mediated, and I attempt to consider that mediation by drawing in Barthes and Sontag—so the fact that they are rendered in black and white, and not as "true" to their original form, is less significant. Fidelity to the original is not where the energy of the photos is for me.

To consider as another example, the Report from the Commission of Truth and Reconciliation, which you reference, and which I use in the last pages of *The Fish & The Dove*. The energy from that document comes not from its physical object-ness. My only engagement with it is virtual—as a downloadable pdf on the commission's website. What I was trying to show from it is the fact of this language, the seeming endlessness of line after line recounting the torture and murder of Korean civilians. What was important about the document was the sense of its scale—page after page, and of its language, so to the extent that you might be able to read it, you know that it takes on this particular administrative tone, a kind of bureaucratic droning. Using the passive voice, e.g., "the investigation was poorly conducted," leaving no human trace, no embodiment of the responsibility. The language is distanced from the perpetration of the act. That distance, and the suggestion of what it was obfuscating, was where the energy of the artifact existed for me.

Perhaps what I'm suggesting is that the more mysteries the object contains, the more enigmatic, the more it seems important to represent it in a way that stays close to my own encounter with it.

Exchange Question

LUCY IVES

I came across Julietta Singh's *No Archive Will Restore You* (2018) via a conversation with a student in the class I am currently teaching (the class is about memory and mnemonic devices). Having read Singh's essay, I started to wonder about the limitations of the concept of the archive, as well as of individual or actual archives, in themselves. I'd be curious to know: Have you ever been disillusioned with an archive—or, with the very practice of materialist historiography that archives seemingly enable? Should we question the ubiquity of the term, as well as the way in which many artists and scholars (myself included) have a tendency to attribute great value and significance to archives both real and theoretical/imaginary?

MARY-KIM ARNOLD

I was grateful to be pointed to this essay, and while I don't have the experience of being a doctoral student that Singh describes, nor have I really had any sustained engagement with scholarly research, the longing for a kind of resolution or redemption that might be presented by the archive, real or imagined, is a recognizable one.

I am not sure I know how else to respond to this provocation, except with the memory that this essay stirred up in me.

After my mother died, we packed up her personal effects—clothing, mostly, some costume jewelry, a few trinkets. We filled six large black trash bags, destined for the Salvation Army.

If I could go back, I would keep them all. I think I might like to take out each item and describe it, write about it. This is the dress my mother wore to the ocean, when we walked the boardwalk at night. This was the coat she bought to wear for Easter, but then that Easter was too warm for a coat.

Here was a skirt she made herself and wore on one of the afternoons I remember her happy.

My mother, in her moment of being, the ordinariness of a woman, moving through her day, choosing an ordinary dress for an ordinary day, feeling a little ordinary joy at the end of it.

Singh says, "The archive is a stimulus between myself and myself."

What can be said about It matters only in the sense of my telling it, my tracing it, my holding it.

She was my mother. She wore a dress. Now both mother and dress are gone.

Rachel Blau DuPlessis

KARLA KELSEY

This forum's conversation around feminist poetics of the archives wouldn't be the same without your intellectual and creative contributions to literature and thought. Your works of criticism have been pivotal, transforming the field of poetics, challenging received notions of whose writing matters, of what a reader might pay attention to, and of how such attention might be articulated. Reading *The Pink Guitar, Writing Beyond the Ending,* and *Blue Studios* not only taught me new things about writers I love but also were transformative experiences on an affective and intellectual level. I can still remember exact physical moments of engaging these books, of holding them in my hands.

RACHEL BLAU DUPLESSIS

[interjecting]: Thank you; this comment means a lot to me.

KARLA KELSEY

Your creative works equally challenge the boundaries of what can be written, of how one might write. For example *Drafts,* your series of 114 poems composed over two and a half decades, combines the epic and the ephemeral in an extensive, recursive long poem investigating the entwined processes of memory, history, and language. And your collage poems *Life in Handkerchiefs* takes up these threads on a vivid, hand-worked scale, combining vintage handkerchiefs and text.

There are so many questions to be asked about your relationship to archives—official archives like the Beinecke Rare Book & Manuscript Library, where your papers are housed alongside H. D.'s, Mina Loy's, Barbara Guest's, and other writers with whom you've been in conversation. Also unofficial archives, like your collection of hankies.

The question I choose to ask here is about generativity and detail. In an interview with C. A. Conrad you call Mina Loy's "Feminist Manifesto" a "generative document,"[6] and in your "Statement on Poetics" you discuss the "social-sensuous generativity" of language and the "ungeneralized detail" that "changes everything because it speaks of the contingent, the intransigent, the odd, the potentially unaccounted, uncounted, unaccountable."[7] What is the relationship between the "generativity" of a document and its "detail," and how do formal and/or informal archival settings play into this relationship?

RACHEL BLAU DUPLESSIS

When I was thinking about how language and historical ideologies worked together—while figuring out my critical book about the early poetry of modernists—I found that the odd detail, the clashing word, the weird thing that rubbed *me* against the grain often was like a pinhole onto large-scale contradictions and social thinking. Those pinhole moments opened whole worlds of debates and ideologies current at the time (of the early modernist poets) and did so in the condensed mode of poetic techniques. Things like the hanging "Klein" in a T. S. Eliot poem (when has a proper noun like that ever jumped both over a line break *and* stanza break?) or the visual-cultural compression of "Pig Cupid . . . rooting" in a Mina Loy poem, or the words "besides" and "then" and "I am" in a Langston Hughes poem. If one stayed alert for those bumps and knots—a lot could be inferred and postulated and found. Word choice, semantic images, syntax and line break seemed to be a point of contact between poetic language and social worldviews in the poets without having the poems be polemical documents. I called this tactic of critical looking, or this lens for asking questions, "social philology." (This all in *Genders, Races, and Religious Cultures in Modern American Poetry*—and I actually do understand why Cambridge did NOT want it called "Entitled New" for the three new entitlements of modernism—New Woman, New Black [i.e., New Negro, in the contemporaneous word], New Jew—but it *was* a lovely title.) Responses inside the techniques of poetry to those formations are found all over in the poetry—not solely as content but deep in elements of form. So I wrote a critical book on that method of looking at poetry.

It's as if the poems, seen in this lens, became their own archive of poetic detail that had large, social rationales, really, and were not just surface word play, or wit, or decoration. This was for me a very fruitful thought—this sense of crystallizations and condensations of gigantic nodules of thought within poetic representation. And, of course, representation (loosely art) is a kind of thinking via forms and tactics (using words and segmentivity in poems).

As the end of a poem (precisely, "Draft 85: Hard Copy") I wrote:

> The poem
> being archive of feelings to come—
>
> And of what else we don't know.
> It is really "quite curious…"

I think this is true, though it is hard to explain. Maybe the poem is a kind of prophecy of future feelings? or it stores feelings we did not know we had until we read them and then we are provoked by the poem to feel them? This is so much the opposite of the more banal, "this poem expresses its feelings so beautifully," that I am almost giggling. Maybe the poem predicts feelings that you will have? Goodness—who knows, except I used the interesting word "archive" in the middle of all this speculation.

I actually think that art is some kind of archive as well as many other things. Maybe it is an archive of feelings to come?

Some art is a definite archive—a still life of your nicest objects painted with all the glisten and shininess and textures imitated (at the apogee of a certain kind of still life in the 17th century, usually by Dutch painters)—what a strange pleasure to see the possessed quality of those possessions.

Or *Life in Handkerchiefs*, a project of collage poems that I did between 2017 and 2018. I describe this as loosely a progress through a female life, told page by page with poems, prose poems, aphorisms, and other texts collaged together with vintage handkerchiefs as the main artistic medium, along with fabric, lace and trimmings, artificial flower notions, string, and paper, including tickets, origami paper, and a photograph. This work is not really *my* life only, not even only my handkerchiefs for all the collage poems, but something between my life as a girl-and-woman at a time and place and a general plausible woman's life of a certain class and social zone with all those negotiations of gender expectations and resistance, doubled self-consciousness and self-questioning. It draws on handkerchiefs that I really owned—and even really used until they were practically rags—and then got salvaged into this art. And as the medium as well uses handkerchiefs picked up by me at yard sales (more salvage of the oddity, the particular, other people's stuff) and saved until I thought of this project. The use of hankies as a collage medium seemed the perfect—if unknown beforehand—culmination of my random collection of these pretty and sometimes clichéd objects. And there were handkerchiefs donated to this project by other women, friends, acquaintances and relatives, who must have been struck in some way at the interest of cleaning their bureau drawers of an oddity that they too had saved for a very long time. And as Karla Kelsey suggested too, it was a chance to pass on an affective object. In fact, some of the notes about the origins of at least two handkerchiefs in the lives of my friends' relatives were included. And now in my notes to the project. Luckily for me, these friends decided to contribute to this art project—my metaphoric archive of womanhood—there was something wonderful about that generosity. An archive of femaleness, femininity (all that lace and flowers), of blood (various) and snot, and tears, of gestures of dress-up, of living loosely through World War II and the postwar years, the knowledge of the Shoah, US casual racism; atomic bomb fears, how women get to be in charge of holidays like Christmas and St. Valentine's Day and Thanksgiving—all memorialized in—handkerchiefs? (And now in their accompanying poems.) This too is, as you say, a work based on an archiving sensibility as well as a respect for and a playing with crafts. I hope that one day the book—or perhaps box—of these collage poems' hankies might be published together.

Exchange Question

DANIELLE DUTTON

I just started reading Valeria Luiselli's *The Lost Children Archive* and one of its epigraphs reads, "An archive presupposes an archivist, a hand that collects and classifies" (Arlette Farge). Archival work (like editorial work, or caretaking, taking care of others or the work of others) often goes unseen and unconsidered. I wonder if you can imagine someone in the future trying to study you through whatever archives you've created or tended. What sort of archivist do your archives presuppose?

RACHEL BLAU DUPLESSIS:

You've asked several questions, because one asks about "the archivist"—a library professional with a degree in archiving, who has been trained in various ways. I'll answer that one first. Often these people intimately know the archive they are in charge of (I know a fine set of literary archivists like this) and can help researchers wonderfully. That's their job, but (as with teachers, or anyone in our general field) some do their jobs better than others. If you go to that archivist with a somewhat vague but earnest question, she might say, "Have you thought of looking at . . . [this file or that file]? It might be interesting to you." So that's the kind of archivist I hope my collection has! The one with useful, informed, pertinent suggestions. The other part of your question is asking about the researcher ("someone in the future trying to study you"). I hope that person is empathetic but astute, understanding that with any document (a letter, a journal entry) one writes in a certain mood, tone, or with a certain purpose, and whatever the tone (etc.), the document reflects only a part of the full "you." A person is also not self-consistent, and if I say something mean to one person about another, and then turn right around and write a butter-wouldn't-melt-in-my-mouth epistle to that other person—a researcher might understand that I have many facets and so does the world . . . and that you can't call me a hypocrite until I have done this in more than 50 percent of all cases! In short (this is an extremely comic, not-really-me example), unless a subject leaves such an obvious train of stale breadcrumbs that it becomes clear she is showing only a carefully curated mask of the self even in an archive (this can happen), you have to take just about everything with wise, empathetic judgment and a nice big clichéd grain of salt. Further, I would like to hope that anyone who researches my work checks her citations four times or more (because citing poetry sometimes becomes rewriting that poetry), gets dates right, and doesn't make funny errors (someone

recently wrote I had taught at Buffalo, for example; nope). Also, think-
ing about the scholarship of other people, I always have that still vivid
negative example of a researcher who published a whole book on H. D.
with a highly overwrought interest in H. D.'s [male] lovers and who
ascribed the parentage of H. D.'s child (Perdita) to the wrong—and
the more luridly interesting—partner. Do *not* be that researcher. As
for "what archivist my archives presuppose"? In this world of woe, who
knows? Perhaps what my archives could be useful for in a century is
finding the butterfly wings or pressed flowers that I have occasionally
put in my journals—because the future will need these to restart species.

Danielle Dutton

KARLA KELSEY

In *A Room of One's Own* Virginia Woolf writes of wanting to see how
the fictious female writer Mary Carmichael might "set to work to catch
those unrecorded gestures, those unsaid or half-said words, which form
themselves, no more palpably than the shadows of moths on the ceiling,
when women are alone."[8]

These unrecorded gestures are nothing less than the "strange food" of
"knowledge, adventure, art," and Woolf shows us that representations of
female engagement with this food are perilously absent in the literature
of her time. Not only are these gestures absent but female lives have
been so over-written by patriarchal versions of female gesture that they
can only by captured by the "talk of something else, looking steadily out
of the window." Each time I revisit these passages I find them perilously
contemporary!

Counteracting this, your books *Attempts at a Life*, *SPRAWL*, and
Margaret the First share a voracious exploration of such "strange food,"
creating windows into the lives of female characters, both historical
and imagined, as they hunger and eat. *Attempts at a Life* operates in
short pieces, vignettes that draw on a cast of characters including Jane
Eyre, Alice James, Madame Bovary, and Hester Prynne. *SPRAWL* is
an ekphrastic response to Laura Letinsky's contemporary domestic

still lifes and pulses with the rhythm of the body as your narrator circumambulates her suburban neighborhood: "I appear to be free from design or discretion. It is an easy discovery of the 'feminine.' I walk through the doorway wearing my aggressively orange hat. I do it over and over."9 *Margaret the First* delivers a complex portrait of celebrity culture through the ambition, sensibility, and brilliance of a 17th-century duchess. What a variety of vital "strange food" you've created for readers, and I have yet to mention the lives of books you've published since 2009 via Dorothy, a Publishing Project!

My question here for you has to do with technique: Woolf suggests that in order to capture the "strange food" of female life, writers need to "look out the window," developing alternative techniques to those used in conventional narrative writing. What are your thoughts on this notion? Do you have any favorite techniques?

DANIELLE DUTTON

For days now I've been trying to think of something smart to say in response to this generous question, but the truth is that I operate as a writer and in some ways as an editor very much inside a space of instinct. There's a kind of silence there. It's something I've spent a decade or so trying to "overcome," because so many aspects of the job of being a writer and certainly being a teacher of writing demand that we articulate how it is that we do what we do and why. But I write the way I write . . . because I do. I'm not trying to *not write* some other way. I'm thinking about how Eileen Myles talks about how most of the interesting work (they're talking about in poetry) is being done by female writers. They aren't saying that all work by female writers is better than all work by male writers, but that—okay, I'll just quote them: "Female reality (and this goes for all the 'other' realities as well—queer, black, trans—everyone else) is more interesting because it is wider, more representative of humanity—it's definitely more stylistically various because of all it has to carry and show. After all, style is practical. You do different things because you are different." I believe I write toward that "strange food" because I am strange and have always felt strange and estranged, as a girl and a woman, for sure, and also no doubt because of certain inherited mental health struggles, and also because I grew up Jewish in a conservative/Christian small town and (despite the presence in my childhood of plenty of good people) was made to feel like an outsider. All of this is as much a part of my technique as a fiction writer as is the fact that I read Gertrude Stein for pleasure and am not very adept at writing plot. Maybe reading people like Stein and Woolf, maybe just that practice is its own way of looking out the window? Looking differently. Maybe I'm saying that one of my preferred techniques is to look past whatever is at the center, to center myself on the periphery instead.

Exchange Question

POUPEH MISSAGHI

How has your work with the archive, this engagement with a remnant from the past, shifted the ways you carry yourself in the present moment or imagine possibilities for the future?

DANIELLE DUTTON

Thank you for this question, Poupeh. There are different ways I could answer it based on different archival engagements, so I'll center it, for myself, around my work with Dorothy, which is active, ongoing archival work, less an engagement with the past than with an ever-shifting present. Each time we add a new book to the press's list there is a subtle rearrangement. An accommodation. A making-room-for. It doesn't feel to me as if this is only in my head. Like when Jen George's *The Babysitter at Rest* was added, suddenly something new could be seen in Suzanne Scanlon's *Promising Young Women*, or how Amina Cain's work speaks to Renee Gladman's, or Leonora Carrington's stories are cast in a new light with the addition to the list of Sabrina Orah Mark's *Wild Milk*. For me this rearrangement, this changing personality of the list, often seems the truly essential work of publishing, a gesture ultimately as meaningful as the particular fate of any one book, and this is perhaps why I feel okay using the word "archival" to discuss what on the surface would seem to be the everyday work of publishing new books. It keeps me engaged both forward and backward in time, and it has practical implications. For example, when we're in the process of choosing books (we only publish two per year) we really do think both backward and forward, to what this body of work wants or needs. We might try to gauge: Does it want a reprint? A translation? A debut? Etc.

It also just occurred to me to add that within the Dorothy archive is a triptych of books by a real-life archivist, Nathalie Léger! Her writing overtly engages archives and archival work in the tracing of women's lives (her own, Barbara Loden's, the Countess of Castiglione's, etc.). Two of those titles are coming out this September (2020) and among other things your question makes me think about how the project of those books rhymes, in a way, with Dorothy's larger project.

Amy E. Elkins

KARLA KELSEY

In your research you employ traditional academic scholarship conducted in libraries and archives along with an experiential approach, shadowing a bobbin lacemaker on the Isle of Wight as well as having yourself 3-D scanned and printed! This has resulted in several essays as well as your current scholarly monograph project, *Crafting Feminism from Literary Modernism to the Multimedia Present*, which draws together literary craft and artistic craftwork, from needlework to poetry and the novel to digital-making.

While your approaches to research might appear to make use of opposite ends of the spectrum—the institutional archive on one hand, the archive of knowledge passed from craftsperson to craftsperson on the other—your writing proves otherwise. For example, your article in *PMLA* about the Ryerson Image Center's new collection of six Bernice Abbott photos of Mina Loy's Bowery assemblages, made in the 1950s, recounts a fascinating story of research and recovery, showing scholarly work to be a collaborative, relational adventure.[10] Editorial projects like the online journals *Decorating Dissidence* (https://decoratingdissidence. com/) and *MAI: Feminism & Visual Culture* (https://maifeminism. com/) extend an invitation to this interdisciplinary, collaborative form of archival scholarship to others.

In bringing together literary crafts and artistic craftwork, what usually catalyzes your process of investigation: the literary text, the craft, something else? On a parallel track, how much does the research technique that you use shape the kind of knowledge any given archive will reveal?

AMY E. ELKINS

My process of investigation often begins with the text because I'm intrigued by the material basis of artistic metaphors. If, for example, I happen to answer this question by drawing on metaphors of weaving, you might be alerted to my artistic practice. I could suggest the ways in which a text and visual art are woven together, how they form the warp and weft of gender and politics in women's work across time, how the idea of agency becomes the shuttle running between the threads of gendered making, and so on. These metaphors tell us something about how folks often make sense of the material world and might approach complex intellectual or existential questions. Similar such metaphors drew me to taking more seriously the ways writers draw on craft in their work—as both figurative or inspirational but also a part of a material, creative practice across media.

In my own practice, art and writing enrich each other, and since I'm often writing about art-making, doing art is kind of like practicing a language, learning the accents and inflections of creative work—attuning my ear (or eyes, hands) to the ways in which makers think. For example, I've been writing about the relationship between Virginia Woolf, craft, and photography. Woolf set the typeface for many of the books published by the Hogarth Press, and because I'm a darkroom photographer, I picked up on the similarity between a photographic negative printed into a positive image and the way Woolf had to set type in reverse, forming a kind of literary negative that becomes positive when printed. Or, as another example, I've been writing about painting and ink pigments in Lorna Goodison's work. As a young woman, she left Jamaica to study painting in New York City with luminaries such as Jacob Lawrence. In her poem "To Make Various Sorts of Black," she cites Cennino d'Andrea Cennini's *The Craftsman's Handbook* in the first line! Goodson describes and gives tremendous meaning to five different pigments of black. I was able to acquire a set of inks made according to these particular recipes, and the poem spoke to me on a completely new level. It is one thing to read about "the black that is scraped from burnt shells. / Markers of Atlantic's graves. / Black of scorched earth, of torched stones of peach"— and another thing to fill a brush with Scraped Shell Black ink and see the way it behaves on paper. Like Goodison's words—printed in black ink for us on the page—the pigments carry stories and work to make us see in a new way. Critically, what all this means is that I'm able to write with attention to medium specificity, grounding my arguments, however transdisciplinary, in feminist materials and processes.

Your question about how my research technique shapes the kinds of knowledge an archive might reveal taps in to the beautiful messiness of working both within and outside traditional archives. I make room for scholarly serendipity—by that I mean a balance of intense investigation and a willingness to let archives, objects, and narratives surprise me. I'd describe my research technique as willfully associative; I relish (and actively create) curious juxtapositions because they often reveal new dimensions of material culture and theory. Even in an institutional archive, I'm looking at the fringes, listening for the stories that might be waiting to be heard, attuning my eyes and fingers to traces of process rather than looking at the finished product as the primary source of knowledge.

I began tracking Berenice Abbott's lost photographs, for instance, because I wanted to write about Loy's assemblage artworks, and I kept running into problems getting access to the few pieces that still survive. The assemblages were created from ephemeral materials, and they seemed to both evade attention while also demanding it—much like Loy herself. I had read that even Abbott had lost track of the photographs and negatives, so I tried to imagine various scenarios for the material life (or afterlife) of those images. They seemed like the sort of thing that might get tucked into a file with other pieces of paper and shuffled around for a while. If someone encountered them, it is likely they wouldn't know they were photographs of Loy's artwork unless they were familiar with Loy's work. A lot of my research depends on an understanding of the persistence of material objects, while also acknowledging archives as sites of power. By thinking in an active way about the borders of archives, I embrace the potential for shifting, challenging, and enlarging those borders to be more inclusive. In my experience, craft provides a model for this kind of intervention because it traverses the personal and political in powerful, unique ways, evading easy categorization and allowing makers on the margins to assert their agency—their survival.

Exchange Question

LISA PEARSON

I've found that shaping a selection of works from an archive is the most challenging task. I'm interested to know how others think about the criteria, the frame, the presentation, the relationships of one thing to another, as well as the accumulation of things, all the big and little decisions that ultimately result in what will become public.

AMY E. ELKINS

This question fascinates me both as a researcher—nearing the completion of my first monograph—and as a teacher. Because I work at the intersection of texts and other objects, the archives I select often emerge as a result of my comparisons between a work of literature and a visual object. In other words, I'm looking at the potential exchanges between the verbal and the visual, which determine my scholarly-curatorial focus. And I usually find myself thinking at least as much about access as about selection per se—trying to recover craft archives as research sources and records of makers' practices across media. In that way, I reassemble like an archaeologist. . . . I like to dig in and see what I find and bring new things to light, and I'm not interested in thinking hierarchically about what counts or merits inclusion along traditional lines. Because my work embraces the fringes of art-making, I'm usually excited about linkages and circulation, networks that fascinate me *because* they are dispersed, queer, excessive, or secretive. I suppose another way of saying this is that I'm really interested in creative practices that are undisciplined. This approach to the archive is informed by craft scholars who have disrupted ideas of high and low work with responses to amateurism, DIY, craftivism, and hobby art. But it's also an outgrowth of my fascination with the neuroscience of creativity, the ways in which writers often make things intermittently across media as a form of inspiration, the impetus to think in new ways with diverse materials (fibers, clay, panes of glass, recycled cardboard, found objects, etc.) and in ways that are more embodied—more haptic, more visual.

For me, assembling an archive becomes something loosened from linear approaches to selection, and I've worked that methodology into my pedagogy as well. For example, while I teach literature using an array of hands-on and multimedia approaches, I've been really intrigued by collage's capacity to bridge theory and practice in the undergraduate classroom. I'm always looking for ways to deepen my students' ability to synthesize, look closely, and articulate the far-reaching creative potential of literary texts. I sometimes ask students to create collage artworks that accompany their final research papers. And as they make their artworks, I encourage them to think about both the content of their essay (its argument, the primary sources, the critical context) and the process of academic writing itself (structure, integrating others' perspectives, enchantment, and labor). In making a collage, they find new and wonderful associations and write with more creative insight and critical rigor. This approach can be really important when I'm teaching courses rooted in cultural studies and global literature. In my courses on "Contemporary British Multicultural Novels," collage, as an instruction model, becomes a medium for political and aesthetic critique, analysis, and public engagement. In my courses, my collage pedagogy asks literature students to theorize—through hands-on making—the ruptures and sites of solidarity in contemporary narratives of postcolonialism, xenophobia, border politics. By creating points of difference (cuts, tears, excision) and transformation (repair, assemblage, unity), students become more attentive to the power structures at work in multicultural fictions. In this way, they are selecting works from massive archives and assembling in the way you describe—the many big and little decisions that ultimately reveal a uniquely powerful mode of knowledge sharing while also testing the limits and potential of kinship, relationality, and the borders of knowledge and experience.

Camille Guthrie

KARLA KELSEY

In an interview conducted for the *Boston Review* you and Ann Lauterbach address the intermixture of past and present as it comes to the surface in language and visual art. The differentiation between history and immediacy is not so much effaced as shown to be different facets of the same object, as, for example, in Ann Lauterbach's articulation that "Paintings and sculptures are present in time and space and are the result of an artist's engagement with another time and space; they are material, formal interpretations."[11]

This idea resonates with creative work, like yours, that draws on archival sources and insists that the world of artistic creation is a reality as significant as other life experiences. Your book *In Captivity* works with "The Unicorn Tapestries" housed in the Cloisters, and *Articulated Lair: Poems for Louise Bourgeois* engages Bourgeois' sculptures, paintings, and drawings. Poems I've read from *Diamonds,* published in 2021, are in conversation with famous figures from literature and culture. The titular poem begins: "Judith Butler, I am calling you / here in the kitchen where I'm unloading the dishwasher / performing my gender as I'm wont to do" and goes on to address Michel Foucault, incorporating Shakespeare's Queen Gertrude and Ophelia as well as Rihanna and other pop culture references along the way.[12]

While these projects all draw on archival sources, you create a distinct range of textures and palettes for each project. I imagine for each project a mind-map that has a central constellation of objects (like "The Unicorn Tapestries") that branch out to related objects and textures (animals in captivity, for example). As such, the works transcend their central figures but don't range so far afield that they get lost or trail off. This focused expansiveness also allows you, like Louise Bourgeois, to take on typically "feminine" iconography (the unicorn, the dishwasher) in complex ways.

I'm very curious to hear your thoughts on oversaturated feminine imagery. What strategies allow an artist like Bourgeois—a poet like you—to reenergize the overly familiar?

CAMILLE GUTHRIE

I love oversaturated imagery and write about many examples of it in poems in my book *Diamonds*—from Sylvia Plath's prom dress to a painting of a Pict woman from the 16th century to Hieronymous Bosch's *Garden of Earthly Delights*. I love overlays (Lucy Lippard's term from *Overlay: Contemporary Art and the Art of Pre-History*); images or objects that are laden, and sometimes burdened, with significance; things that are overlapping, reintegrated, overinterpreted, misread, or encumbered with projection. When I read that the Smith College library holds Sylvia Plath's prom dress in their archives, I lost my mind with excitement. A colleague of mine, the playwright Sherry Kramer, teaches a course called "The Magical Object," and to me, that prom dress glowed with magic. It's one of my dreams to visit it in the library; I don't know why I haven't done it yet. I wrote a poem called "Magical Object" about wishing I could wear the dress during my divorce, when I felt powerless. I think many poets who come to poetry through Plath at a young age think of her as a witchy, ambitious, and iconic figure. Her life and her poems became surfaces for projection and fantasy, adoration and criticism—palimpsests for our interpretations. My poem was another attempt to touch the hems of her image.

Exchange Question

RACHEL BLAU DUPLESSIS

Given that the metaphor of an archive is so powerful in contemporary thinking, can you trace for yourself how you entered the zone of that metaphor, what influenced you in thinking about that metaphor; how you would define "archive" for yourself based on that metaphor; and how that definition figures in your work?

CAMILLE GUTHRIE

As I haven't used the word "archive" when thinking about my work, I can speak to how I research and respond to sources. My first experience using sources as a beginning to my own work occurred in my college thesis; I wrote into Nabokov's *Lolita*, which I adored, in a version of the voice of the character Lolita, which I felt at the time had been misread by many readers. A slant way into my admiration and exploration of that widely read and commented-upon text, as famous works always acquire an archive of conversation around them. Much later, in *Articulated Lair*, my poems for Louise Bourgeois were responses to her work and life—an imagined conversation in which I certainly described her work, yet what most compelled me more as a strategy was what poet and literary critic B. K. Fischer defines as a hallmark of feminist ekphrasis:

> Less oppositional than aggregative, feminist ekphrasis comprises acts of description and interrogation, improvisation and analysis, homage and backtalk. It frequently draws on all three critical motives I've mentioned: it destabilizes gendered hierarchies of value, engages in collaboration and aesthetic exchange, and adumbrates rich alternatives to conventional binaries.[13]

I love that she includes backtalk! Another new poem of mine takes a similar route—backtalking to Keats's traditional biographers, who often disparage Fanny Brawne. In my poem "My Boyfriend, John Keats," I take on a voice of rivalry for Keats's attention in order to examine how women compete for male attention and power; how girlfriends, wives, and daughters are overlooked in history; and how I found that I've been in more than one conversation with other women poets in which we stake claims to love Keats the most.

Lucy Ives

KARLA KELSEY

Each of the eleven books that you've published is utterly its own, unique entity that observes and reinvents relationship to genre. Each book sits squarely in its room of the archive while at the same time teasing out nuances and transcending boundaries until—voilà!—the floorplan has opened. For example *Loudermilk,* your novel set in an MFA program in Iowa, not only invites us into the trials and tribulations of your young aspiring-writer characters but also includes some of the poems and stretches of prose that they write. When I imagine you at work I imagine you sit before the entire Western (and some of the non-Western) archive of literature. As you write, you rearrange the walls and the furniture.

Added to this are your editorial projects, most recently *The Saddest Thing Is That I Have Had to Use Words: A Madeline Gins Reader*, which collects this extraordinary poet-artist-philosopher's transdisciplinary writing. You end the book's introductory essay with the following thought on the undervaluing of poetry, which has stayed with me for months: "Poetry may be writing, of course, but it is not necessarily that; it is also image, performance, gesture, song, social life, gossip, furniture, food, shelter, dance, research, email, garments. This is not to say that poetry has no determined or identifiable form, but that it suffers when it is confined to a stanza. It may well need all the room of a novel, if not the room of an actual room. Madeline Gins is the one who taught me that."[14]

How has working with Gins's archive shifted or solidified your sense of genre—shifted and solidified not only what might belong in what genre, but also the usefulness of the concept of genre for the creative practitioner?

LUCY IVES

Thank you for this question. I wrote in a recent review of a collection of writings by the artist Moyra Davey,

> . . . there is a certain "magic circle" drawn around the authors Davey prefers. "Magic circle" is a phrase that the critic Walter Benjamin applied to the act of creating a collection, and with it he implies at once the synthetic quality of collections and the collector's selectivity, according these a mildly occult valence via his chosen metaphor. The collector is a creator not just of piles of stuff, but of categories, genres. And with new genres come new aesthetic possibilities.[15]

In my opinion, genre is a way of speaking about conventions of reading and looking, where you sit or stand and whether you're allowed to talk to other people or move around while you're communing with an object or text. By combining different or new sorts of things into a given work, the author of that work is suggesting different affects and behaviors to the reader or viewer. Gins, for one, was very good at this sort of thing. I think that this is part of why it's taken us such a long time to really be able to "read" some of her unpublished work from the late 1960s and 1970s, because the habits and behaviors of mind and body suggested by her writing from this time are really more those of a more densely mediated, projective society (a society like our own), a society to come.

However, as much as I am able to observe what Gins does here, in this writing from her archive, and as much as I've learned that this sort of thing is possible (and I marvel at it!), I'm not sure I partake of the same logic in my own work. I am primarily interested in writing speculative texts that are expressly very difficult to write, because of the sorts of mimetic skills they require. I'm interested in teaching myself to imitate different genres of writing—that are not, strictly speaking, important or canonical. For example, for *Loudermilk*, I taught myself to write a style of poem that would have been written in an academic workshop setting in the US circa 2004. It's not exactly significant that I was alive at this time and also hanging around these contexts; I didn't want to write a poem that *I* would have written at this time, in this place. I wanted to write a poem ("the" poem) that would have been written by a young man in his early twenties, in this time and place. So I made some studies and sketches, and I developed a technique to write as this person, writing at this time. It's a projective exercise. In my novel *Impossible Views of the World*, I did the same for a minor novelist of the nineteenth century in the US, and I also created various other documents written by other people at other historical moments.

As stated, I'm interested in very challenging kinds of writing—kinds of writing that are not precisely personally expressive and which are deeply informed by research, theories of material culture, as well as theories of affect and psychology. I don't believe that I can or should attempt to counterfeit every kind of writing or every point of view; my choices are specific and have to do with a style of historical learning that interests me at a given point in time. A more recent example of this sort of work is a short story included in my collection *Cosmogony*, which is written in the style of a Wikipedia entry for the word "guy." It's a strange and synthetic point of view, the "objective" or algorithmic tone of these entries, mixed with the voice of a person who's struggling to compose this entry, along with themself.

Exchange Question

ASHLEY LAMB

The artist, writer, and illustrator Maira Kalman created an archive of her mother's all-white wardrobe and accessories after she passed, with the aid of Kalman's son, Alexander. The installation was called "Sara Berman's Closet" (https://www.metmuseum.org/exhibitions/list-ings/2017/sara-berman-closet) and was exhibited in the Met's period room, in conversation with other meticulously curated domestic spaces from the 1800s.

Think of someone who has had a profound influence on your own life, living or otherwise. This can be a person whom you have known in-timately, or a person whom you have been in relation to in some way but have perhaps never met. If you were to make an archive in their honor (or to shame them), what would it look like, and where would it be displayed? This question can be answered through language, by drawing, a song, etc.

LUCY IVES

I think that the best way I can answer this question (having been to Sara Berman's closet on several occasions!) is to point to my two recent novels, *Impossible Views of the World* and *Loudermilk: Or, The Real Poet; Or, The Origin of the World*, in which I am at pains to create archives of institutional experience—indeed, I am drawn to the use of the verb "shame" in this prompt. Part of the usefulness of speculative writing (if, indeed, it really needs to be useful) inheres in its ability to embody forms of experience that do not make it into traditional archives; in this sense, it's a bit like the installation in question here. Although I never set out to shock anyone, it has been interesting to me to see the ways in which readers have responded to my choice to "hand it to" (as a friend wrote to me) a large institution, a family member, and an academic program I may have attended, via these two fictions. Yet, what I believed (fallibly, to be sure!) I was doing in composing these books was talking about aspects of experience that it seemed to me no one cared much about. My main goal was simply to record these feelings and experiences for posterity.

Ashley Lamb

KARLA KELSEY

The ruffle of a dress, a tendril of hair, a torn image of embroidered fabric juxtaposed with monumental architecture and winter trees. Your visual collages explore the swift cut between interior and exterior, nature and culture, the abstract and the pictorial. They thrive on expression through detail, reminding me of Rachel Blau DuPlessis's articulation of the poetic detail as "the situated, the historical, the fact now and not at some other time, tonalities of the current, sedimented and incipient."[16]

Your use of domestic objects and complexity of form create a feminist practice of archival work. Your collages stand alone and also richly accompany texts, for example the images you created for books in Litmus Press's Leslie Scalapino Award for Innovative Women Performance Writers series. In tune with materials, you also manage the metal shop at the School of the Art Institute of Chicago and find time to co-teach woodworking classes for women, introducing them to under-recognized female artists like Lina Bo Bardi, Charlotte Perriand, Mira Nakashima, and the Shaker inventor and toolmaker Tabitha Babbitt.

Engaged with so many different materials—images and textures of collage, the grain of wood, structure of metal, traditions of crafting—I think of you as a walking archive of matter and technique. You remind me of the exciting decisions any artist has to make in terms of the raw, found nature of material and the object the material is slated to become. What is the value of leaving a material raw, obviously cut from another source? And what is the value of smoothing away edges? How do you—how does any artist—decide?

ASHLEY LAMB

Thank you for such a generous and thoughtful question and reflection upon my work as an artist and educator.

I have often been accused of staring. In the museum, on the train, in the grocery store . . . . I am trying to read the image, the person, the object, in order to gain a greater understanding.

I love when I look at an object and can comprehend how it was made. It is satisfying to know an object in such a way, it fosters a deeper bond or appreciation, I believe. This is particularly true for me when it comes to wood- or metalworking—appreciating the skill it takes to create a complex joint, for example, or beautiful welds. The *raw*.

I have tried my hand at many art forms, but I have always (it feels like) made collage. There are so many things to love about the process. There's always material, you don't need much to work with, and it's very mobile. Leaving such material largely unaltered, the viewer is able to guess at the life it once had, while examining it in this new relationship. When it comes to understanding how it was constructed, it's fairly straightforward. There's a humility to collage; it is the sum of its parts, which may include an old newspaper or a receipt from Target.

I like that the collages are somewhat self-possessed. I haven't taken away the material's thingness, rather I see my role as helping its voice come through in a different way. In my work, the raw found material is always in relation to what is not there. What remains of an image implicates the parts that have been cut away or hidden by another layer. So, life is like this, with parts we choose to show and parts we keep for ourselves, but they are nonetheless both there, always, in relation to each other.

How does anyone decide what to show? I think it's mostly instinctual. If I am making a collage in direct relation to a text, I try to capture the feeling of the text through visual imagery. This can be through color schemes, specific images, the way a line intersects with another. I know that it is "done" when it speaks to me in a similar tone that the text spoke to me.

My work has always, in my mind, had a relationship to writing. I love poetry in particular, which so often implies what it means to be a person, in and in relation to the world. I try to hint at those notions as well, through almost-figures and suggestions of partial scenes, sometimes titles that implicate them. In fact, many of the collages submitted for the viewing gallery were created as cover art for specific texts. Karla has asked me specifically about how I found a resonance between each text and image, but I feel I can only answer that question for myself. That is, perhaps it would be more interesting to hear if and how the collages feel in relation to the texts from their original authors. I hope that they can identify something of their own work there, that it speaks in a voice harmonious with theirs.

As far as my process goes, I usually read halfway through a text before I start making something in response so that it's fresh and I understand the consistent tone. I highlight (literally) specific visual imagery that stands out to me as central to the text in some way as I am reading. When I revisit the manuscript, I reread it through the specific visual elements that I've pulled out, and then try to craft something that accentuates them. Sometimes the details are very literal, but often they become abstracted through interpretation. It also depends on the materials I have at hand, and how they fit (also literally) into the bigger picture. If I am creating something for an unpublished work, as most of these were, I almost always offer the author/editor several options, and give them permission to crop the work if perhaps only a certain part really speaks to them. A text and its cover can often become associated in one's mind, and I would never want an author to publish a work of mine unless they really felt they belonged together. I think both poetry and visual art can transport us to someplace that is both otherworldly and deeply internal, the way that spiritual experiences can also be.

Exchange Question

MARY-KIM ARNOLD

In writing about her work in 18th-century French judicial archives, historian Arlette Farge observes, "One cannot overstate how slow work in the archives is, and how this slowness of hands and thought can be the source of creativity."

Has there been a time in your own work where "the slowness of hands" or the body's response to this slowness has provided unexpected insight or inspiration?

Farge goes on to say that because of the "inescapable" labor, "your patience will inevitably be tested."[17]

As an alternative to the above question, has there been a time when laboriousness, tedium, or frustration with archival research has sent you into a different direction from where you began?

ASHLEY LAMB

I'm sure we're all thinking about slowness right now, those of us who can afford to, and the way our once hectic lives have been contained within the domestic spaces we find ourselves within. I know I have benefited from the opportunity to use some of this hush to take stock, reconnect with friends and neighbors, with my own needs and wants, the good and the bad.

I've always been a slow maker, despite a desire to be another way. I am drawn to process-oriented work, which necessitates a clear order of operations. Metal and woodworking, printmaking, even collage—there is a very specific place you must begin most of the time if you want to arrive at your imagined end. I think there's pleasure in each phase, and that the different steps help break up the monotony of the collective time a work may take to complete. Moving this way through something, be it an art object, a piece of furniture, an archive, whatever, allows you to get into the "flow," as it is often described. The flow is for me a kind of spiritual experience, something I chase after. If I don't feel it, then the work can begin to feel like a chore, a labor. Those projects often get cast aside into an ever-growing pile of unfinished beginnings.

Slow work is flow work. To be fully present with an eye toward neither the past nor the future is such a wonderful feeling to have pass through you, and part of its pleasure may well be its fleetingness.

I enjoy the slow work of repetition, making an embroidery for example. This to me feels like going on a long walk you've been on many times before. You notice new things each time, but because you know your way you don't have to focus so much on the immediate world around you, and can drift into your own thoughts while still engaging in the work at hand. When something begins to become familiar to you, even the motion of laying a stitch down can be satisfying, much like the act of walking itself.

But I have perhaps not answered the question. I think what I'm getting at is that almost always when I have the opportunity to engage in work that is slow going, I find it soothing, and if I'm lucky, inspirational. Especially in the present day when our attention spans have been lessened by digital technology and our fast-paced world feels like it's only always getting faster, engaging in slow work allows me to once again hear my own thoughts more clearly. For me, it's the difference between reacting and being really intentional about what you have to say.

Poupeh Missaghi

KARLA KELSEY

One of the many richnesses of your work is the way in which narratives, images, and concepts shift and deepen. This happens, for example, in the very title of your novel, *trans(re)lating house one*. With "trans(re)lating" you offer us "translating," "relating" and "retranslating" as simultaneous parts of a larger process. This is mirrored by the structure of the book. The right-justified pages, written in the third person, are cinematic and relate the journey of a young woman through Tehran as she looks for missing statues in the aftermath of Iran's 2009 elections. Left-justified pages are first-person meditations on this woman's quest, affirming and questioning the act of writing within and about trauma. Laced throughout are "corpse" sections, which provide statistics of individual deaths of those associated with the 2009 protests.

In an interview with Yanara Friedland in *World Literature Today* you eloquently propose that "personal events and questions from the past live inside you and haunt you, in both positive and negative ways, until you can find documents of them, hear stories about them, speak about them, analyze them in different contexts, archive them. It is only when they are materialized that they leave you, opening space for new things to come reside in you. I feel a similar thing exists on a collective and national level, and thus the obsession with the past."[18] These thoughts resonate with the experience of reading *trans(re)lating house one*, and also speak to the work you do as translator both into and out of Persian and as Iran's editor-at-large for the literature in translation journal *Asymptote*.

Your novel is generous and challenging as it draws out difficult questions surrounding art-making, trauma, and the many mediated forms of witness available in the twenty-first century. It is also rhythmic, imaginative, and cinematic—I couldn't put it down. Do you align one of these poles—the intellectually challenging vs. the aesthetically absorptive—to different aspects of archival work? What role does the creative mind play in cultural memory?

POUPEH MISSAGHI

Karla, thank you for your readership and for such beautiful wording of my work.

As to your first question, I want to resist separating different aspects of archival work from one another and allocating them to one pole or another; at least not in the creative realm that I practice in. For me, an exploration of the archive demands a simultaneous coexistence of the intellectually challenging and the aesthetically absorptive. It's their togetherness that sheds new light on the material of the archive and invites a more active open engagement with it, both by me and the audience.

This ties to the role of creativity in archival work and cultural memory. To move beyond mere consumption of the archive and the past, I believe the creative mind needs to play a key role in our approach, both for the writer/artist who dives into the archive to produce her work and for the reader/audience of that archive-based work. It is the creative mind that allows us to listen to the possibilities of the archive and to become participants in the making and shaping of cultural memories, rather than simply receiving them ready-made. It offers ways to connect these memories from the past to the present, understand what we are in the midst of, and be enabled to imagine new possibilities for our future beyond the realities saved in the archives and carried within us through these cultural memories.

Aren't we all the collectives before and around and after us called forth into this one body that defines itself as "I" in this particular temporal and spatial vortex? Is there any way to extract the collective from the individual, the individual from the collective? Such a circular labyrinth, this "individual collectivities" you speak of. Let's pause for a second and meet; if not here, there.

Exchange Question

CAMILLE GUTHRIE

How does your writing and its relationship with the archive connect with your activism or your work on social justice?

POUPEH MISSAGHI

In most of my writing projects, particularly the longer ones, I find myself drawn to archival work and this oftentimes ties to some form of activism. I'm interested not only in exposing injustices but also in thinking through the process of exposing them on the page.

In *trans(re)lating house one*, my aim was to be witness to the unjust killing of my people by the Iranian government following the 2009 presidential election fraud while also contemplating what it means to be a writer/translator/witness.

In my current writing projects, some of the archival work I'm doing centers around topics such as embezzlement and socioeconomic disparities in Iran as well as methods of interrogation and torture throughout the past few decades. I am heavily invested in finding new creative modes that would invite a more participatory engagement with these issues, through which we could go beyond revisiting particular incidents and rethink the complex sociopolitical—personal, collective, domestic, and global—webs around them. I believe such an approach can potentially create more fertile ground for ongoing expansive involvement in the multifaceted social justice practices we all need to be part of, both as writers and citizens.

Lisa Pearson

KARLA KELSEY

You founded Siglio Press in 2008 and have gone on to publish over thirty volumes of image-text works that want equally to be looked at and read, defying genre categories and throwing into question what it is to engage literary and visual art. In describing Siglio's list I want instead to press your books into readers' hands because the objects you create far transcend any description—which may well be an essential component of feminist making. Siglio's website articulates this border crossing as mission: "Siglio is a small, fiercely independent press driven by its feminist ethos and its commitment to writers and artists who obey no boundaries, pay no fealty to trends and invite readers to see the world anew by reading word and image in provocative, unfamiliar ways."[19]

This refusal to obey boundaries includes those between the archival and the immediate, between public reservoir and private collection. For example, Anouck Durand's *Eternal Friendship* collages together photographic archives, personal letters, and propaganda magazines to tell a story of friendship and history that crosses from Albania to China and into Israel during the Second World War, the Cold War, and the end of Communism. Bernadette Mayer's *Memory,* which you just published this May, brings into book form Mayer's 1971 month-long documentary project of over 110 photographs, two hundred pages of text, and six hours of audio recording.

With books like *Memory* and Nancy Spero's *Torture of Women* you move work that exists in other forms (the archive, the gallery) into book form. How does your sense of the material you are working with shift as you carry it into a new vehicle? How does the book form inform the impact the material has on the viewer-reader?

LISA PEARSON

Particularly with these two books, but often with many other Siglio titles, I see the work I do as publisher, editor, and designer as the work of a translator. But rather than translating from one language to another, it's from one form to another. As this different species of translator, I need to understand the original work as deeply as possible, confront what will be lost or sacrificed, locate equivalences (or approximations), and stake out what might be gained.

With *Memory* and *Torture of Women* in particular, the challenge was to take works of art that have great spatial and public presences and find new forms for them in the very private space of reader and book. Both works are monumental installation works (Spero's comprises fourteen panels that each measure about nine feet across, and Mayer's thirty-six-foot installation of 1,110+ photographs also included a six-hour audio recording). A book obviously cannot replicate the experience of being in the gallery or museum and seeing all of the work at once (not only by standing back, but also by looking closely while being aware of what's in your peripheral vision) or the experience of seeing and listening as with *Memory*'s audio component. But "the book" gives the reader *time*. Not only can the reader spend as much time as she likes on a single page, but she controls the pace of moving through the book and its direction. With a book, the reader can also return to it, read it again and again, in different ways. This creates a different kind of, and I'd argue a deeper, legibility as the reader has another means to experience and contemplate works like these that particularly need time. And, in both of these cases, these are works with which people have not had much time. *Torture of Women* rarely travels from the National Gallery of Canada (and when I saw it installed at "WACK! Art and the Feminist Revolution" at MOCA LA years ago, the panels were stacked from floor to ceiling, rendering most of it infuriatingly illegible, particularly for a *feminist* exhibition). *Memory* was not seen in its entirety for more than forty years after its initial installation in 1972, and then for a short time in Chicago at The Poetry Foundation in 2016 and at CANADA Gallery in NYC in 2017. Time—and thus visibility and legibility—is the gain when space is lost.

With all Siglio books, the "book" is not a transparent delivery device (or a glossy coffee table statement that calls attention to itself) but a form that can very deliberately and specifically shape the experience of the reader—which, I believe, has an extraordinary potential for intimacy.

As it happens (because both have deeply feminist intentions), *Memory* and *Torture of Women* use monumentality to stake a claim to a larger space while subverting that monumentality with a certain demand for intimacy. *Torture of Women* is 125 feet long in total, but the paper is fragile and wrinkled; there are seams, raw edges. Spero creates almost private spaces for the first-person testimony of the torture of victims by collaging smaller pages with typewritten text onto larger pages. She leaves vast fields of space empty for the silences, for the pain that can't be described. The book makes sure those seams are revealed, that the empty spaces are honored. It repeats and changes the crop of an image to see it differently or in relation to something else, to read it more closely—or to ask the reader to read it again.

With *Memory*, the experience of walking the thirty-six feet down the gallery wall to "read" the first line of photos in sequence, and then returning to the other side (a bit like the motion of a typewriter carriage return) to read the second line all the way across, and so on, could not be replicated or even hinted at (an accordion-fold edition would have been unwieldy and too expensive). The audio (while it's available online to listen to while you're reading, if you like) is also impossible to include in the book. But the text (100,000 words) is Mayer's voice, and it is "the sequence" that governs this work (as an actual experiment in time). So instead, the text and images flow opposite each other on most spreads, sometimes aligning, sometimes diverging, but both strictly chronological. The page turns: time passes. And the images, in grids of nine, have chance-determined compositional relationships, just as the larger installation did. The original photographs in *Memory* were snapshots made from slides, many overexposed or underdeveloped. In the case of making the book, it presented an opportunity to pull detail through intense color correction (which Mayer was pleased to have happen), to render legible what might have been obscured in the original: memories extracted from the shadows, as it were.

I should also say too that my work as editor and designer are deeply intertwined, and both depend greatly on collaboration. I was able to work with Spero on this book in the two years before she died, and I feel very fortunate to have been able to work with Mayer, who lives just forty-five minutes from me, so (at least pre-Covid) I could pop over, we could look and discuss, and I'd always get to have tea and maybe a meal with her. First and foremost is the intention to honor the integrity of the work, which means listening, reading closely, paying attention on multiple levels. In most cases, the artist-writers I've worked with, or their estates, understand "the book" offers possibilities that the exhibition space does not, and that there are ways to work beyond "literal" translation. It's perhaps the most gratifying aspect of what I do.

Exchange Question

CHET'LA SEBREE

This August marks the 100th anniversary of the ratification of the Nineteenth Amendment—recognized by many as a key success of the women's suffrage movement. I am often reminded, however, of what Frances Ellen Watkins Harper stated at the 1866 National Women's Rights Convention: "You white women speak here of rights. I speak of wrongs," underscoring racial inequality.

The reality is that the ratification of the amendment only ensured the vote for a specific subset of white women. Women of color—despite their contributions to the suffrage movement, including marching separately for the same cause while leaders like Alice Paul thought it important not to alienate racist, white Southern suffrage supporters—continued to be disenfranchised.

Although we go into the archive with a commitment to discovery, sometimes we are confronted with complex realities. In your archival practice, how do you grapple with this? How do you grapple with "wrongs" in an archive you seek or develop as an act of celebration, commemoration? How do you engage with intersectionality and/or your own positionality as you engage with the violent histories?

LISA PEARSON

My archival practice has been limited to looking at the works and personal histories of individual artists and writers, so whatever might be problematic is generally very personal in nature. This raises other sets of questions about how to grapple with the questions that surround the systemic wrongs that you refer to. In working with personal histories of individuals, I intend to amass as deep a knowledge of the author's work and life as possible. And much of the knowledge I gain is never transmitted directly to the reader; rather, it might inform decisions I make as an editor and a publisher, it might infiltrate an essay (or press release) that I write, or it might not. My credo—as publisher, editor, and designer—is to let the work speak for itself and to allow the reader to engage that work as directly as possible. And yes, the resulting book is a celebration, but not hagiography.

Many of the artist-writers I publish work very much in the domain of the oblique, the ambiguous, the contradictory, so the reader is challenged to navigate in whatever ways she knows how and, hopefully, will discover in the course of reading a book that invites very different modes of reading. I prefer afterwords to forewords—or sometimes no accompanying essays at all—so that nothing impedes that discovery, and if anything, invites multiple interpretations/readings. I see the works Siglio publishes as round and deep, and I am thrilled when a reader or critic gets a 360-degree view (or a takes a very deep dive), which inevitably means seeing flaws and weaknesses. In fact, I'm particularly excited when a reader/critic finds her way in-between the lines. In other words, what might be complex, messy, or even "wrong," is allowed to surface, to be revealed, and the reader/critic is offered the opportunity to wrestle with it.

Chet'la Sebree

KARLA KELSEY

By creating a cross-generational conversation with Sally Hemings you open up the portal of time, allowing readers to experience a space where past and present converge. In taking on the persona poem you also open yourself to convergence, which allows us not only to see the psychic and physical landscape inhabited by Hemings, but in many ways to taste, touch, and feel this space as it acts on the individual body. For example, "Extraordinary Privilege, August 1792" begins: "I smashed his favorite pale blue pinwheel pearlware— / a gift—a soup tureen for whomever I am serving / a pound of meat, peck of cornmeal."[20] This language absorbs me in the material world of object and action as well as the complexity of Hemings and Jefferson's relationship: the agency of giving and smashing. The complication of a gift that can only be used in the act of service.

As I was thinking about your use of the persona poem I was also thinking about something Poupeh Missaghi has written about the process of writing about Tehran, the city of her birth and a place she knows well but in which she no longer lives. Poupeh writes: "I think the process of writing the book, engaging with the city on so many different levels—intellectual and emotional, conscious and unconscious, on an axis of past-present-future—as well as contemplating the after-writing impacts of it, has resulted in the city being ingrained in me in ways I never expected."[21]

In the course of writing *Mistress,* you spent six years researching the life of Sally Hemings. Has this experience mapped Hemings into your life in ways you didn't expect, and do you have advice for writers who find themselves embarking on creative archival research?

CHET'LA SEBREE:

When I first started writing about Sally Hemings, I was twenty-two. I started writing about her as a response to a prompt in a creative writing workshop on formal poetry. I was instructed to write a sonnet from the perspective of a historical figure. I combed my memory for what might interest me and Hemings came to mind. I'd read Ann Rinaldi's *Wolf by the Ears* in fourth grade—a historical fiction about Sally Hemings's daughter Harriet.[22] The gleeful, research nerd in me immediately went in search of more information—realizing I knew no more than whatever sanitized version of history a novel assigned for a ten-year-old would present—only to realize what should have already been apparent. There were no records by Hemings—a woman enslaved in the late 18th and early 19th centuries. Something about this gap, this secret, this silence (or silencing) drew me in. I was and always have been interested in investigating silence and secrecy as a writer—invested in being present in the gaps.

After graduate school and before it was clear that I was embarking on a project about Hemings, I wrote proposals for a poetry project in which I gave "voice to voicelessness and voiceless experiences"—a direct quote. I wanted to write about love and loss and women's bodies, but I couldn't shake Hemings. From 2011 to 2014, my fascination with her only grew as I better understood the complexities to her story: that she and Jefferson's wife were half-sisters; that she accompanied Jefferson's daughter Maria to Paris—where Hemings became Jefferson's "concubine,"[23] according to her son Madison Hemings—at the behest of Maria's aunt, as the enslaved woman Jefferson selected to make the journey couldn't because she was pregnant; that she struck a deal with Jefferson to return to the United States on the condition that he would free her children. The more I learned the more I felt she'd been robbed by history, that history had rendered her solely a voiceless victim. Within the confines of slavery, she managed this sliver of agency that would impact her family for generations. And the more I learned, the more I tried, largely unsuccessfully, to write about her.

The reality of the project, however, came into full view when I received a fellowship from the Robert H. Smith International Center for Jefferson Studies. In one of the first creative projects funded by ICJS, I was invited to conduct research for a month at Monticello, Jefferson's plantation and home to his presidential library. Even though I'd written a proposal that said I would work with *Getting Word*—an oral history archive started by Lucia Stanton and Dianne Swann-Wright to record the histories of descendants of families enslaved at Monticello—I still didn't know what I was writing about Hemings or why. I'd been writing about Hemings for five years at that point and none of the poems were working. They all felt forced or as though, through them, I was merely trying to offer a history lesson.

I arrived at Monticello in August 2016 with few successful poems in hand and then was faced with the weight of research and writing about her on Thomas Jefferson's land. It was more emotional than I could have imagined. It felt like a haunting—walking the grounds where she walked, being paid to live on land on which so many with similar ancestry to me had been enslaved. Amid the haunting, I felt the gravity of what I was proposing—to render this realm a little more real for my contemporaries.

So, I read books on Paris and papers from Jefferson's retirement series. I took tours of the house at different times of day to catch the differences of light refracting. I asked for selections from special collections and artifacts from archaeology. I tried on a replica of an eighteenth-century corset in the University of Virginia's Department of Drama costume shop and felt the tight press of boning against my ribcage. I wrote in Jefferson's bedroom in the morning before tour days, listening to the clock's methodical ticking. And the poems still weren't coming. My journal was littered with fragments—descriptions of stoneware, the feel of the pressure shifts on the mountain, the scratch of raw fabric. It wasn't amounting to anything, or at least not anything I could see clearly.

About halfway through the fellowship, I was asked to have a recorded conversation about the project for ICJS. In preparation for the conversation, the ICJS community engagement officer—a descendant of those enslaved at Monticello—asked what everyone kept asking: *why Sally?* It was a fair question. It was one I had been asked over those first five years of the project. I yammered on about my investment in voicelessness. A trained journalist, though, she kept asking.

When I taught first-year composition, I encouraged my students to see research as an act of discovery, to go into a project with questions as opposed to expectations. It gave me great anxiety to have spent five years researching and writing without a clue of what I was doing. But in that conversation, I found my answer. After her prodding, I eventually blurted something to the effect of "maybe if I can save her, I can save me," and my voice cracked. The emotions I'd been trying to stuff down those first few weeks swelled to the surface. There it was. I saw something of myself in Hemings. Separated by time and the unparalleled inhumanity of slavery, our existences as young women were suddenly linked—the way our worlds talked about us and our bodies, the way the world never wanted us to succeed. Even more frightening, in her I saw one version of a future.

Hemings made a difficult decision to return to the United States, to remain enslaved to ensure the freedom of her children. What complicated decisions would I have to make? How would the color of my skin be a factor in them? In this way, Hemings was more than mapped on me, she brought into focus the realities of what I was grappling with in my twenties. How would I, one day, be forced to protect my future children? What would I be forced to give up to do it? What decisions would I make about my body in the face of uncertainty, in the face of violence? Most of the persona poems in Sally Hemings's voice that made it into the collection were written after that conversation, which led to a pivotal poem in the collection where Hemings speaks directly to the contemporary speaker who bares my name: "Chet'la, I cannot save you. You must."[24] A simple lesson. Perhaps an obvious one, but one that feels rooted in me now.

It is important to go into the archive as an act of discovery, to see how the research presents itself. Trust that there will be something if you keep an open mind, even if it's not what you're expecting. But I also encourage a good self-care practice. Usually, whatever with which we find ourselves obsessed, whatever leads us to the archives in the first place, is something already gnawing at us, something already mapped on our existence although we may not understand how or why. For me, it was exhausting to explore this history, to be on this "axis of past-present-future" as Poupeh Missaghi put it, to allow this archive to occupy my mind and spirit. I think part of what took me six years to research this book and really eight years in total from initial poem to publication, was finding the time and space to wrestle with the gravity of it all, to understand what I was seeking from the archive, to accept that what I was seeking it could not give, and to make my peace with that. As you enter the archive, for so many reasons, tread lightly.

Exchange Question

AMY E. ELKINS

In *Living a Feminist Life*, Sara Ahmed describes how books become "spaces of encounter; how we are touched by things; how we touch things. I think of feminism as a fragile archive, a body assembled from shattering, from splattering, an archive whose fragility gives us a responsibility: to take care." She proposes a survival kit—"To live a feminist life is to live in very good company. . . . I encourage you as a feminist reader to assemble your own kit. What would you include?"[25] What are the texts—broadly defined—in your feminist survival kit? What do you include in the archive of inspiration, strength, care, etc., on which you draw?

CHET'LA SEBREE

My feminist survival kit would include:

- Alison Saar's *Coup* (2006)

- "There Is No Hierarchy of Oppression" by Audre Lorde

- "White Privilege: Unpacking the Invisible Knapsack" by Peggy McIntosh

- *The Bluest Eye* by Toni Morrison

- *Wide Sargasso Sea* by Jean Rhys

- "Everyday Use" by Alice Walker

- My great-grandmother's gold locket

- A photo of my niece and nephew

I first encountered Alison Saar's work in July 2016 when she gave an artist talk at Vermont Studio Center—an artist residency. *Coup* (2006)[26] isn't the work that necessarily caught my attention most then, but it is one that stays with me. In the sculpture, a seated woman is tethered to more than a dozen suitcases by a long braid. In her hands, she holds a pair of scissors. There is power in her, a will to change. For me, it is an acknowledgment both of the struggles of Black women as well as our power and agency. I mourn for the "baggage bound to us by our braids,"[27] while also feeling empowered by her scissor-wielding hands—poised to sever herself from this burden.

I feel a similar mix of emotions when I turn to the work of Audre Lorde. She starts her "There Is No Hierarchy of Oppression" essay, "I was born black, and a woman." I read the essay for the first time in college, a decade before I ever saw *Coup*. In it, Lorde asserts, "I simply do not believe that one aspect of myself can possibly profit from the oppression of any other part of my identity," and "I cannot afford the luxury of fighting one form of oppression only."[28] At eighteen, it was the first time I read something that really acknowledged in plain language the complexities of Black womanhood. Lorde's work would begin a larger journey for me, which would eventually lead me to Kimberlé Crenshaw's work on intersectionality. Honestly, almost anything Lorde-related would go into my survival kit: "Poetry Is Not a Luxury," "Uses of the Erotic," "The Master's Tools Will Never Dismantle the Master's House."[29] I draw from her work both inspiration and care; her words balm wounds I knew were there but to which I hadn't attended—a deep cut where you can see the spliced skin before blood and pain present themselves.

In the way I feel seen by Lorde, I keep Peggy McIntosh's "White Privilege: Unpacking the Invisible Knapsack" close by to pass like a pamphlet in spaces where white people have not acknowledged their white privilege in any genuine way. McIntosh writes that she "was taught to see racism only in individual acts of meanness, not in invisible systems conferring dominance on my group."[30] Often, the people with whom I engage who need to read it are people who consider themselves progressive and open-minded, but have never considered that the "flesh" color of Band-Aids are a manifestation of said systemic racism and white privilege—that we live in a society that normalizes whiteness and others my Blackness. Having this in my kit is both a way of taking care of myself, like protective equipment, and a way of educating, which has always been important to me.

As a child, one of my favorite make-believe scenarios was the classroom. I was the teacher and my stuffed animals were the students, so naturally my survival kit includes the convocation speech Adrienne Rich delivered in 1977 at Douglass College, "Claiming an Education." The essay taught me not to be a passive recipient of information but to be active in my own critical consciousness, to "demand to be taken seriously," to seek criticism, and to do the "*hard work*."[31] As an avid reader and intellectual, I still follow this guidance. For instance, I thought critically about whether or not to include Carol Hanisch's "The Personal Is Political" in my kit. I couldn't get past the politics of *whose* stories were allowed to be politicized—Rosa Parks over Claudette Colvin—but that's a conversation worthy of its own essay. Rich's speech, however, not only implores me as a seeker of knowledge but as an educator; it requires of me "a pledge of mutual seriousness about women, about language, ideas, methods, and values."[32]

The other books and stories in my survival kit are less manifestos by which I try to live and more narratives that spoke to me. Toni Morrison's *The Bluest Eye* presents the complexities of Black girlhood and the challenges of coming up in a world that didn't, and at times refused to, see me. I'd include Jean Rhys's *Wide Sargasso Sea* for the bold way it pushes against the established and celebrated narrative of Charlotte Brontë's *Jane Eyre* and Victorian conceptions of the "madwoman"; from Rhys I've learned to retell narratives as an act of resistance, to remember that there are so many versions of one story. Perhaps she, in part, led me to Hemings. "Everyday Use" by Alice Walker also falls into this category. I read the short story with my mother when I was a teenager. Every time I think of it, I am reminded that my mom encouraged me to be a voracious reader. The story also brings me to the penultimate item in my survival kit, which is an heirloom from my great-grandmother: a gold, four-picture locket.

I feel very lucky to have known three great-grandmothers and one great-grandfather during my lifetime. My great-grandmother Ruth (my mother's mother's mother) died when I was fourteen. When I was in my twenties, my grandmother gave me Ruth's gold locket. Apparently, my great-grandmother left it to me when she passed away, but I was an irresponsible teenager, as many of us were, so my grandmother waited to give it to me until after I graduated from college. In this way, in my survival kit, I bring with me my ancestors. My great-grandmother was a governess for a white family in the 1960s. Grandmom Ruth, as I called her, cooked the white family's meals, managed the children's nannies, and maintained the house. A couple of generations later, I am a college professor. I am who I am in the world so that I can honor the matrilineal sacrifices that these women—my great-grandmother, my grandmother, my mother—made so I could be where I am. I carry my Grandmom Ruth with me to conferences, to readings, to my classrooms. I wear her around my neck in this locket. I, like Mama in "Everyday Use," see the value of carrying my ancestors along with me, in my heritage being transparent in my journey.[33] They give me strength.

And just as they give me strength, my niece (age four) and nephew (age nine) give me purpose, which is why I would include a photo of them. They remind me, when I'm exhausted, devastated, seemingly defeated, that my intersectional feminist practice is for them, so that they can hopefully live one day in a whole where my niece will survive a routine traffic stop and my nephew can go for a run.

---

1   Susan Howe, *Spontaneous Particulars: The Telepathy of Archives* (New York: Christine Burgin and New Directions, 2014), 18.

2   M. NourbeSe Philip and Setaey Adamu Boateng, *Zong!* (Middletown, CT: Wesleyan University Press, 2008), 191.

3   Patricia Saunders, "Defending the Dead, Confronting the Archive: A Conversation with M. NourbeSe Philip," *Small Axe* 12:2 (June 2008): 63-79. Accessed 27 March 2020.

4   Gayle S. Rubin, *Deviations: A Gayle Rubin Reader* (Durham, NC: Duke University Press, 2011), 363.

5   Ibid., 370.

6   C. A. Conrad, "A Visionary Practice of Cultural Critique: Interviewing Rachel Blau DuPlessis," Philly Sound, http://phillysound.blogspot.com/2008_03_01_archive.html.

7   Rachel Blau DuPlessis, "Statement on Poetics," in *Inciting Poetics: Thinking and Writing Poetry*, ed. Jeanne Heuving and Tyrone Williams (Albuquerque: University of New Mexico Press, 2019), 13–37, 23.

8   Virginia Woolf, *A Room of One's Own* (London: Hogarth Press, 1935), 127.

9   Danielle Dutton, *SPRAWL* (Seattle: Wave Books, 2018), 3.

10 Amy Elkins, "From the Gutter to the Gallery: Bernice Abbott Photographs Mina Loy's Assemblages," *PMLA* 134, no. 5 (October 2019): 1094–1103.

11 Camille Guthrie and Ann Lauterbach, "The Poem is a Human Artifact," *Boston Review*, April 2010, http://bostonreview.net/poetry/camille-guthrie-ann-lauterbach-poem-human-artifact.

12 Camille Guthrie, "Diamonds," *Boston Review*, April 2018, http://bostonreview.net/poetry/camille-guthrie-diamonds.

13 Link to Fischer's article: https://lareviewofbooks.org/article/feminist-ekphrasis-example-louise-bourgeois/.

14 Madeline Gins and Lucy Ives, *The Saddest Thing Is That I Have Had to Use Words* (Catskill, NY: Siglio Press, 2020), 37.

15 "Moyra Davey Captures the Photographic Impulse of Writing," http://www.lucy-ives.com/arts-writing/on-moyra-davey.

16 DuPlessis, "Statement on Poetics."

17 Arlette Farge, *The Allure of the Archives*, trans. Thomas Scott-Railton (New Haven, CT: Yale University Press, 2013), 55–56.

18 Yanara Friedland and Poupeh Missaghi, "Mapping Tehran: A Conversation with Poupeh Missaghi," *World Literature Today*, February 2020, https://www.worldliteraturetoday.org/blog/interviews/mapping-tehran-conversation-poupeh-missaghi-yanara-friedland.

19 Siglio Press (2020), http://sigliopress.com/.

20 Chet'la Sebree, *Mistress* (Kalamazoo, MI: New Issues Poetry and Prose, 2019).

21 Friedland and Missaghi, "Mapping Tehran."

22 Ann Rinaldi, *Wolf by the Ears* (New York: Scholastic Paperbacks, 1993).

23 Madison Hemings (transcribed by S. F. Wetmore), "Life Among the Lowly, No. 1," *Pike County* (Ohio) *Republican*, March 13, 1873.

24 Sebree, *Mistress*, 69.

25 Sara Ahmed, *Living a Feminist Life* (Durham, NC: Duke University Press, 2017), 17.

26 Alison Saar, *Coup*, 2006 / wood, wire, tin, & found objects / Overall: 52 x 168 x 52 in. (132.1 x 426.7 x 132.1 cm).

27 Sebree, *Mistress*, 30.

28 Audre Lorde, "There Is No Hierarchy of Oppression," in *I Am Your Sister: Collected and Unpublished Writings of Audre Lorde*, ed. Rudolph P. Byrd, Johnetta Betsche Cole, and Beverly Guy-Sheftall (New York and Oxford: Oxford University Press, 2009), 219–20.

29 Audre Lorde, *The Master's Tools Will Never Dismantle the Master's House* (New York: Penguin Modern, 2018).

30 Peggy McIntosh, "White Privilege: Unpacking the Invisible Knapsack," *Peace and Freedom* (July/August 1989).

31 Adrienne Rich, "Claiming an Education" (convocation speech, Douglass College, New Brunswick, NJ, June 2, 1977).

32 Ibid.

33 Alice Walker, "Everyday Use," *Harper's Magazine* (April 1973).

PROSE

Kate Bolton Bonnici

On Emily Dickinson's *Gorgeous Nothings*: Responses in Miniature

—for Maureen Rose Murphy, 1951–2016

1. Poems and Toys, Poem as Toy: A Photograph

2. Poems and Toys, Poem as Toy: An Essay

On Christmas morning 2015, I took the photograph above of the first poem in *The Gorgeous Nothings*, an art book of facsimiles from Emily Dickinson's envelope writings.[1] My body sits outside the frame but is part of composition: I hold the book open to the manuscript facsimile, the first line of which reads, "A great Hope":

A great Hope	The mind was
fell	built for
You heard no	mighty Freight
noise	For dread
crash	
The Ruin was	occasion planned
havoc	
within damage	How often
Oh cunning	foundering
Wreck	at Sea
That told no	Ostensibly, on
Tale	Land
And let no	
Witness in	

The facsimile envelope (doubly photographed) upon which the line is written echoes in photographic silence the tan of the kitchen table and chairs, the white space around the facsimile the same as the white coffee mug and sweatered arm across the table and the disheveled stack of papers and glare of light from the kitchen window facing the garden. For all its silence, it is a photograph dense with text—Lego instructions, yogurt container, coffee mug, sports schedule (such records of recurrent desire)—and layered with toys—plastic bricks meant to be assembled as an ice cream shop and four dolls foregrounded on their backs in various periods of dress. Miniaturized forms philosopher Giorgio Agamben would call "the cipher[s] of history."[2]

My husband and children gave me the book when we were celebrating my mother-in-law's last Christmas. Already she could not speak. She died of complications from ALS the week before the following Easter, preparations for her funeral rushed because no extra masses could be said during Holy Week.

In R. W. Franklin's reading edition, *The Poems of Emily Dickinson*, "A great Hope fell" is regularized as No. 1187.[3] On the printed page it falls neatly into two stanzas:

A great Hope fell
You heard no noise
The Ruin was within
Oh cunning Wreck
That told no Tale
And let no Witness in

The mind was built for mighty Freight
For dread occasion planned
How often foundering at sea
Ostensibly, on Land

There is no impediment to the smoothness of the line—indeed, not even punctuation pauses one until the last—all breath managed at the level of phrase, which is mostly equivalent and equidistant to the level of the line.

Although I had the reading edition, I read this particular poem first in envelope form contained in a book received in the home of a woman who struggled to breathe. Franklin's clean version is not land, not sea, but the black surface of well water; the envelope is a conversation or conversion or the converse. The envelope at the morning, not yet mourning, table is the "havoc" drowned in the printed form.

I understand, of course, the constraining expectations of real or assumed meter. I understand, of course, the impulse to resolution as intention or as the breakdown of matter. I understand misunderstanding resolution for salvation.

Omitted: crash, havoc, damage.

Revised: the line.

No longer: "The mind was"—a line that breaks itself open as it breaks the reading heart. "The mind was"—former being and we leap the ditch, as Mary Oliver explains, to "built for." "Built for" as a contained—or if not contained at least reckoned—line maintains the possibility of questioning.

Skip a line and "built for" becomes the inverse of "for dread—or "for dread" makes an equally plausible answer to the question of the mind's construction, the dead dark of "mighty Freight."

Can hope as an act of desire recur—wave-like, oceanic—once fallen? Can the poem as book brought to the table not be a document or a replicated antique, but a toy through which we, remade in the early light of Christmas morning, gather to play with history?[4] That is to say, can it hide? Can it pretend?

3. Ars Moriendi[5]

What is the meaning of a good death and does it count if near the time of such dread occasion you ask to go to the hospital? What if you cannot say hospital and must write the word and is the word alone enough or must it be accompanied by a noiseless grammatical plea? Or what if the hand muscles lie down together like old laces, and you must gesture or press the button on the voice machine to prompt another wording of place and all this only means the answer must be no because the hospital is where you go to live and it's too late for that. Here, the answer becomes more morphine. The hospice nurse says give more to keep you from thinking you are choking or drowning, which makes you need to lean against someone. When you foundered and I held you, I promised to take care of your son and your grandchildren, and I knew that this was a promise made for me.

4. Dramatis Personae[6]

You.　　　Formed as language in the writing mind means mostly
　　　　　Maureen and sometimes the poet. Means no longer here,
　　　　　means bounded by dates, means new or other ways of
　　　　　making presence from memory. Can address sustain its
　　　　　object, or is the object, as Glory, overtakeless?

Me.   [Here the curser waits. It blinks. Remains undefined.]

Husband. Refers to your child who is no longer but always will
          be. Yours and child, that is. Title imbued with weight, with
          freight, this companion in all restrictions, failures, and
          longings.

Children. Mine. Yours. Somewhere in between or both or neither.
          Infancy as transcendental opening of "the space of history,"
          these "unstable signifiers" closer to ghosts.[7]

Infant.   Possible addition, or not. Also Agamben's boundary
          "between the human and the linguistic," so defined as
          experience, and at the time of this list the plastic babies with
          which the den is adorned. I first wrote "strewn." When does
          adoration become adornment become litter become glitter
          become gone?

Book.   The more urgent question: Is a photograph of writing
          rendered in language or does it render language image? And
          by this I mean the book came wrapped in green with a pale
          gold bow. The failure of hope on cut paper rendered
          photograph rendered gift rendered permanent like stone.
          Once you were a teacher, but you'd long ago stopped being
          able to squeeze a pair of scissors. The more recent past: you
          could not read to your students. Surely only a strain in the
          voice. Surely only.

Poem.   AKA: words handwritten and bound by the envelope's edge.
          AKA: memorial. AKA: toy. AKA: crib of the spectral infant.
          Each word written, as Agamben says of the Nativity scene
          reconfigured, "a whole in itself . . . welded into a single
          structure"[8] through participation in the imagined event.
          Proof that the absence of the witch does not invalidate
          the spell.

5. Ars Moriendi[9]

My daughters were born in hospitals. The second time, I was assured
I would not be strapped to the bed with fetal monitors, watching the

light only of that inhospitable pall. That I could move around, sit down, even shower. How cordial. The first time my mother was there. The touch of her hand on my calf as if beckoning made me unable to concentrate. You came the next day and stayed some number of days less than a week because on day eight of my first daughter's life your first son died, and when you called to tell your second son, the one who was with me, he fell where he stood standing by the bed and could only say, Oh God, and I held the baby who was a jaundiced, breakable mystery. In my memory of the moment I cannot picture holding a child, only something so light it could float upward. What I do remember is being beside the bed, trying to kneel down to your son while I held your granddaughter. My episiotomy hadn't healed and I must have felt that as I squatted. The unbreaking, breaking body, how pompless no life can pass away.

6. Letter, Unaddressed[10]

You've said we shall not harm her magic pace, but how? How do we do no harm? Such a charged directive at which we daily fail.

In the trace of said failings, how do we keep hope small—alive, but closer further simply merely finer? I like the last—granular. Keeping awe on the scale of the speck. Not planet, but astral dust, not flower but pollen grain.

Gorgeous these Lucretian atoms incapable of love or otherwise, only able to compose.

Is this how the breach is filled? What was once held I hold in other form—fondled fire swerving to the embers of another years-past uncovering.

In the *Nicomachean Ethics*, Aristotle calls pleasure perfect—that is to say, "within each now something whole and complete."[11] Simultaneity of alternatives is a form of pleasure outside of movement and thus reconceiving time. This is the making, the made-ness of your poems.

Absence, or the possibility thereof, is agony in the body. In the poem, both are pleasure. Pleasure down to the smallest particle. Pleasure even now.

7. Critical Apparatus

The Gorgeous Nothings was a gift—the site of pleasure in an otherwise grievous time because we were preparing for my mother-in-law's dying, preparation for which I felt wholly unequipped, not only as an individual mourning human, but as someone capable of helping my young children and my husband with this passage. The book allowed for a way into Dickinson's poetry not separate from but part of the messiness of lived experience. At the same time, it provided a critical frame for thinking about the "poem"—in particular, the spectral nature of handwriting, the mediation of photography, and most importantly, the simultaneity and multiplicity of words that seem to be alternatives co-existing in the space of a writing. It was this simultaneity/multiplicity that helped break the spell of linear finality for me, and in breaking that spell, re-cast the poem as necessarily including a multiplicity of simultaneous "alternatives" so that it might expose its unbounded-boundedness, its potential and instability, the myth of fixity in composition.

Agamben's writing on the nativity crib, following his work connecting children to ghosts and funeral games to rites, opened into a way of re-conceiving the spectral. His thinking about pleasure acted as a further lens through which to enter poetic interpretation more fully. Agamben argues that pleasure is "an experience so essential to human beings" that it is pleasure upon which a new concept of time can be founded, for pleasure and "quantified time" do not correspond:

> This does not mean that pleasure has its place in eternity. The Western experience of time is split between eternity and continuous linear time. The dividing point through which the two relate is the instant as a discrete, elusive point. Against this conception, which dooms any attempt to master time, there must be opposed one whereby the site of pleasure, as man's primary dimension, is neither precise, continuous time nor eternity, but history. . . . True historical materialism does not pursue an empty mirage of continuous progress along infinite linear time, but is ready at any moment to stop time, because it holds the memory that man's original home is pleasure. (114–15)

Holding this in mind, or in memory, I found myself accessing the poem as a site of pleasure—if not in time, then interrupting or re-encoding time so that the pleasure of the poem becomes a memorialized time-stop, a chiasmus against which linearity cannot proceed in its stream unto death (and the poem as likewise not moving into a final eternal state). Here, pleasure bears the weight in the form of a book removed from an opened box and occasioned by celebration of recurrent, unful-filled messianic time, which is to say a book of a woman's writings once and always laid upon the toy-strewn table opposite the room wherein stood the scene of miniature nativity. There, we looked and talked and read and played—and we still do.

8. Ars Moriendi[12]

Seven months after you called to tell us your son had died, when we were traveling to come see you with the baby and I put her on the bed, she rolled off, hit the ground, and had to be taken to the hospital for a CT scan. Was it the same bed? She neither died nor was injured from the fall; she fell from the other side of the bed. I think it was the new bed, the king-sized bed in the same room. When you were dying you bought a new bed that stayed until the very last when a hospital bed became necessary. The new bed elevated your upper body so you could roll yourself out during the night. Beside you on the new bed the partner you loved could lie with you so that your body was not a body alone on that specific pillow. Your grandchildren liked the new bed too, ushering you up by remote, turning your rest to play, your surface to a toy. In a final photograph you wear a BiPap mask and the red flannel nightgown from Christmas, with four children flitting around you, and though the picture does not tell this the bed would have been lifting you up and up again, funeral games before the rites. All of you together, rising.

---

1   Emily Dickinson, *The Gorgeous Nothings*, ed. Marta Werner and Jen Bervin (New York: New Directions, 2013), 16–17.

2   Giorgio Agamben, *Infancy and History: On the Destruction of Experience*, trans. Liz Heron (London and New York: Verso, 2007), 81.

3   *The Poems of Emily Dickinson: Reading Edition*, ed. R. W. Franklin (Cambridge, MA: Harvard University Press, 1999), 472.

4   See Agamben, *Infancy and History*, 79–83.

5   Includes text from *The Gorgeous Nothings*, 16–17.

6   Includes text from *The Gorgeous Nothings*, 38–39, 66–67.

7   Agamben, *Infancy and History*, 58, 60, 93.

8   Ibid., 144–45.

9   Includes text from *The Gorgeous Nothings*, 88–89.

10 Includes text from *The Gorgeous Nothings*, 38–39, 66–67, 160–61.

11 Agamben at 114 quoting Aristotle.

12 Includes text from *The Gorgeous Nothings*, 80–81.

Lesley Jenike

The Birthmark

I think, if she were to see a little girl who behaved in all respects like herself, it would be a continual horror and misery to her, and would ultimately drive her mad.
—Nathaniel Hawthorne, on his daughter Una

It's a brisk October morning. I've driven a half an hour outside the city to act in a student film. I'm to play a housewife and I'm to do it in a cornfield.

It's a low-budget affair. No dialogue.

One of the actors wrote the music and someone's girlfriend styles my hair like Kim Novak's in *Vertigo*—a classic chignon, swirled not tucked, so the coil becomes an aperture at the back of my head.

The tray I'm told to carry on the director's mark is filled with broken glass and a serving fork. I walk, my heels sunk in the dirt.

A young woman follows me at a distance.

And as the field reaches deep space, my figure becomes a dirigible by which I pull her into our mutual fable.

Wait—

In a description of his after-hours living room, Nathaniel Hawthorne writes,

> [A]ll these details, so completely seen, are so spiritualized by the unusual light, that they seem to lose their actual substance, and become things of intellect. Nothing is too small . . . to undergo this change . . . . A child's shoe; the doll, seated in her little wicker carriage . . . . Ghosts might enter here.

It's not unusual for the artist to make the usual strange. It's not unusual for a film to be uncanny, or for family to become like a film.

This film I'm in, it's called *A Strange Dinner*.

//

Hawthorne named his oldest daughter after a character in Spencer's *The Faerie Queen*—Una, meaning *truth-seeking, virtuous, the first.*

But what he got was a child whose character was not unlike an eighteenth-century lantern show.

I suppose what I mean is, we all begin as a desire to commune with the dead.

And that's how movies began too.

Étienne-Gaspard Robert scared the hell out of late eighteenth-century Parisians. He'd usher his audiences into catacombs and abandoned churches (Catholicism was outlawed in postrevolutionary Paris), building suspense in the spirit of clandestine theater and ancient ritual. These happenings were like the séances of the nineteenth century and the speakeasies of the twentieth; with literal smoke and mirrors he summoned drifting, moving spirits to the great amazement of the middle classes.

The Phantasmagoria show not only conjured the recently dead heroes and villains of the Revolution, but it conjured even the yet-living. Napoleon arose with his laurel wreath. Lady Macbeth, who is never dead but lives eternally, arose with her red mark.

The trick was Robert's magic lantern technology, what he renamed the Fantoscope—a magic lantern on wheels; by rolling it further or closer to the screen, the images appeared smaller or larger and, most importantly, they *moved.*

To the throng of thrill seekers, Marat, Robespierre, Voltaire, and Rousseau, banshees and skulls, demons and cherubs, hovered and swooned like women in whalebone—as ephemeral, as easily devoured by the eye. Soon, people were asking for specific ghosts. Someone wanted Shakespeare. Someone else wanted Marie Antoinette. *Now that,* Robert said, *is out of the question.*

The trick was to envelop the senses. Think of the mass—the paintings, the incense, the singing, the bread-into-body, etc.; as such, the

Phantasmagoria was an immersive experience:

Fantoscope // glass armonica // image // sound

In respect to sound, Ben Franklin invented a strange instrument a decade or two earlier when, after delighting in the hum of a wet finger on the rim of a wine glass, then a wet finger on a series of differently sized wine glasses, he thought—I might turn those glasses on their sides and nest them inside each other and concoct a machine that would turn them automatically, then one could play them like a keyboard!

Mozart wrote music for what Franklin coined the "glass armonica," but for our purposes, Robert used it specifically to mystify and terrorize his spectators.

It is a sound that poisoned its players, people said. It's a sound that even killed a child practitioner who fell down dead due to that intoxicating, otherworldly tone. Perhaps the glass armonica ripped a hole in the veil and that child tumbled through.

//

A child's development is as circuitous, strange, and as disputed as the development of film.

A child perhaps in fits and starts gains a selfhood—so much more lurching for a girl in particular toward what she *is* in contrast to what she *should be.*

British psychoanalyst D. W. Winnicott describes childhood play as a paradox—a "joy to be hidden, but a disaster not to be found."

What if we applied Winnicott's theory of the *True* and *False Self* to the work of play:

To hide the True Self can be pleasurable—as in *Hide and Seek*—but for the True Self never to be found is a recipe for disaster.

A self is forged in a paradox of seeking and waiting to be found.

A self is forged in the primary relationship between child and caregiver.

A self is forged in the illusion of omnipotence, and the disillusion of reality.

A self is forged once the mother is diminished

or

Self is forged once the mother is raised up.

Winnicott says,

> The baby quickly learns to make a forecast: "Just now it is safe to forget the mother's mood and to be spontaneous, but any minute the mother's face will become fixed or her mood will dominate, and my own personal needs must then be withdrawn otherwise my central self may suffer insult."

What happens, then, if the mother is depressed, damaged, out of reach, static, stiff as a photograph, and immovable? Winnicott, who had such a mother, says,

> The mother's role is thus first to create *illusion* that allows early comfort and then to create *disillusion* that gradually introduces the child into the social world.

My daughter looks in the mirror and says—mainly to herself—"I am beautiful," then she asks me, "Am I beautiful?"

"Of course!" I say.

She screws up her face and shakes her head, rifling through her hair with both hands so it frizzes, bristles, stands up, is wild.

"How about now?" she asks.

"Still beautiful," I say.

She is disappointed.

//

Some say it was the magic lantern, the camera obscura, some say it happened inside Edison's Black Maria, or with Muybridge's trotting horse—in Paris or California or London or New Jersey, to whomever stopped to look first.

How does a person *show*? When do we know there's a *person in there*?

Some say it's a potential sense of humor, taste in food, preference for a particular toy, or when she discovers herself in the mirror. Some say it happens long before then, in the darkness of space onto which the illusion of movement is projected.

Some say we're born marked, if we're marked to be marked.

Some say we're born creased and some say we're born clean.

Men and women have died over hypotheses like these.

//

In "A Strange Dinner," a woman wakes up barefoot in farmland, follows a maniacal version of herself (me) to a dining table tucked behind a copse of trees, and finds her husband, son, and daughter busily eating nails and pills and shattered china.

I play her False Self, lifting a roaster's lid to reveal a live rabbit.

And as the music boils, she does too—finally overturning our chairs, knocking us all to the ground as a shorthand, filmic equivalent to a psychotherapeutic triumph.

The final sequence begins with a match cut from my tray laden down with its blood and screws and bolts and shards to hers with its pristine teacup.

Once the film is complete and we've gathered in our little art college's auditorium to watch, I'm struck by how, in my late thirties, I'm suddenly someone else's bad trip.

The affable college president walks up to me after the lights come up, and slaps me on the back. "Nice work," he says, and laughs.

//

The affable college president was an abstract painter. I hardly knew him, but I love his paintings, his diagnostic citations in biomorphic shapes. I love his whimsical view of cancer—as almost funny, bright in color, a weird, wall-sized valentine to an unclear future.

We went to see his last show at our college's gallery just before he died, and a short film of him painting played in the screening room on a loop as people milled and chatted with their drinks.

In this documentary—made by a film professor, with help from students—the college president wears death in his face. His face *is* Death. It's not a trick. And Death paints.

I think we all felt pained to see it. There was an audible suck-in of breath when he first came on the screen.

Some of us may have rifled through our mental catalogues of famous film images to settle on Death on a beach playing chess in Bergman's *Seventh Seal,* only in this case, Death paints. He paints and he paints. Sometimes, his paintings come alive and move around the canvases, breaking free of the canvases all together in a filmic feat of live-action and animation commingling—one of the oldest collaborations in cinema—see: *Out of the Inkwell* (1918) and *The Alice Comedies* (1920).

In a kind of metacommentary, Death watches the painting begin to move. He says, "The thing kind of pulses and moves across the page and drops some babies . . . they're full of life because we're reproducing, you know."

Encaustic is an old technique, Death tells us, using beeswax, pigment, and heat. It's the medium of first-century Egypt's mummy portraits, a series of death masks art critic John Berger describes as painter and painted both "living at that moment, collaborat[ing] in a preparation for death, a preparation which would ensure survival."

Death kept painting because painting is life and he'll keep painting until he absolutely cannot, but the footage will continue, played on a loop in the gallery.

Death says, "It's not about the cancer, but it's certainly about the joy of being alive, and the playfulness and reverence I have for life."

//

I remember only this snippet of a talk a famous old poet once gave in our university's library—how he claimed film was a kind of Seventh Seal—by which I suppose he meant the grand finale, the final stage of our technological/spiritual development/deterioration that encompasses and surpasses all our other art forms—a Coming-of-the-Lord people saw pending for generations.

Think about it:

The elements in Shakespeare's *The Tempest* appear at Prospero's command. His is a cinematic magician adept at his own cosmic lantern show; Prospero, yes, was the first auteur.

Nathaniel Hawthorne surely knew this and knew what magician Étienne-Gaspard Robert was up to all those years ago when in his short story "The Birth Mark," he describes the heights of distraction the scientist/husband goes to in order to simultaneously confuse/entertain his wife whom he is soon to poison:

> Airy figures, absolutely bodiless ideas, and forms of unsubstantial beauty came and danced before her, imprinting their momentary footsteps on beams of light . . . as if her thoughts were answered, the procession of external existence flitted across a screen. The scenery and figures of actual life were perfectly represented, but with that bewitching, yet indescribable difference which always makes a picture, an image, or a shadow so much more attractive than the original.

The scientist is hell-bent on erasing his wife's birthmark—the size and shape of a fairy's hand on her cheek. The wife's simple-minded former lovers thought the birthmark was a charm, a gift, so she did too. Nature isn't perfect, the birthmark says, but imperfection is the mark of nature. The era, however, is a Romantic one; the wife's fetishized birthmark is Ariel's mark, the mark of the elements, and a gorgeously bad sign. No matter how obedient the wife is or wills herself to be, she's *touched* by the sign of wildness and intractability, and with his magic he forces her into stasis a.k.a. *perfection.*

//

My husband has a strawberry-colored birthmark on the back on his thigh. He remembers, as a boy, how his parents drew it on a child's outline on a piece of paper to be kept in a drawer at his school and at the police station, so if he was ever kidnapped, lost, found comatose or—worse—he'd be identifiable. They were the kind of people who put his name in every piece of clothing, on every toy: Return to sender. If found please call:

Thinking of that outline of a boy—like the taped shape of a crime victim—fills him with dread to this day—and the birthmark, the thing that will say he is himself, also exists outside himself, and is on file somewhere.

Death the Painter, a.k.a. the Affable College President, says,

> I've got this outline in my head of what I intend to do, but just an outline. This is an improvisational process . . . each painting influences the one that's going to follow it.

Birth // Mark.

There's no mistaking Hawthorne's space between the words, emphasizing both the *birth* and the *mark.*

When babies are born, people say they are *perfect,* that they are *beautiful.* But birth is awesome and disgusting; whether pushed or cut out, babies are marked by the experience—made red by it, squashed, angry, hurt, maybe even terrified; in this way, they are in communion with the woman who gives birth to them.

My daughter was born *perfect.*

After some months, however, I noticed a little dark mole on the backside of her right knee. I remember staring at it, mesmerized, as if it were an aperture, a torn hole in her white fabric, a portal through which I might fall.

To ask where it came from is to ask how stars begin—I'll never get it straight. Or how Ariel was born. Or who can claim to be progenitor of moving pictures.

//

The very first filmed production of Shakespeare was *King John,* in 1899 (a portion of an English stage play), but the next was *The Tempest*—produced in 1908 and directed by Englishman Percy Stow—and it was wholly different, shot partially on location, dynamic and poetic, rife with magic, utterly silent.

We begin with Prospero's escape/deposition with toddler Miranda to his island empire; we watch as he discovers Caliban (a hunched tramp) and rescues Ariel from her tree.

Yes, Ariel is a girl—pubescent, wild-eyed, wild-haired, dressed in rags. She skips everywhere she goes, barefoot. She's the kind of girl we both long for and dread.

When her job is done and she's finally unbound, she returns "to the elements," untroubled and un-troubling. She is Miranda's crazy potential mitigated, carefully put away, so Miranda may rejoin the "somber fabric of humanity," as Hawthorne described it.

//

Someone called me up. Someone made me into this woman, stuck me in a cocktail dress and heels, and made me walk through a cornfield.

The woman in the film isn't the me to whom this happened.

Do you see what I mean?

Every one of us is born with a double. Una Hawthorne may have been *One*, but she wasn't. There was another Una too.

And to my daughter I say, there's probably another you. I've even seen her from time to time, screaming to be unbuckled from the car seat, wearing pajamas to daycare.

//

Someone called me up, and I drove, predawn, an hour outside the city in an obscure direction. It was a curly-headed, gender-fluid student from my Eco-poetics seminar who messaged me—"Hey, you wanna be in a movie?"

I'd just lost my first pregnancy the previous May. I was willing the next little spirit down, but nothing/no one came. And I was frayed—having trouble threading myself into the *somber texture.* "I used to act a little," I said. "Back in the day. So yeah, sure."

But I felt hysterical driving down that two-lane highway with a blue sateen fit-and-flare dress in the back of the car like a second body. The dark outside was so dark.

Finally, the sun came up or, rather, we all turned toward it, turning onto a gravel drive toward a farmhouse someone's professor's sister owned, the whole outfit already in gear, and the director—a lanky blonde student in an olive-green parka—looking over the shot schedule. "We're taking the actors up to the location in an hour," she said.

As the somebody-or-other's girlfriend did my hair, she talked to the young guy who was to play my husband about sleep paralysis and back-combing and why she doesn't smoke anymore. I still didn't know what I was doing there.

Then we rode in the back of pickup up a hill to a stand of trees. At thirty-seven, I felt like a hick teen going cow-tipping.

"Hold this tray, please," the director said, and her DP—a guy with a phenomenal mullet—got the shot cued-up.

Am I describing this right?

On the tray is broken glass and a serving fork.

"You're going to beckon to yourself," the director told me, "I mean

U___ who's basically you in real life (she gestured toward a pretty twenty-something in a green velvet dress and bare feet), then you're going to turn and slowly walk toward the trees. And she's going to follow you. Ok?"

//

I would like to tell my daughter:

We will watch all the movies. Movies can sometimes feel more real than what's real.

You'll see, sometimes it takes what feels like a lifetime of watching movies to get at one truth, and even that truth is suspect.

There might be a way to exorcise a filmic body, only I haven't found it yet. Think of a film as a person. Inside every film a myriad of spirits, and only some are good.

You'll someday be born, grow up, and leave me. You're the movie I've swallowed. You have all the words, all the pictures, all the sound, though you don't know them yet, nor the story.

//

When Hawthorne took Una to Italy in 1858, she contracted "Roman fever—another way of describing malaria + a resulting nervous disorder—after she lugged her pad and pencils around the city, sketching the Forum, the Coliseum, the Trevi Fountain. She wanted to be a girl-artist but was marked instead for sickness, melancholia, spinsterhood, hysteria, the convent, and finally death at an early age. I have to wonder if Hawthorne inspected his infant Una for the signs, having named the fictional child in *The Scarlet Letter* Pearl as a sort of wish for his own imperfect daughter. He described her illness like this,

> . . . attended by fits of exceeding discomfort, occasional co-matoseness, and even delirium to the extent of making the poor child talk in rhythmic measure, like a tragic heroine—as if the fever lifted her feet off the earth . . .

so that in the throes of her fever, Una briefly becomes Shakespeare's Ariel—spirit of the air—and sails her shadow across the screen.

Now, in the retroactive, Phantasmagoria show that is the Underworld's Art School, Una (the phantom, the moving image) is giving her artist's talk, and she tells us, in response to a certain slide, that "This does not exist."

We all look up and see a picture of the Via del Corso, except abstracted into blues, greens, violets—no discernable form except maybe a little red mark at center like a fairy's hand.

She'd scrapped it, she says, to make room for what comes next—that is, wifedom, motherhood—and look where it got her?

After the next slide, she says nothing. And the one after that—nothing. Not every human gesture requires comment.

//

You can still find some production notes for *A Strange Dinner* online. The student set designer kept a blog where she toyed with the color palette, configured place settings for the dinner table, posted pictures of her travails at local thrift shops, mused around about her mood as influenced by the weather, her petty conflicts with advisors, and most poetically, "Notes to Self" that include:

> Ask Dad about roaster.

> Ask Morgan about rabbit.

What if we thought of parenthood this way, Hawthorne—as similar to the kind of collaboration we bring to bear in filmmaking—a collaboration between truth and illusion, and, most importantly, between people?

Hawthorne and his daughter Una collaborated on a letter for Sophia, Hawthorne's wife. Here is Una's quotient:

> All Rose's side of the hawthorn is covered with buds, and my wild violets are rampant. I water hawthorn branches every morning,

and as yet they have showed no signs of fading, though Papa, with his usual hopefulness, declares they will. We found today on the hill a lonely violet, the first of that sisterhood. Julian appears well and jolly, but yesterday we were all killed by eating newly-dug horse-radish, which was as pungent as a constellation of stars. Papa stamped and kicked, and melted into tears, and said he enjoyed it intensely, and I bore equal tortures more quietly; the impregnable Julian being entirely unaffected by it, laughed immoderately at us both. Papa wants me to leave a place for him, so goodbye.

Your loving daughter, Una Hawthorne

The mirror = [Haw]thorn; wild violets

Sense of humor = "no signs of fading // Papa *with his usual hopefulness* declares they will"

Objective correlative = "lonely violet" // "first of that sisterhood"

Figurative language//Synesthesia = "as pungent as a constellation of stars"

Self-restraint = "I bore equal tortures more quietly"

Familial submission = "Papa wants me to leave a place for him"

//

In the 1908, silent *The Tempest*, Ariel frisks through a meadow and as Ferdinand tries to catch her, she slips through his hands in a cinematic disappearing trick we now call the *cut*. Laughing, she leads him to Miranda; in lieu of language, Miranda kisses him.

In *The Strange Dinner*, I end my screen time in a heap of sateen in a meadow, shaken out of my chair by the young woman who is really me, though I am really her. She has triumphed over her own predilection for cruelty, I guess, by dumping me into the grass, disrupting the dreamy dinner party, letting the rabbit out of the roaster. Someday—though I didn't know it then—my own daughter will do the same to me.

My daughter now has a pink, plastic-wrapped digital camera for kids, and there's a video function, of course. I sometimes pick it up and look to see what she's made, and she's made, inadvertently, a movie of our floor, our walls, our staircase—the immovable—as her little brother, her father, and I, blur against them in a panic of impermanence.

Let me put it this way:

Once Miranda found Ariel sunbathing, slathered in sunblock and nearly eclipsed by her giant white sun hat and sunglasses too big for her face. She was reading a collection of Hawthorne's letters.

She must have heard the backdoor glide on its track and with her strange, almost preternatural collection of senses, known it was Miranda. She said, without looking up, "I find it necessary to come out of my cloud-region, and allow myself to be woven into the somber texture of humanity."

"Ariel," Miranda said, "Daddy wants to see you."

Miranda, in her fevered recollection of those days on the island, often pictured Ariel sprawled on a towel by the tub of cat litter they kept just outside the backdoor, her skinny arms straining to hold up a cheap paperback edition of *The Scarlet Letter*, her face mostly hidden by her hat, her red mouth unsmiling. Everything that spirit did was calculated. That Ariel seemed to have come from nowhere, to be eternally eighteen, to have been fragile enough to pop like a bubble, strong enough to lift heavy weather with just a finger, eternally nonplussed, effortlessly odd, perpetually intellectual—struck Miranda as *no-fair*. To be like Ariel, to have Ariel's access to Prospero's mind—that was Miranda's greatest wish.

Looking back at that particular moment, and at a beaded strand of moments just like it, Miranda at last understood. What came to mind was the vision of a nineteenth-century writer, pants legs rolled, astride a creek, plucking from its sucking mud a fossilized child's shoe, as he says to himself, "Ah! Now *there's* a tempest!"

Christina Milletti

Composition Axe

—an excerpt from Choke Box: a Fem-Noir

An experiment. I type six simple words:
"Everything my husband writes becomes true."
My assignment?
Verify this claim. For my children. The Board. Myself.
Even though it may be impossible.
But I will no longer deny, I can no longer deny:
What my husband writes on the page, now takes place near my person.
Wherever he is, Ed doesn't need to write a word.
Can you hear him?
He's laughing.

Let me explain:

Not long after my husband began to write his book (from the first, he called it a "memoir"), I noticed an eerie correlation between scenes taking shape in his papers and odd incidents that began to occur in our home—as though Ed's solitary work at his desk upstairs was directly influencing our downstairs behavior. The effects were subtle at first. The cat went missing. Then my Volvo's transmission died. Later, the IRS showed up for an audit. Nothing unusual or extraordinary. Each event on its own merits was merely "inconvenient." Cats stray, after all. Cars die. Is it surprising that I at first believed that the sudden abundance of ill-timed events in our lives was no more uncommon than a hair clot in a bath drain? A temporary obstruction that—with the right tools, a bit of patience—was entirely resolvable? I'll admit I was slow on the uptake. It took me much too long to see the connection between my husband's work and our daily troubles, and, by then, as with most things in marriage, it was much too late to stop what was happening from spiraling out of control.

For once I think my mother was right: the most dangerous place a woman can be is in the so-called "safety" of her home. The statistics don't prove her wrong.

I'm aware that my "explanation" (the Review Board at Buffalo Psychiatric has pressed me to call it a "confession") won't satisfy the committee of six that is responsible for overseeing the small discretionary movements I once controlled myself. They're a humorless lot—huddled and scoliotic in their mismatched plastic chairs. Yet for all their oily cynicism, they've never ignored me, never lied to me. Never even raised their voices during our weekly meetings. True, they're hard to fathom, to get a rise out of. But at least—at the very *least*—they are reliable. That's more than I can say of my family. Certainly of Ed.

At night, when the hall lights dim (they never go fully dark here), and my most morbid thoughts surge against the rising chemical swell of my last Dixie-cup dosage, I fear I've come to find the Board's unflagging equilibrium so soothing that I must have changed as irrevocably as they accuse. After all, they don't nag or bicker. They don't lash out. They don't even roll their eyes at my (admittedly) snide assessments of their limitations: the ill-fitting suits, the mottled, over-fluoresced skin, the predictable short-sightedness in vision as much as intellect. To them, I'm just one case among so many others, and they've heard enough lies and exhortations—from small fibs to outright rants—to make them stony and steadfast, as if rigor mortis were a condition they've become as accustomed to sporting as the tweed coats with patched elbows they all like to wear. Under any other circumstances, I might have respected their dour commitment. (I have a helpless and embarrassing admiration for authority figures.) But when someone like me comes along—educated, devoted, and, truly, still somewhat naïve after all that has happened—it's evident they're at a loss. They've already decided that *my* behavior is an act.

My story? A desperate woman's fabrication.

"You've read the statistics on domestic violence?" anonymous Board Member 4 asks, for instance, referring to the pamphlet he'd given me at our last "progress" hearing. When I nod but then go on to explain (once again, I might add) that I did not kill my husband of ten years—that Ed simply disappeared—he sighs a great breathy chortle that shakes phlegm from his jowls. His meaning is clear: I remain a source of great disappointment to him. If only I'd admit what I've done, he'd finally be happy: they'd *all* be happy.

What he really means is that they all could go home.

Board Member 6 chimes in. His hair is short, his glasses large. He wears woolen trousers even in the unbearable summer heat.

"Do you miss your husband?" Beneath his question is a subtext with which I've become all too familiar.

"Of course," I retort. "We were a happy family. At least," I said, "until Ed started writing that book."

"And then?"

"And then," I say, "it was as if Ed had left us."

"You mean," he says, his eyes on my file "that he *died*." With greater emphasis now: "That you *killed* him."

He levies this insult without once looking up from his notes.

"I mean," I say more firmly, "that he *disappeared*."

I get flustered. Anyone but a murderer would in the face of such blunt accusations. Fortunately, my counselor steps in on my behalf.

"As the Board well knows," she says politely in her light, carefully child-like voice, "Edward Tamlin hasn't yet been located."

"True enough," #4 jumps back in, his fleshy nose quivering over my file. "But that's precisely why we're here."

With a unified nod, they break for lunch, naturally without consulting me. They will decide my fate in the town nearby over seared mahi mahi and pinot noir or a ribeye steak and a nice rioja. But I already know what their verdict will be. I can see it in my counselor Celeste's face: Celeste—such a sweet girl—who has, from the first, fought for me harder than anyone else. Even my own family.

It was at her request that I began to write what she calls my "counter-memoir." I resisted at first. I'd had enough of authors and books, the queer energy that Ed's work had led to. But with Celeste's encouragement—not to mention the pen and paper she regularly smuggled into my room during her consultations—I relented. Ed, after all, was no longer around to correct his book about our marriage and his life before we met. And while the memoir he wrote—incomplete at the time of his disappearance—will never see the light of day as long as I refuse to sign the release forms Celeste delivered to me, I also learned long ago that lawyers have a nasty habit of worming their way through even the tiniest loopholes. They'd never allow an alleged murderess like me to stand in the way of their share of a profit. So here I am: composing myself. Steeling myself against a book that has changed the shape of my family: a memoir that took Ed away, sent my children downstate. A book that managed to get me locked up without cause. ("Civil commitment," Celeste corrects in the margins.) All that before it's even in print.

At the time of this writing, my motives aren't yet wholly clear to myself. Naturally, I'd like my side of this story to be heard. I'll even admit I crave recognition for my efforts on behalf of my children, my brother. Even my husband. But I've learned enough in the past year to know that airing one's dirty laundry on a line doesn't make it any cleaner: it just elevates its altitude. And, really, what good is that?

What I truly desire is what all mothers desire: for my children to understand me. For my children to one day realize the full extent of what occurred in our home. How I was led astray by love. Done in by betrayal. And—finally—ruined by the peculiar "factors" (what else can I call them?) that altered my admittedly incomplete understanding of natural laws. Not to mention, my relations with Ed.

Perhaps—if I'm lucky, if I get this story straight—my memory of those missing six seconds that brought me here will return. I'll finally know what went down at our farmhouse. And maybe? What the future holds for me too.

Of course the cynic in me whispers something much different. More dire. A warning that even now is hard to write down, as I just now have, since it once was so easy for me to have faith—to *believe*—in the simple life I was living:

Women, don't trust the men in your lives.

And trust the women even less.

Darien Hsu Gee
from *Three Wives*

my grandfather's first wife (name unknown)

b. 190–
d. 19—

dongping village, shandong province, china

totem

Here are the items she brings to her husband's home: clothes, a silver comb, a pair of ivory chopsticks, a small ring set with an orb of carved jade. *Not for the family*, her mother whispers. *To keep. For you, just in case.* Her father has disappeared without a goodbye. Maybe he went to the teahouse, or for a walk along the river, skipping the flat, smooth stones across the water. Maybe he is haggling for five more *jīn* of coal briquettes for the winter. Already she is becoming a faint memory. Her husband-to-be is an intellectual from a good-enough family. Later, alone in that strange bed, she will pull the ring from her underclothes and slip it onto her finger, raise it to her lips. She searches for home with each probe of the tongue. She will wonder if she can swallow it whole.

courtyard

Her new family has her dowry—her chickens have become his chickens. Clipped wings fly the short distance to nowhere. Her future husband has returned to the village. His parents had sent a message to the university: *Come home quickly. There is an emergency.* It took several days to make the journey and he arrived weary, expecting an ailing father. Instead, a wedding ceremony with him as the man of honor, and her, sitting on the bed, dressed and waiting, vision obscured. She tries to imagine what he looks like. When he lifts the heavy red veil from her face, she sees kind eyes. She lies with him that night, spreads her legs and consecrates the marital bed. The next morning, she is alone. Her new husband has returned to school in Shanghai, a city she has only heard of. Her husband is an educated man, she cannot read or write. He is *Jīdūjiào*—a Christian. No one in the village understands this, not even his own parents. She tends the graves of his ancestors, looks after his mother and father as if they were her own. Nine months later, a girl is born, company for a short time—the baby dies an infant. Still he does not return. All that remains is a handful of chickens, the rest slaughtered for her wedding banquet.

first position

She could have been a dancer—anything is possible. No one remembers how she looked, her hidden talents, her gifts. Before she became his first wife, she was known for her alabaster skin, her long arms, her mischievous smile. She could have danced the emperor's dream, donned feathers and silk, held court as others watched in envy. She was not the favorite but the first. The first to marry him, the first to lie with him, the first to bear him a child. My grandfather mentions her in passing to his only living daughter, my mother, when she is a mother already. *When I was in college, I had an arranged marriage.* At the table sits my grandmother, his second wife, the one I'd always thought was the first. *Womanizer*, she teases, but she is matter-of-fact—she has always known about first wife. *A village wedding*, she says. *It doesn't count. He left the next day.* These are my grandparents smelling of camphor and ginger, with skin spots and grandchildren, knit cardigans, black cloth slippers, gold crosses on delicate chains around their necks. What they have been through—a first wife, a dead baby, a third wife, a dead baby—and let us not forget the war, one more page in their secret shared history. My mother mentions the first wife in passing, when I, too, am a mother, a footnote to a conversation I no longer recall, a detail missed when spoken in a whisper.

your husband's second wife's granddaughter
has some questions for you

When did you die? How did you die? Did you stay in the village? Did you think about your husband? Did you think about your daughter? Did you wonder why he left? Were you angry with your husband? Did you hear stories about his life? Did you think about finding him in the city? Were you waiting for him to come home? What happened to you during the war? Where are you buried? Did you ever sleep with another man? Did you re-marry? Did you have more children? Did you leave the village? Did you get sick? Was it easier being alone? Were you lonely? Were you afraid? Did you feel you had failed? Did you want a different life? Did you feel it was your fault? Were you punished? What was your childhood like? What were your parents like? Did you have any brothers or sisters? Were your parents poor? Did you ever see them again? Were you relieved your husband was gone? Was it easier? Were your in-laws kind? Did they gossip? Did you care? Did you find passage on a ship to Taiwan? Did you have another life? What name is on your tombstone? Who do you watch over? Who watched over you?

refrain

Some days, I imagine, first wife looks back and considers. Perhaps she passed each day with the routines of a woman bonded to a man she may never see again. The stirring of the morning porridge, scalding hot and dotted with seeds, dates, and pickled vegetables stored in porcelain jars, ready for his possible homecoming. It's never spoken of—her husband's unexpected departure, his unlikely return. She keeps company with what is left: the sewing, the stories, the familiar laughter of women who may or may not have taken her in. She sits among them, waiting. On days when children wander the dusty patches of dirt, small clouds rising to cover their faces and clothes, they clap one another on arms and legs to avoid a scolding when they get home. Might her daughter been among them, had she lived? Small twigs woven into braided pigtails, the smell of sweet sweat, young arms circling her neck. She does not allow herself to contemplate another life. She has no choice but to make this living enough.

my grandfather's second wife (my grandmother)
hsu shiu ying (po-po 婆婆)

b. 1903
d. 1994

shanghai, china
qingdao, china
taipei, taiwan
white plains, new york

a woman of god considers her husband's first wife

You ask: Who? Where? Your new husband shakes his head. She might still be in the village, or maybe back with her parents. He doesn't remember her name or what she looked like. *It was a long time ago. I saw her only one night.* This should bother you—it does, a little—but such old-fashioned village thinking is not for modern women, not for Christians. That marriage had been a trap, not a union under God, and he did as he was told to please his parents. *All arrangements had been made and I left the next day.* No matter there had been a ceremony, no matter he had planted a child in his village wife's belly. *I heard later the baby died.* A sign or a curse, if you believed in curses, but you are a woman of God. Such things are not for believers, or so you tell yourself.

rumor

Your husband is sleeping with his secretary. The other wives say it is because of the distance, the long separation, the war. They are certain it will not last. *She is young and modern. Your husband is just lonely.* A Christian man, your husband works for the YMCA and is stationed 1,500 kilometers away, inland and to the southwest, in Chongqing. You are in Shanghai with the children. Your young daughter might have jaundice from being indoors, your son might have TB. You surrender your fears, give them all to God. But. You try not to imagine them together. You know the feel of his hand in yours—you wonder about his wedding ring. You are not a romantic. You are an English teacher—well respected, well liked. Many people call you *Hsu Laoshi*—Teacher Hsu. When you are promoted, you become *Hsu Xiaozhang*—Principal Hsu. You are not one to cry or shout. Instead, you write your husband a letter, tell him everything is good. You talk about the children though there is nothing to say. *They are bored but well behaved.* You tell him you miss him, that you trust the Lord to deliver him back to you, safe and sound. You don't mention Julia, a name you've only heard. You don't pin him to the spot. *Who is she to you?* Perhaps that was the mistake. Perhaps your silence was the only permission he needed.

likeness

Oval mirror, square room. Your reflection returns your gaze, sees you in this new place, a placid neighborhood in a suburb of America. *White Plains.* You are the same woman and yet. Your husband travels between Taiwan and New York where you now live with your son and his family. Julia is not here. Marooned in Taipei, she is so far away that some days you forget about her. Some days you feel as if your life has always been this way. You brought one suitcase, left everything else behind, including him. Julia would not let him move with you, permits visits only as agreed upon. It must be fair—no more, no less. In America, no one asks about your past. They don't care that your husband isn't with you. *Widowed*, they might think. *Possibly an immigration thing.* Or: *Maybe he didn't want to come, preferring the old country.* Never mind that you are not from Taiwan. Never mind that you fled the country of your birth (China), you by boat and Julia by air because she was carrying your husband's next child. These details are lost to foreigners, though, wait, it is you who is the foreigner. The stranger stares back and wonders what she sees.

hospital corners

You teach your granddaughter how to make a bed—a triangle of sheet, tucked beneath the mattress, pulled tight. *A well-made bed means good rest.* You teach her how to make paper-wrapped chicken, how to play Johann Sebastian Bach's Minuet in G on the piano, how to knit an afghan. With your own daughter, there had been no time for such things. Air raids trapped her in the bedroom of your dark house in Shanghai while you went to work, ducking between buildings, your husband miles and miles away. Your Chinese-American granddaughter helps you, holds the yarn while the needles click. A teacher, you consider what else she needs to know—what is essential, what is necessary. Also—what to keep, what to let go. When you open your mouth to speak, the words do not come.

an act of repair

When the phone rings, your husband's voice is ragged on the other end. You are seventy-two years old. It takes a moment to understand his words as they travel the 8,000 miles from Taipei to New York. *Julia jumped. She jumped in the early morning when we were asleep. She went to the balcony and she jumped.* Julia was gone. Julia is gone. You replace the receiver in the cradle, your slight frame wavering. Your glasses fog up. You sit down, you stand. You are in the living room, you walk into the kitchen. You begin to make dinner. You tell your son, maybe you call your daughter. Julia is gone. Your lips move in silent prayer. You are an old woman but have nineteen years ahead of you before you die at ninety-one—still, this feels like the end. Over half a lifetime with Julia on the periphery, edging in until your own boundaries collapsed. *What choice did I have?* There is a name for women like Julia— *Kàngzhàn Fūrén,* Lady Wife of the Resisting War. In English, this makes no sense—how else to say who Julia was to your husband, who Julia is to you? Many husbands returned from the war with new wives, new children. Some women were happy to be rid of their men. You wanted yours back. Julia is gone. You remain in the wake of her unanswered questions. That night, you think of her unhappiness and how it eclipses—even now—your own.

my grandfather's third wife

chu li shin (julia) 朱禮信

b. 1913
d. 1975

guangdong, china
chongqing, china
qingdao, china
taipei, taiwan

at the quay

Julia flew on the army plane from China to Taiwan because she was pregnant and the Communists were coming. Her husband and his other family journeyed by ship, bringing her son, not even three. The women on the plane ignored her, wives of other officials who whispered loud enough for her to hear. *Not the real wife.* At the ceremony in Chongqing, Julia had worn a gown of white. When he slid the ring on her finger, she cried. Witnesses signed their names to the paper, declaring them husband and wife. He had gathered her in his arms and she thought his love could suffice. As the ship approaches, Julia imagines leaving a letter for her young son. *He promised to divorce his other wife. He promised it would just be me.* Leave the leather satchel, a gift from her father, a man her son will never meet, because her family has disowned her. *They said I brought them shame.* Leave the Bible with the tissue-thin pages, the bent corners, the underlined Scripture. *Be completely humble and gentle; be patient, bearing one another in love. Ephesians 4:2.* If she walks away now, maybe she will live to eighty-eight, or even 100. She might make it to America, and this moment would become a memory, a tale with a different ending, the story of what she had to give up to save her own life.

lucky number

Count the days, he comes home tomorrow. The new piano has claimed its place by the window—dark, immovable. Julia thinks of his other house, sees his other wife sitting upright, fingers at ease over the keys. Their husband stands behind this other woman, hands on her shoulders, smile on his face. Three days here, four days there—or is it the other way around? The houses so close they could be neighbors, yet far enough away it takes effort to glimpse this other life. Concealed in the shadows of a plum-blossom tree where she has been spying on him— on her—Julia closes her eyes, tries to forget the woman she has become. At home, alone on the wooden bench, she taps a finger against the ivory, hears each note in turn. *A single tree makes no forest; one string makes no music.* She cannot play, wanted it only because the other wife had one, too. *Bāshíbā*—eighty-eight keys in total. *Bāshíbā*— eighty-eight, a symbol of good luck and fortune. *Bāshíbā*—each one an empty kiss, a reminder of how she is not enough. *Bāshíbā*—eighty-eight chances at happiness, lost.

afterlife

After the war, there was just enough room to start over. How easy it would have been for Julia to disappear, a corporeal reminder of what can happen to any modern marriage. She could vanish—an apparition, a wisp of thought, a question mark. He might doubt she ever existed at all. It's not the money. Both Julia and the other wife work, manage their own expenses, their separate houses, their children, their desolation. They live parallel lives that cross at a single point—him. Julia accepts her fate, she does not leave. Her few friends question her judgment. *Why suffer? You can take care of yourself. Go while you're still young!* Julia does not expect them to understand. Her life has been built this way, there is no tearing it down now. They have all been through so much, why not make it forever? They could stay tied together in the afterlife— three plots, three souls (make that four—don't forget the village wife). Company for eternity, one big happy family.

a night at the movies

Alone at last—the two of them, arm in arm, dressed for an evening out. Julia has been asking for this time, just her and her husband on a date. A neighbor will watch the children. They will have dinner at a restaurant, then see a movie. Maybe an American movie, dubbed in Chinese, though they both speak English well. They will hold hands and they will kiss. She will tell herself again, *I can be happy like this.* Her husband laughs at something she says—she can always make him smile. Julia rests her head on his shoulder as they walk home—a perfect, starless night. They arrive, door open, the neighbor frantic. *It's not my fault, she doesn't know how to swallow properly!* The doctor, bag in hand, turns to her husband with a shake of his head—Julia, on winged feet, to the kitchen. There, her daughter, two years old, blue in the face, unmoving. Her wide look, almost surprised. *My luminous pearl.* Julia gathers the child in her arms, but she can't hold it all—her daughter, her marriage, her loneliness. Some things she must let go.

fairy tales and ghost stories

Name on passport: Chu Li Shin

English name: Julia

Derivation of transliterated name: "Chu Li" = Julie = Julie-*ah*

Place of birth: Guangdong Province

His promise: to marry Julia once the war is over

His second promise: to leave his wife and children

His third: to start a new family with Julia

Outcome: he keeps both women, both families

Fallout: Julia's birth family disowns her

Offspring: one son, one daughter

Complication: daughter is born with Down syndrome

First obit: daughter chokes to death as a toddler

Doctor's report: Julia has depression, may be manic, may be bipolar

Daily rant: why don't you leave her when will you leave her you promised you would leave her I hate you I hate you I love you please leave her

Authoritative response: it's complicated

And also: how can I choose

Finally: I love you both, differently

Simple math: Julia has been with him for over thirty years

Fact: he will never leave her ("her" is subjective)

Fact: Julia has had enough

Second obit: Julia dies at age sixty-two, death by [omitted]

Brandon Shimoda

from *Tomb Model of a Noble's House*

I could keep the book a very long time,
by gradually changing each of its fragments—
—Roland Barthes

short
minutes spell out
the glimmering,
grave
directive
—Paul Celan, *Bedenkenlos*, Benighted

<u>The walk to school</u>: the anxiety is that cannonballs scattered on a road or in a field—aim has been taken, some bodies have dropped—resemble grapefruits, which, sparkling, inspire hunger before sorrow.

A rabbit in the alleyway. It gives a few steps before turning and dodging north through a bush . . .

People, known by their homes, keep their projects and cleaning supplies out back.

Bamboo, hollow and cut into chimes, in the wood, can summon a world, but the world is a mirage, is not music, but nature. Late afternoon wind, it comes from nowhere, ruffles the papers, dives into the ground. The alleyways. Haven't been in the pool yet. Ate a banana at 1:30, two thin slices of cheddar, 5 o'clock. Finished a novel this morning, thought: What if I am a character named Midori? Is the old man or young man or young boy me, going through the plotless experiences I am, or is he him, yet in this life, the writer, aware of being written? At one point do our names lose us?

Where before there was one palm tree standing above the mesquite tree, same coordinates, there is again one, and how the wind sounds—same plants beside me too, whose name I don't know, as those that grew alongside our last apartment on 5th Avenue, at the kitchen window.

A said the last time he cried was when his piano was stolen. Somebody had stolen his piano. When I asked him who, he said, *I don't know.* When I asked him again, he said, *My sister.* He has a sister and a brother. He eats his coleslaw very slow, and is the last in his class to finish lunch. He says he's good at the piano, which sounds like his virtue elevates when he is near it. When he stands up, he smiles, then laughs—not laughter, it is a single laugh—like a pianist rising from the bench to meet the audience's applause after a perfect performance.

scotomization

K wants to start a radio station called FT. When I ask her what FT stands for, she improvises *Fun*, hesitation, *Talents*, but it's clear she's not convinced, and confirms it by saying, *No, it doesn't stand for anything, it's just FT.*

K touches a small pink flower on a bush growing along the eastern wall of her school, and says, *It's a blossom. All flowers are blossoms*, I say, to which she replies, *It's a spring blossom*, and adds, five seconds later, *Spring blossoms are the most beautiful flowers in the universe.*

Like Someone in Love, a film by Abbas Kiarostami. An older man's white mustache, trimmed straight, the moles on his face, white hair, the skin around his eyes. Among the most abrupt endings, though the crisis needed an escape . . . within the parameters of the film, the man lost. He was moving frantically around his apt. holding a cotton swab, checking constantly the window while the girl, Akiko, buried her face in a couch pillow. No explications, we get instead faces, which are Kiarostami's obsession—film exists to obsess over the face, the face as planet and satellite –> the metaphor for film, every film being a face, a registry of emotional content. Faces are what we study, though they are easily and ultimately elusive, beyond memory. So we put them into situations –> the person is the artist, the face the creation.

None of us had seen the asshole, then all of us had seen it. We all saw it; we're seeing it now. It is the sun. There was no expectation to see it. We were, in fact, sleeping. The dream of the asshole usurped many hours of wakefulness, though really it was a return to the dream. Everything could be reduced to the denouement of the asshole: life, the decision to write, go on living, etc.

to *disclose* space –> He did not have to believe what he was seeing or even what he was painting, he just had to move his hand in such a way that was as new as what it was attempting to disclose by feeling.

the position of our bodies in bed every morning strikes déjà vu every morning strikes déjà vu.

Man w/Alice Cooper face tattoos leaves a brown paper bag on the bench of the bus stop.

Riding east on the bus, it is the most normal-looking people who turn out to be the most feral . . .

The thrill of the people who ride the bus midday. The pure madness in their eyes, or the decimation of the flame of madness, which you know rose tall through the top of their heads, burning everything.

Our most reliable companions are the birds. Ironic that we rarely see them, though we could set the days of our lives by their ceaseless zajal.

A chainsaw started, now there is a chainsaw. I am in the woods or it is spring. It is the sound of wood being opened. The trees are full and green and yellow with pollen. What is six? Green. Is six big, medium, small? Birds are crying for food in the eaves of the warehouse. The chainsaw idles. The mesquite tree in the yard is motionless. Its wood is dark brown and divided. There's a faded pink trailer parked by the sound of wood being opened with its two windshields shot through in the center. Translate that cry to the unthinking melancholy of humans, when they are hungry and feeling neglected. We can no longer say *our* or *we*, as in the movie the young boy in Kagoshima asks his father, *What is the world?* The world is a sign. Literally, you can see it. One bird is on top of the rusted wrought-iron wall, and the chainsaw has stopped.

To walk two miles exposed in the sun to arrive in a windowless room . . .

The looks of the houses; lethargic, inscrutable. A patio umbrella, closed, becomes a squid. Trees that have unburdened themselves of oranges—a small radius of oranges drying out. I have, so far, included, in my essay on Etel, the oranges we ate after dinner our first night together.

The arrow-shaped rainbow on the seat of the toilet reminds me of my father's big glasses.

An old man emerged from behind a formidable door in the wall and, with his baseball hat not quite fitting his head, pulled himself onto a new, gleaming blue bike, and pushed off.

The dead pigeon one foot to the south.

The reflection of white lights on the bald man's head suggests the place where his horns used to be—

The shadows of the readers on the wall behind them resemble hunch-backed dictators delivering the news . . .

The man who rises with a look on his face that says, *This is not what I came for.*

The Bible is redundant.

A man outside the post office in a Panama hat and a t-shirt that says *FBI, Suk It*, reeks of perfume as he passes . . .

I weigh less when I speak. Unless what I'm saying is stupid, then more.

When I'm silent, stone of air.

All that pain, that manifests originally as a smile . . .

The environment is often a book; I abstract myself in reading. I divide myself, at least; go invisible. Do I become larger? Does my mass change?

The jacks of giants keep the ocean from surging the coast and are thrown through the air to make a sucking, martial sound.

On a deserted university campus, the smell of deep-fried fish.

The illumination of negative space

Pouring a substance of hybrid and subversive makeup into a form to illuminate negative space, to make a body within a body . . .

They are reminders, reminders of the dark trees and flowers –> a revelation of the laborers that constitute the fleeting moments of a free country-life's evolution (staggering foundation).

Sitting on the small brick patio outside K's bedroom—beneath the wooden eaves, a perfect mesquite tree, wide-reaching limbs that resemble the limbs of a tree damming a river, an elephant's tusk or a memorial to a snake. The ground is yellow with pollen. There's a green hose uncoiled in the yellow and an orange electrical cord slung over the wooden eaves keeping a festoon of small white frosted lights on throughout the mesquite tree. Mourning doves are in the trees and on the wires. The mesquite tree is reaching over the cement brick wall into the neighbor's yard. The sky is clouded light gray through the mesquite leaves and the trees are tossing with wind. I'm going to water the dead geranium .... What are the bushes with white flowers becoming, innumerable trees? I could let my eyes go limp upon the whole think [sic] as if I'm going to drink it. I saturated the dead geranium with water. Pretend it is going to come alive or buy a new geranium. Every so often the pool cleaner rises above the water and sucks desperately (mechanically) at the air. The most voluble trees in the wind are palms. What did Susan Sontag say about palm trees? She rated them high . . .

civic performances

vs.

civic rehearsals

Book of Friends

But they are more than either situational or ecstatic intonations –> they are recollections of the earth and startled, shimmering clock faces passing up on it . . .

Five silver balloons loosed from a used-car lot separating in the air in the exact formation of the stars in Cassiopeia.

Dreamt last night that militant shepherds were herding muddy sheep through a narrow street in a border town. We had to press ourselves against the walls of ramshackle, shooting gallery-like buildings. The shepherds were armed with large, black guns. We were entering Nebraska.

I pass by a chicken coop in an alleyway. I hear chickens, but only realize I do when I see egg shells among a mound of straw. I wonder if any are whole. A rooster. Then a cage with two hens. In another alleyway I admire a cactus garden. Seems composed specifically for the admiration of a single person. It is a lonesome pursuit: the admiration of a cactus garden . . . suddenly everything is revealed as if washed by a high rain. There were two makeshift benches in the cactus garden, where someone could sit and stare at the cactus and grieve inwardly. An old man walking a large dog giggles lasciviously when his large dog barks at me. The man's yellow teeth. They appear from behind a white wall. A second dog barks behind the white wall. Men and women of no clear category are running suicides near Tucson Ave. I can't hide in the park, in these alleyways.

I woke up so quickly all my dreams were erased. Only a film on my teeth remained of my dreams.

A young woman in a white pickup stops in front of an old shoeless man sprawled out in a park and shouts *Wanna salad?*

I woke up at 5:42 to take Mom to the airport. Shortly after returning home, she called to say she was sad and already lonely.

The corn is brittle.

Genius becomes ozone.

Metamorphosis of the *Moment*
Metamorphosis of the *Document*

A mourning dove becomes, in the afternoon, a mammal. It hunts without moving. Its call is a riddle and is closer than one would think.

The task of the poet is to act as steward over the metamorphosis of experience into _____.

Or we have the potential to lock history up within riddles. Our ambiguity too must be clear.

poets—being outcast and exiled by the present (time)—have more in common with the timeless substance of history than with the people with whom they, however superficially, live.

The poet is the archive. The person is the archive, but the poet (in the person) is the person who activates and makes use of it. It is more than—or can be more than—a (so-called) nonfiction poetry . . .

There is something of the apocalypse in every immersive documentary poetry.

The anus (asshole) of a mourning dove resembles, from below, a small ottoman.

Poetry is not a dream.

Van Gogh's art was a *substitute* for this faith.

Leonardo's drawings of clouds.

My lecture description is due tomorrow. I know what it is but I'm stalling. I want a force to exert itself as a surprise, surprisingly. L says to make it *short and to the point*. The difficulty is that there is no point. Dancing, for example. A hole might be worn into the floor if the steps are forceful and unending, but even then the floor will be worn around the waist or the dancing will continue underground—which is the ground or the new underground.

When we walked along the wheel ruts through the jungle and into the clearing, I thought: this is the perfect place for him to kill me.

The lady pulled a long sac of small, uniform eggs from the womb of the iguana and handed the sac to us without saying a word. The iguana lay bleeding from her womb on a slab of wood beside that knife that had killed her. Her expression was indistinguishable from that of the lady.

The urge to pee in a stranger's yard is strong, esp. if there's a bush in the yard made yellow by a streetlight overhead.

(They hung his head).

Driving a large truck slowly through the curve of a dirt road beside small evergreen trees. The sensation of swinging wide, or either the truck or the trees are on a slowly spinning platform as in the window of a department store during Christmas. Movement in memories becomes partly mechanical. Our . . .

Working for many hours on a poem that feels as frivolous as ludicrous. Writing many pages of prose in the dark realizing the day after the pen had run out of ink.

In the poem, I begin to recount people who actually lived, then reduce them to characters It's a misappropriation of lives and ultimately throwing the book onto the roof is not the subject: it's the action hysteric out of the emotion and sound is something far greater—Why was I obsessed with roofs? Not obsessed, possessed, they stayed with me for over thirty years. The bar and I shared a (general) birthday. The arm slips—the memory of faling [sic] asleep in a tree.

Leaving Tucson tomorrow. The leaving feels only vaguely routine. We've left innumerably—here and elsewhere—though this leaving feels darker, less certain. We're going to Taiwan then to commune with the States. It's that the abyss at the far end is more genuine, though the horizon appears the same, in view and in mind. And it's not that we're motivated by a dichotomy in needs: immersion vs. dispersion, or maybe it is: a holdout. We know this and have based ourselves on this, but have not been successful in establishing ourselves within some governing vision. So we exist, and our existence, even if not the same, is based on intuition.

Last night I spent three hours on a couple of stanzas of a new, perhaps self-indulgent poem. My mind was not committed enough, though it is one in which I'm putting self-knowledge and discovery to the test: what can the poem learn beyond what I have, thus far, learned? Can we foreclose upon the tedious wondering of where the words are coming from; we push thoughts through by synthesis—we live at all by synthesizing what remains after a moment is passed. Largely what is left is large . . .

The ceiling fan has been spinning for two months. Two milk crates— one red, one orange—are empty at the foot of the bed. There are two gloves on the bedspread. One pillow is embroidered with a large-leaved flower and an explosively colorful flowerhead, devilish: orange, red, and, from a distance, I cannot discern between blue or green, though I blame the mustard for compromising those colors.

April 2013–May 2013

Don't touch the cloud-dweller. (Stalin's order re: Pasternak)

What if we were to go ahead and become beginners, now that much is changing? (Rilke)

Without reminders that you're here, would you be reminded that you're here.

The chimes confirm not only that you are hearing—in a soundless landscape, the mind seems to fold the ear in—but that you are: a peaceable sound, as things gathered in passing and hung above, or in, a void, that reminds you of the wind, the shore, silence after death, how could you know, the silence before the arrival of someone who frightens or saddens you, the inability to communicate, all of which confirm the bottommost elements of what you are, for in the desert, as at the bottom of a lake or ocean, it is not certain, because there is little, or no, relation. People were, once, here, or people are, anyway, here, so that the reflexive inclination is to shoot the chimes free and return all supposition to silence. Did you finish your book, Brandon?

What do I see first. The poem, the photograph, tells me. It flattens what I see, first, so I may see the forms of what I see before the thoughts that exist *out there*, for which the poem, the photograph, is an instrument of invention. The complement of forms, ocotillo culminating eight feet in the air, hanging on the understanding that its limit is fixed within itself, that it goes further and that *our* understanding of, our encounter with, ocotillo is based upon all the ocotillo we have seen, that we will see, even that we have and will not ever see . . . We're listening to Christmas music, the music is culpable. The holiday has its genuine moment with the man who came riding down the drive on a horse wrapped in cold green holiday lights.

I experience how little sound is made by the movements of people, as opposed to the more illusory sense of the movements of people creating a tidal cacophony. Silences layered upon silences produce noise, and only by making them white, which is a psychosomatic trick, can we make it bearable. Many say *this* is unbearable, and only by layering silence into sound can we make not only the movements of people, but all existence, bearable.

A landscape we know first from dioramas. Photographs produce nostalgia for those first encounters, or are produced out of them.

A (The) sound of gunshots, muffled, repeated, coming up from the valley, the sound of stiff wooden boxes being hurled, blasting earth, or the earth exhaling, bluntly, from a sodden, vegetal nostril.

A book comprised of all the things I didn't say:

You become curious to know what it is like to deal with things you have not, for fear or incapability, dealt with.

Clocktower in Nogales: paused at 1:41

To be with one faceless old woman in a boat fit for one in a small mire of piss in the middle of which is an evergreen tree bedecked with red ribbons and bows, the small boat turning lethargically in the winds and when the evergreen moves. The old woman is mute, you hang your arm over the side of the boat. You neither increase nor decrease your drunkenness. It is your permanent bearing. The old woman is a book you feel need not end, but catch you up on one sentence after another, psychological, ritually observant, the book has lent its face to its content, its story. The evergreen is a slim pyramidal stack of wreaths and the red ribbons and bows are flecked with gold. The bows are ornamental flowers, carnations, poinsettia. The piss is turquoise. You turn and turn, or the small boat turns and turns, and the piss stays somehow fresh, while also turning cool, and there is two of everything, but the tree, megalithic; it sits on an island in the middle of the mire that supports only it.

An evergreen tree on the edge of a cliff overlooking the border between Nogales, Mexico and Nogales, Arizona, is an old woman, unsteady, though she carries a small child on her back, and both she and the child are featureless. A woman of memory, reminiscence.

Singing is the punctuation *and* the sentence. Pauses, inherent, between passages lacking in exposition and detail. Little can be developed in dialogue, the characters emerge through song, which are at their most pivotal and profound when solo, so the characters are detached from each other and from the governing narrative, which becomes a skeletal support for the songs, when they come, and I hoped that they did, while listless when the narrative was left to knock its bones together. All of my *visual* memories are of the faces of those who were singing.

The recurrent vision, memory: sitting on a grassy ledge overlooking Frenchman Bay. The bay is a sensation and a void, the view has no bottom, I am in my own ear. There are paintings diagramming my body and the scene. I return there, no date, all time exists as a place, without purpose, but to sit in the grass at the edge.

I see at least two new ways into the maze . . .

Two roots of (for) resurrecting the dead: constant dissatisfaction and a florid imagination.

The song is a passport. It's meaningless [sic] is turned into a message, that the song wd seem to be telling you something, have encoded within a warning. And the more frivolous the song, the more urgent the warning within it.

Coming into the bedroom late at night, L already asleep, the only light is slatted and of a waning moon resembling snow that has yet to be broken.

Primary on my mind: not the actual scenes, the objects and moments and faces I might be able to describe into a scene, but my own inability to set to any one: woman planting spinach, the dream of a house, the reduction of a life into trivialities, etc.

All the poems yet written are readymade set decorations, miniaturized to hang on the walls of the miniature house. The book is a maquette for the sculpture that is life, though which is catching up with the other?

We went for a walk and looked at trees. Helicopters are crisscrossing the thin, underlit clouds. The Chinese pistachio, the European olive. M said the olive trees looked like eucalyptus, and L said, *Eucalyptus leaves are shiny.* We ate steamed buns, ten, pork and spinach, and fried rice. L knocked the ice cubes onto the menu.

I woke up after 10. Around 5 I woke up fat and sweating and threw up in the toilet. I did that three times. The third time I was retching. Nothing came out but saliva. My stomach was a skin bag . . . I've the body of a ten-year-old. Maybe also where the voice comes from.

As like Rembrandt, start with the gesture, then go back into the gesture to add (the) information.

It's a _____ day realizing you hate your grandparents.

People's recurring dreams.

All the people in the book return as people on the street: strangers.

Asses: more real than me.

We sleep on the floor and always have the blinds drawn. So when we go to sleep or when we wake up, we are deprived of looking out the window. We have no view of *the world* from our bed. In Maine, we saw the trees, the lake, and snow. We were greeted each morning with light and the ways of the world in the stilled arrangement of things: tree limbs, sky. Here in Tucson, we've had no view. We've been sleeping on the floor for a year. Our windows have either been too high or blinded. What does that do to us? The bed—sleep—is even more of a tomb because a view is life, continuance. Permission. I know it forecloses one freedom of being alone . . . .

I started writing this book on my thirty-third birthday. I wrote, "

EVEN TRANSPOSING GRANDFATHERS, as it is a book about old people, who will soon not exist, so the amalgamation multiplies their longevity in the mind as ONE ELDER against their impending extinction: THE TOTEM. CROSS-DRESSING GRANDFATHERS.

The time I electrocuted myself for hours unplugging a lamp in the living room. It was a voice that interrupted the circuit and through [sic] me off the socket. P was there, I her [sic] J's voice calling P, his name is Paul, the name of K's older brother. . . . It was P, with mom, who walked through the front door and interrupted my execution with a VOICE, I was embarrassed, like I had been caught masterbating, [sic] I ran upstairs, I heard MY voice say I am fine but it was a simulacra of my voice like the one I hear when I am stoned, my pockets eat my hands and I feel, always, like I have to take a shit or that I've shit my pants.

The time, in the days following an acid trip, I could see, clearly, with my eyes closed.

A man pushing a shopping cart half-filled with mismatched plastic shopping bags stops before the window of a coffee shop, spreads his arms wide. A girl on the other side of the window, facing directly the man and his embrace, acts as if she does not see him. Half of us pride ourselves on our ability to see everything, half on our ability to see nothing. The man wears a blue hooded sweatshirt that reads, Balboa, California. Two girls eat salads and laugh with their mouths closed. A young man looks at apartments online. A young girl across from him asks where. Brooklyn. It's my favorite thing: looking at apts. Three people share three Apple laptops. They're having a meeting. The man has a big head and close-cropped goatee. The women on either side of him both where [sic] thin green sweater-shirts. Their meeting is over, now they are chatting. The man has a monkish haircut. The two women in green sweater-shirts are bored, but are doing their best to maintain an attitude of relaxed professionalism. The man is moving his index finger around the mouse pad of his laptop. One woman asks, *Where did you learn about all the codes for* . . . but before finishing the question (1) the man has already thrown himself into an answer, and (2) she has ceased caring, and wishes she were elsewhere, in the hallway between her kitchen and bathroom where the air blows. A girl in an off-white cable-knit sweater is Skyping with her friend, whose head resembles, on the computer screen, a gopher emerging from a hole in the ground.

A woman in Montana feeds carrots to her favorite horse and plays it Peter Tosh's *Greatest Hits*. *He likes reggae,* she says. *And Gatorade.*

A blonde woman wearing a denim shirt says, *You have to teach the camel a trick that other people will find annoying,* then emends that to say, *that other people will laugh at,* adding, *something saucy, flirtatious.* The woman she is talking to says, *Like throwing nuts at them?* The city could be regarded as home, for some, even, if one were in the mood, and perhaps, standing on the top of a moderately-sized mountain, a beautiful home, a home where one could get nice and full and die and everyone would love them forever in death. Camels have durable lips. *I have these two camel trainers who are always playing tricks on each other, betting each other who can play the better trick.* The women discussing camels and camel tricks and trainers are sharing a tomato-basil-mozzarella panini. Every bite sounds like they are biting into sheets of bubble wrap. Then they are alone in a bamboo cage eating insects with their hands, while a young boy wearing a red bandanna over his nose and mouth and holding a thin machine gun watches over them. A bird explodes from a tree and thousands of small leaves fall onto the roof. The two women in green sweater-shirts are leaving. They've been sitting with their associate, the man, for three hours, and now, saying goodbye to him, he does not lift his gaze from his mobile device.

If there's a frog in a toilet and you sit on the toilet, the frog will jump into your ass. I once dumped a bunch of flowers in a toilet. Newlyweds dance on the roof of a bar. A man puts his hands in his pants pockets and furrows his brow when he wants to think but lacks thought and knows that he will spend the rest of his life following someone around whose face he will never see . . .

the final act of adoration

a secretive (daimyo) cabal called sonno-joi, or "Revere the Emperor, Expel the Barbarian" (12).

The general idea is of a REACHING OUT when falling, even before, and as falling includes also death, the hand reaches, that is the reflex, though the hand proposes human connection: physical, communicative. We reach for the earth and for others. Often there is nothing there: no earth, no other people.

Every poet becomes accustomed to being singled out as The Poet, and so adopts, in her mind, the position, for which finding herself in a community of other poets, who have also been, at some point, singled out, is disconcerting. The Poet, in an unconscious attempt to retain the status of singularity runs as far away as he or she can in/to a place or wilderness where that status is unquestionable: the dangling one, for whom all the others, the community of individuals, becomes a dream of the past. The Poet, even in exile, is never not working, and her exile only amplifies the truth of that: no people, but the insinuation of corpses that contribute to the environment half as myth, half as compost. The Poet can be pure, as long as she survives, with or without reports sent home, either because The Poet has transmuted the writing of poetry into thought and observation, or because there has ceased to be a home to which reports could be sent. The cessation of home resides in the mind and the heart of The Poet. The world is green and dark blue in the evening. The sun is yellow and when interacting with night, becomes green, which is the wilderness, and brown, and the sky is blue, gray, and white.

The floor beneath a painting, where the painting was painted: the expression of where it, the paint, wanted to go: like milk from a goat, it comes naturally when and how it does. A goat, for example, named Elvis.

Don't dwell too long on the dying gesture, i.e., the reaching of the hand. What is of interest is the hand is [sic] space and one's imprint on space, as well as one's imprint on a surface, the impermanence of heat. This was the last thing I added.

Somewhere within the flattened depths of nine decades comes a smile to mind . . .

I have (been) for years sleeping beneath (below) the level of the window so that my vision's been genuflective and I've woken into walls . . .

January 30, 11:15 p.m. G died twenty-three hours ago. No one was there when she died. The doctors, nurses. No one. Mom and L had already gone back to the house. Mom called me at 12:44 in the morning. We had just gotten home; I plugged my phone in. When she was a child, my mom was ready to love and be loved. It was inborn, this readiness, her love. Her mother was proud, but depressed. Her daughter, no matter how splendid she was, could not fix it: her depression. Nor could her other three children, though by the time she had them, her sickness had already begun to calcify. A photo taken at the beach. A photo taken in the hills above the valley. I write what I remember if I cannot name it. Mom was eating ice cream last night at 9 p.m. She was sitting with G in the convalescent home. G was not responsive. We were her first grandchildren. What did my mom do with her rosary? Did she see heaven? She looked out the window and smiled. My mom looked too but could not see anything. Children run from one side of the gym to the other. A man is hiding behind gymnastics mats stood up on their ends. I cried when P cried, when I heard that P cried. It was P's sixtieth birthday. They had removed the feeding tube from G's [sic] stomach. It wd then be a matter of time: nothing was entering into her. She could not speak but you could hear her breathing. A river in a forest, the hills rising from the river thickly forested. Long wooden boats, long slippers. P now lives alone and will until he dies . . . . K is upset she did not have the chance to say goodbye.

This is what I want: to continue to write passages into which I can enter repeatedly until there is no room left for me: until I have painted myself out . . .

Night: when we walk above the sun

I am not in the mood for frivolities though neither am I, apparently, in the mood for gravities. I've reached no mood. It is neither equilibrium nor achievement. The space between me and the book, the infatuation that comes and goes.

Mariah Carey was in the ceiling.

Lychees will soon be good.

December 2012–March 2013

Michelle Phương Hồ
To Hold an Integrity

My parents sacrificed everything to seek a better life in America.

My parents sacrificed everything to seek a better life in America.

My parents sacrificed everything to   better   America.

My par   ts   thin   k   better if in America.

          rents   iced every   life in America.

                  f ed   s   t r ife in America.

                cri ed   thing   see   li e in America.

My   s cr   e   a   m   .

My parents sa   i d   n   o   better   in America.

              sacrifice   every i   to   America.

My   sacr   ed   s   ett l   er .

My pa   s s   verythin   .

My   r   a   ced   thing to   better   in   .

     pare   every hin   t   i   Am   .

My   if   to   be   li e   .

To arrive at the house in one piece, thinking it yours, and there is your mother, and there is your father, and there is your brother, and there is the altar. To take your seat by the severed stump of a tamarind tree and soothe the edges with your fingertips.

To say the first sign of splintering began here is to try tracing a mist, like aiming the finger toward a dissolving center, or weighing down a cloud with a fist.

Whatever happened, I can tell you the quake began at the center, a center which was no center but an open-mouthed, bottomless weep.

What I remember most is the carpet—red, made of something like velvet, spilling from the tongue of a wide staircase. Bố's soft steps as he cushioned my cries. My brother and I, feet pounding as we raced upstairs to drop parachutes of plastic bags from the ledge, chasing our breath—*again, again, again!*

Outside, a pair of swings. Rusty chains my father gloved in blue plastic so our hands wouldn't bleed. My brother and I, clinging wild and weightless. I remember no intention of leaving.

*

We caught wind of a better life out there somewhere—somewhere being noiseless streets and white children. Well-behaved. Promising.

So began years of weekends of open houses. Just looking.

When we left, I told Trinh, *Don't cry.* To not see a person again was a concept I hadn't yet considered. Loss I didn't know to weigh.

In 1975, a two-hundred-year-old tamarind tree was axed in the gut. Its trunk was dragged across the parking lot of the U.S. Embassy so that the Jolly Green Giant could prepare for landing. Hundreds of Southern Vietnamese clambered to enter the embassy gates.

We had no future there, my aunt says, mouth all panic and flight.

A new place meant new configurations of people, new faces to greet with first impressions.

Surroundings change, but the body remains.

This is how a polished place hides the aftermath of a bomb.

In the dream, I wake up inside the house of my mother's dreams.

She runs a finger along the granite countertops, maplewood cabinetry, and satin brass pulls. Tốt.

Outside, children laugh, a dog barks, and parents discuss some matters. Their voices languish, muddy through water. I never learn their names.

Where my body ends, and her dream begins, I don't know. I exit the womb: a flat note, after a long crescendo. I try wriggling out of stillborn skin, but it clings like a widow to ashes. I am nothing but repetition, but grateful beneficiary, I inherit a purpose which is to keep the dream alive at all costs.

Location, location, location. We settled for the house with the blue gate that dangled open on windy days and an ill-placed dividing wall that darkened our rooms after two. Meanwhile my mother hoarded copies of *Better Homes & Gardens* discarded by the library. Dog-eared visions of someday. *Mẹ ngắm thôi.*

*

Eventually, my parents gutted the thing. My mother handpicked every detail: French farmhouse cabinetry, stainless steel appliances, crown molding, granite countertops, a top-notch security system, and an iron fence to guard the garden.

The day my father died of cancer, she burst into a botched surgery of exposed plumbing and skeletal beams, construction workers caught mid-hammer by her shout—

Finish the house! Finish the house!

There are facts I can't ignore:

How my grandmother walked from Tuyên Quang to Hà Nội to sell
yams and potatoes, the day the French bombed the road back home,
and that's why we don't know that side of the family.

Or how, after eight years in re-education, my grandfather re-entered
Saigon through an unmarked gate and found the city flipped on an
axis of allegiance.

Or how the night I found out about my father, I wept not for his
goneness, but because he never got to go back.

Or how a lone mother raises a fist and cradles her child, and a family
disappears into marble.

Or how, to deface someone, you need to look them in the eye.

A common mistake is to scan the crowd for familiar faces. Black seas of fine hair forming tight-knit giggles. When a girl who looked like me—Sylvia—swung around in her seat to bare teeth in one bright tree-lined smile, I learned how a body seizes in the glaring sun. By twelve, I knew how to run. On picture day, I faced the mirror, and nobody noticed how many times I lied. I brushed my hair, and my vision filled with bruises. I saw only blondelike smiles. If Sylvia could, why couldn't I?

*

Please. Under the fluorescence of TJ Maxx, I begged my mother for necklace: three strands of plastic stars, iridescent. *Thôi! Vỡ va vớ vẩn.* Why couldn't I? She peeled me away by the wrist, but the stars hung in my hunger.

And I obeyed—wandering back to the aisle, in some kind of trance—
the stars, a siren's call, while my mother deliberated the cost of
second-hand soaps. I fingered the beads in my pocket as the exit doors
opened. The stars—I could nearly feel them kissing the nape of my
neck.

When my mother found the necklace, she wept. Clutching the strands,
like rosaries.

*

I imagine desire like this: roots greedy for ground, toppling buildings and cracking asphalt, veins prowling the dirt and swallowing everything in its path—first little sprouts around the trunk, then the grassy knoll, then the city beyond it, finally the whole earthface.

I take 101 South, 87, 280, and finally exit on Story Road. The clerk sing-songs me inside. I'm hoping to buy a block of bánh chưng. He laughs, turns. *Không!*

Too late, by the time I learn. How, *in Batesian mimicry, a non-defended, edible species protects itself by copying the warning colors of a defended, toxic species.* Over time, the golden teeth of my pebbled leather reveal *spectacular similarities,* dangling by forearm, dainty with leisure. *Model, mimic.*

*

> *I need to, I need to, I need to*
> *I need to make you see*
> *Oh, what you mean to me*
>
> —The Beatles, "Michelle" (1965)

When Bác Tuân belts out a rendition of "Michelle" after family dinners, he is singing for me and his own daughter. *I will say the only words I know.* To name a child is to make her known.

When I ask Sylvia why her parents changed her last name, she speaks in highlights and sheen. That night, online, I study photographs of Sylvia smiling from inside the white-knit bond she shares with white-like friends. *I love you, I love you, I looove you!* I look them whites in the eyes, like a child, looking to her mother. For recognition, a face to mirror: am I shadow, or alive?

On Wandering Souls' Day, Buddhists pay tribute to those for whom no incense burns, no family to remember them, *desolate, seeking, every night and all.*

Bác Lan's apple cheeks brim with two streams that spill into the corners of a smile. *Có thể con không nhận ra.* She presses the pits of stone fruit into my palms, riverbeds breaking: it is possible my father's body is not how I will remember him.

*

Ten years pass. I visit my grand-uncle, who sponsored my father to America. *Ông ơi, Ông có biết đây là ai không?* The same hefty, sagging head. Embroidered curtains, velveteen blankets stacked on the bed, a portly figure depressing its surface. Heavy as I remember. And the long pause he takes. *Không!*

Your eyes are failing, isn't that right, Ông?

Isn't that right?

Hold the integrity of the space you leave behind, my dance teacher warns.

Otherwise, your limbs

        flail

     the body

         spirals

Who is the real you and who is the fake you, asks long-limbed, blue-eyed friend. Distressed blonde blade of grass lilting. She notes my eyes, my eyes she has never seen my eyes like that, she means evil. Bad girl bad girl.

Two-faced crook wants honest connection wants no special accommodations I am rather confused, a stressed mimetic. She wants avatar to match real life she means either predictable or exaggerated my whole ethnic self she says she wants but please, no evil eyes. Stressing her sensibilities, *Don't you know who I am?*

*

Now, how to leave at the door the aftermath of a bomb. Consider the terms of entry: pomp and circumstance, sunbaked heads bobbing with salvific possibility, wide open arms of gracious host. Either folded into the bosom of America or *desolate, seeking, every night and all.*

cranking the steel groan grinds me either/or. either lose
a loved one or lose a loved one. either lose a family or lose

a family. lose your face or lose your face   why
these not be one/the same?

to tame my heehee hyena hysterics, i   fumble
nervous nervous for the right face

which one is it now?

this peculiar bothness: a hug here, a cheer there, a cavity
welling. laughing and weeping   i do   i do   i do.

In 2008, the United States and the Socialist Republic of Vietnam arrive at an agreement on the ACCEPTANCE of the RETURN of VIETNAMESE CITIZENS. A *precarity.* A *processing.* It costs $150 to return. A wish to establish *friendly relations,* ejecting then ejecting again please make up your mind. Now: a unilateral interpretation: wishy-washy / comrades / criminal aliens / wanting / not wanting / flip-flop / hopscotch / ashes / ashes

We all fall down!

Upon return: a xe ôm driver says, *Call me Chú,* and *let me take that—* bag full of belongings—gone. *Khờ quá.* My mother suspected I would lose everything, either here or there. I'm left in the middle of the souvenir market with a handful of facsimiles.

*

Disownment: dis ownment: what I feared most: no longer being possessed. *Cứ việc* shoo shoo and the back faces you, bosom over colander, water running cold.

Accommodations: a room, group of rooms, or building. For example: The cost includes accommodations. Also a convenient arrangement, settlement or compromise. For example: I am happy to accommodate you as long as you are willing to accept the terms.

I try twice to express my complaints. First, in abstractions: I play dead, pray to fall asleep, really to disappear. Okay concrete, I try to name the child: *white culture,* white hosts and white house, *not you, no offense* gently here and there.

To bear, to hold. To go all evil eye, sassy raw rubs on the accommodations. Starts to wear on a body alone. I wake to the blank stare of cream-colored walls and my eyes water, my throat closes, I shove off both shoulders heaving.

Gracious host, alarmed by my whole self hurtling out of nowhere, pivots her whole self into the bedroom and shuts the door. Impossible.

I see clearly my severed body and the whites of her eyes, the inconvenience of both in the same room, an arrangement, a compromise, what we pay for.

Sướng không?

Nightfall descends on a path I can't cross. Behind me, an excruciating blankness, no hook to hang my coat. I linger in the doorway of my childhood bedroom. Just looking.

I leave anywhere I don't feel at home, the young girl tells me. I see right through her vow. She wants someone to say, *Come, be home here, belong here.* I promise none of this. I'm afraid she will keep leaving, creating places where she doesn't belong. I tell her all I can remember are the stars. That the ocean between places where we lose everything is the same ocean that holds us afloat. I say the ache home is long, but she'll see it soon—not distant shore, nor phantom limb, but the sufficiency of the stars.

Jose Felipe Alvergue
hogtied

Convict Leasing

"Juvenile convicts at work in the fields," 1903, Library of Congress.

convict (n). from the verb form, convict: to convince in argument; to "over come"; to impress. From the Latin, convincere. The proof of guilt is carried over into a physiological realm by the mere presence of the body whose address is at once the utterance of the charge [convict] as well as a recognizability of the ethos that keeps the convict separate, working. The public identity of this ethos, even if classified across multiple genres–Which is to say, naturalized. Liberal democratic conviction, a staging of conduct, is the artifice of a false monstration—the forced revelation that criminality exempts the same freedom which is an energy by another name: spirit, History, the imperative, the contract, altruism, faith in whatever will result from the process.

Between the mid 19th and early 20th centuries states declaring them selves too impoverished to maintain prisons and prisoners would lease out convict labor to railway and mining contractors or large plantations. The practice became especially prevalent following the Civil War. False convictions, theft of bail money, and identity fraud supplied the lease system with so-called convicts

The convict becomes recollection, which labor gives over
to the grammatical. A body is bent and turned weight
on the shovel, a muscle pulls an arc an extension at the
hoe, the hammer. A stance upon the ground shaken by other punish
strike and arranged by the pull of ties and spikes utters ments
an optical situation for which discipline, as we are taught documented
it, offers itself without endangering the objectivity of include the
American liberty.
                                                                rack, where
                                                                in a convict's
                                                                arms are
                                                                pulled infront
                                                                of them
                                                                while they
                                                                stand in the
                                                                sun
"Convicts working in unison by singing," reads a caption until their
by John L. Spivak in 1932, whose description of the im body forms
age makes an aesthetic predicament out of the ethical a
paradox depicted by the chain gang. "Rhythmic move ninety-degree
ment is necessary," he continues, "to avoid injuring one angle.
another while bending or rising." The way history some
times projects memory forward, erasing the breach of
the moment that is the present, makes of the scene a
                dimension interpreted objectively as the

Children often become frustrated when building on a macroscale.
Their hands, better suited for focusing on the touch and manip
ulation of individual objects, can't keep pace with the vision
of, for instance, a corral for their elephant, or a seemingly
endless highway of wooden blocks for their train. I
know that children's hands have built America. Its

naturalness of a state,   *infrastructure, commerce, universities, govern*

of being in such a pose, the *ment houses, etc. The invisibility of what*
naturalness of law to keep the *transpired, which is to say not only the*
body there under watch, near ***work but also the death, and also all***
death like the gray pixelated skyline. *the other fidgeting and research*
To work toward that death, to overcome ***that is the physical world of a***
it, sing it, to praise a faith in it. Recollect it. ***child's body, this is all a lost***
Cast it forward, in front of us, to recollect it, and ***opportunity for a new***
so on, this becomes the work that convinces us of ***language, for educat***
the physical grammatical legitimacy. The image turns ***ing parenthood.***
to brush and the song to syncopation. Convince before the ***All unknown***
heavenly angels and the screen through which song projects ***scenery.***
with blurred echoing boundaries that there is no childhood, no
age, no voice, no status with which to declare no, no recollection and
no iteration, no life which the courts precede with examples and history.

One star in the east,/ One star in the west,/ and between the two there ain't never no rest.

The lease system signals a theatricality to American ab olition. The staging of rights and the commitment in performance belie the reflexive self-awareness of faith in being liberal, being a people of rights. A culture of belief.

While it leaves behind black and white photos scattered around archives [stories of possibility, of a forwardness to memory, of the uniforms overcome, of progress ac commodated] the transformed land, the built carceral networks squat like stumps throughout these states. The benefit and the reward of work made invisible by clas sification still circulates. Forced incarceration is coeval to labor without contract | but the contract is a legality, but the legal is a logic premised on crime, but crime is a racialized grammar that we learn as we build :

Lost childhood is a ghost in every echo of public discourse.

Alabama Arkansas Florida Georgia Kentucky Louisiana Mississippi Nebraska North Carolina South Carolina Tennessee Washington

there are blocks, pillars, and slabs of beams. A is building with buildingstones there are blocks, pillars, slabs and beams. B has to pass the stones, and that in the order in which A needs them. there are blocks pillars slabs beams For this purpose they use a language consisting of the words block, pillar, slab, beam. A calls them out—B brings the stone which B has learnt to pass

chained by neck and

feet to iron cage:

　Muscogee, Ga.

　near Columbus, Ga.

This convict had had the

iron collar around his

neck for 2 months, and

was forced to lie in his

bunk all the time except

during working hours, where

he was chained doubly and

"kept under the gun"

image caption in Spivak's hand, c. 1930, courtesy of the Harry Ransom
Center, University of Texas, Austin

I was
not prepared for my child's own act of definance to this
world. To be gray at birth. To hold her breath. To pause
upon her entry into this fortress, labrynthine and confu
sing as to whose fingers will hold you and whose will
want to squeeze you and convince the breath of its re
striction. As if she looked upon this photograph with
me and paused, holding herself by the diaphram in an
ticipation of hearing the young Black man scream out
in some human actualization of order and sense, not
wanting her own breathing to obscure the photograph's
rationale, evidence that the method of torture might
not undo the project of humanity, which, in the hi
story of her own awareness cultivating inside her moth
er's body, captures everything. The anticipation was like
warfare I imagine. Though one where you are either
unarmed, holding nothing but another person or your
tied to an object you might creatively subvert, as if to say improvise with, if not for being bound to it
ownself, or where you hold a weapon you don't know
how to use. With nothing but a determination that is life itself

The gravity of a prisoner's convictions in the Lease System could range from mere fisticuffing, hog-stealing, or other misdemeanor crimes like carrying a concealed weapon—a crime, as noted by George W. Cable in 1880, common among whites though often overlooked.

My child's voice at times, pressing as it does to the limits of her body, is an investigation. How far will ribs expand. What is hers. Who is it that is that hers. Who is the one feeling skin stretch or the bones move. A word without contrast fills the rooms during her research. Like a cheek, or greasy finger imprinted against windows facing the street. Fills the smallest spaces between fur on cats, surprised by how voice might travel like fingers along their spines. Her language is a filling that seems to not end until spontaneously consonants break the song of a voice. One that until then was the universe itself.

While some 1,200 convicts during the year 1880 were leased in the system fewer than half were serving sentences of 10 years, many sentences of less than 1 or 2 years. 10 years was the maximum amount of time an over worked convict in the system was expected to live. In Tennessee, Cable uncovered 12 boys under the age of 18 leased in the system, with each serving sentences of less than 1 year. In North Carolina there were 234 convicts under the age of 20 lease d in the system.

Our sound is a field sometimes. One where things are
moved by their influence on each other. With no
judgment as we know. To witness is to give it
Captu
re.   **to detain that sound in a camp of tortured stillness.**

Because I am Willful is a word often used to be kind without *Sometimes my*
discipline kindness. To be generous by capturing in a word. It is *students ask*
categorical. Do we learn about paternalism through *how I*
histories of violence? To have been violated? To be *can read*
one who studies violence is seeing influence. What is *that word*
influence by other names. Learning them. What is *outloud,*
truly another name is another language. Another *and I say I have*
place.   *to,*
                                                                       that the
                                                                       writer
                                                                       meant for it
                                                                       to be there
                                                                       for us
                                                                       to have
                                                                       to reckon
                                                                       with.

My kid pushes a small plastic lawn mower so that
bubbles are coaxed from a spinning yellow sprocket.
The faster she pushes it, the more excited the bubbles
seem to float ino the light, bursting into the palms of
maple leaves forming a canopy above the scene of us.
Her pushing. Me watching.

our life blurring at the edge of becoming an aesthetic
                                moment predicament

She pushes her lawn mower until her skin becomes
rosed and it seems to glow, to me. *One time a student*
                                asked if I would
                                feel the same
                                if I were
                                White,
                                and I said "but I'm
                                not. "
                                stone
                                beam
                                pillar
                                slab

I would burn every acre in America

touched by dulled glops of sweat from my child's burnt face.

I sit watching her push and feel weighed and immense and immobile in an anger that is mine. That has frothed among pages of study and that has no counterpart and clouds my ability to be neighborly.

Privilege and too much
television at a young age makes this anger a heroic
passion. The just. The burning vengeance. *Fo*
r a reason
I do not know
John L. Spi
vak, a phtographer and journalist
chose to
fictionalize his document the risks he took,
ing of Southern   stealin
convict camps. He ca   g docum
lled it Georgia N*   ents,
****. *He had to*   lying to
include an   gain ac
appendix of   ces
atrocity   s
to acc
ount
for the
sto
ry.

The fiction moves in where the absence of real reckoning
leaves a space unaccommodated with the words
                                        we have
                                        for naming the
exertion taking place there. The commons

Yet, the document speaks because a camera hanging
around his neck was not used to bound the occasion,
but rather reveal events occuring and give them,
speechless from discipline, the power of conse
quence. Spivak's photos stage an unstaging.

We look upon images accompanied with what we bring with us

Some images need coaxing from the archive. Some
images need pause, a meditative withholding of their
act, a mindful demonstration of what is present.

Sara Veglahn
from *The Monsters*

Although not actually tethered to the rail, he walked as if he were. I gazed up at him. I laughed into air. I laughed in his face—his face so serious with the effort of balancing. It was grey and hot. We'd just come from the beach, our bathing suits still wet with saltwater. He leaped and landed. He was suddenly above. He didn't say, but I knew he wanted me to look and admire, to look and look, to gaze up at him with awe, to see him as remarkable, to see him as extraordinary, significant, notable, the daring young man on the flying trapeze.

When I think of him now, this is what I think about: the graceful movement of limbs, the bare chest, the serious face, and how he was always performing, always balancing precariously on a thin rail, one arm suspended above his head perpetually, one leg outstretched behind perpetually, he is high above the ocean, high above the ground, he reaches forward, always moving along, always steady and serious, and higher than I could ever reach.

I admit that I was lonely. So I set the house on fire. It was the best thing I've ever done. It was the most satisfying thing I have ever experienced. I want to set every single thing on fire. Every house. Every thing. Watching that house burn was like nothing I had ever seen before.

I sat on the fence watching. I was watching from afar. I was not interested in watching the fire stop. I wanted the fire to go on forever.

It was like falling myself when the roof caved in. There was a wave of heat that came toward me when it happened. It was like being under water. It was a lot like water, this fire, this burning, this thing that I did, this fire I set on purpose, I made it happen, and it was glorious, beautiful, perhaps the most beautiful thing I have ever seen, I never wanted it to end, I wanted to continue on, down the road, taking this fire with me.

Listen: I have something to tell you about leaping off the edge. About standing at the gate and breaking the lock. About moving away from the space that was created within a hot and heavy breath. About the way in which I could now only stand to look at him when he was facing the other way.

Like a preacher he was, in those moments of pronouncements, those moments of let-me-tell-you-how-it-is, I am the knower, I am the one who understands, you haven't got it figured out the way I do, and so I'll just go ahead and tell you about it.

I will tell you that in those moments I wanted to push him down. I wanted to take out his tongue. I would have set him on fire if it meant I wouldn't burn too.

Instead I turned everything off. His voice became a slow rumbling then. Static. Gravel. Then I filled his drink and then I smiled in his general direction and then I vaguely brushed crumbs on the table into a pile and then I looked at the stain on the ceiling and then I examined my fingernails and then I thought about pushing him off a cliff and then I thought about setting him on fire and then I would hear the finality in his voice and I came to with a jerk of my entire body, as if I were poked with a stick, and I got up to refill the glasses.

"Show off."

"Practice makes perfect."

He made it look easy, diving into the vortex. He stayed up all night practicing. He stayed up all night diving into the water. All day, he was waterlogged and vicious, barking orders at me like a wolf. This larger-than-life-ness he was cultivating was overwhelming. He was becoming the motion, becoming the water, becoming a copy of himself. Larger than life. It's true, he was doing the impossible. There's something to that. But it was brutal, living this way. I wasn't sure how much longer I could witness this performance. I wasn't sure how much longer I could participate in this battle of wills.

X marks the spot. One moon in the sky and one moon in the water. A third moon hovering between. The great wave made a mountain. The great wave made steam. The difference between water and fire is not so great. I can't tell you how much I wanted to propel myself inside it. This water avalanche, this steam volcano. It became an architecture, an echo that makes a staircase on which one can climb to the pinnacle of an idea. This is how to understand the mysterious.

I threw everything into this space—every word, plate, stone, tree. Every match. Every new thing I had. I was looking for a place to dwell or I was looking to disappear. There doesn't seem to be much difference.

If I got through it, to the other side, perhaps I could make sense of things. But when you're tossed asunder, when you're diving out, it is difficult to understand dry land.

I was laid out. I had a funny feeling. I could give no response.

Tonight. Tomorrow. Yesterday.

What was. All the old-timers. The tower across the street.

If I could tell you I would tell you how every time I saw him I wanted to reach down my throat and pull out my lungs.

There was a time when I was upright. The music I made was an approachable hum. I was way beyond a white picket fence. There was nothing I had done so I decided to make something up. A crime. A disaster. All around me.

There were days I couldn't speak. Days of utter silence. Abandonment to the other senses. What I wouldn't give to go back and do it all over. It was happening to all of us—every day, another one, flat on her back, out by the pool or on the beach. Stuck in a bathing suit for the rest of her days—no matter what the weather.

But we had our own weather, our own houses, our own messes to clean.

I pass through this arc of knowledge. I pass up all kinds of opportunities. The only thing now is to rest, and all of this rest is exhausting. I fall down in the most inopportune places. I fall down and just stay there.

And the expense. I could have never imagined the expense. If I had all day to do what I wanted, I often thought. If I had it all, was never something that crossed my mind. I would never, I often said. I would never do that, I said once. I'm not interested then, was a response I often heard and often thought to make. If you could believe in just one thing, that would help, I was told. I was always told something. What I did understand was obvious. I won't bother to repeat it—or maybe it's important to do so. What I understood was that whatever you think, or believe, or desire is wrong or, if it's not wrong, it will be taken from you. I know this because it happens over and over. And in the time I have left, I expect this won't change. This is the way of the world. The way of the world in a grain of sand, an approach from land. I gave up my ideas long ago. And every time I think about it, I want to tear out his heart and roast it slowly over an open flame.

I saw the explosion before I heard it. A long finger of light lingering. Then the crash of the waves and then a different crash that traveled toward me and made a strong breeze that moved my hair onto my face. I was briefly blinded. When I saw again I saw the column of water still on the horizon, glowing a sick green. As if a mountain were made and it was growing while I watched it. As if it were a place you could get to. I stood on the cold sand with a towel around my shoulders and looked. Each moment I expected it to disappear and each moment there it still was. Ice-like. Majestic. Pathetic.

I wasn't sure which I desired more—its presence or its disappearance. I stood there until the sun gave way. And at the moment of near dark, it seemed it finally gave up its elevation. Another moment longer, and then it was gone.

I left. I walked slowly back to the house. I thought of how I could be like it was. There, then still there, then gone. I wanted to slide over to this other plane. This mountain of light could be my home. This mountain that no longer exists. There I would build a room of water. The webs of light streaming through. A single prism hanging from the window. A table, a chair. This place would never have speaking. Never noise. Only the low hum of waves outside it, serious and cold. I would sit there, still. No thoughts of sticking a knife in his eye. No thoughts of anything. I will kill him if I'm not careful.

When I came to, I was fully clothed and flat on my face. The blast I followed across the water, the pillar of light I saw on the horizon, seemed so harmless. I thought it could not reach me. I thought it was too far away. It seemed it would dissipate over the expanse. What I remember is watching the light, a finger in my eye, the sound only a memory of sound. Everything was muffled, like I had water in my ears. I felt off-balance.

But it wasn't the explosion across the water. I was no longer at the beach. I lay there, my face pushed into the carpet, my favorite dress pushed up my thighs. Then the footsteps in the kitchen. Then the door slamming. The smell of coffee, newly brewed. It was another morning and he was leaving for work.

How long I had been here was anyone's guess. How I was supposed to get up and get on with the day seemed impossible. The waiting until he got home, then his arrival. It seemed clearer to me than ever before that this time was going to be different. I hauled myself up and started to prepare.

I plunged and stayed there under the water, beneath the blue swirl. A new perspective was needed. Music was playing in the house. I could barely hear it—*I'm gonna make you mine, make you mine, make you mine.* The evening was coming down hard and the scent of rain was already in the air. A shift, distinct and dark. I thought to wait there until the storm came. I wanted to stay as I was. I was indexing my thoughts, building a kind of religion, a kind of new prosperity. Here, I had the occasion to think, and this was a new way of thinking. Muffled sounds of below the water. In terms of history, I had these facts: there was a time before me, there is my time, and there is a time I will not know. Let me try to be more clear: here, it was as if I knew the past and the future, but the present was erased. *Sha la la la la live for today.* It was clear to me that the present had no relevance other than here, beneath the water. My inverse-ness had changed my way of thinking—I used to think the present was the only thing that mattered. But here it was different. Was this a joke? The thoughts that came to me were unfamiliar. They were hard to hear. I felt I had a daughter and that daughter was myself. What is the price of loyalty, she asked. And I saw her there, a mirror image, hair swirling around her face which was my own. The sky had no relevance. The earth was only a faint idea. What is the price of loyalty? It was something I hadn't considered before. It was a language I did not speak. What was the answer? To whom had I ever been loyal? As soon as she arrived, she vanished. I could feel the water move around me, could feel the storm's arrival. I was nearly out of breath. I couldn't remember much about the old ways. I thought of the idea of walking on solid ground. I was this close to giving myself over. Then a crash, and without thought I emerged—no longer beneath—no longer the wrong way. I thought the crash was thunder but soon realized it was a deck chair thrown against the house by the heavy wind. It kept happening, hurling itself against the wall.

Hala Alyan
Everyone Removes the Thorn

She missed the funeral. To her mother and aunts, Arwa pretended she had a big gig booked in LA, *a lead in a multicam pilot*, but of course there is nothing, just the same internet company commercial that she'd booked three years ago, which did surprisingly well. They've asked her to do two more since then. The concept is simple: she is part-superhero, part-vixen, trying to outpace the competitors' connection speed. The pay is fine. The rest of the time she temps, going from one overly air-conditioned office to another, veterinary offices, spas, rehab centers. The staff never learns her name, nor she theirs.

Her mother and aunts don't know about the internet commercials; they don't get them in Beirut. She tells them that she does a lot of theater work, which is sometimes true—she was George in a feminist adaptation of *Who's Afraid of Virginia Woolf?* last year—but mostly they don't ask questions. Anyways, Arwa's great disappointments had come early: theater major, a move to California, hundreds of failed auditions, the rained-out ceremony to Tag at a friend's backyard. Tag himself. Sometimes Arwa pictures the Atlantic and Europe like stalwart bodyguards, protecting her from her family.

"But you'll come right after?" her mother had asked. Her voice was nasally and weak. Her own mother had just died, after all. Arwa felt the lance of guilt rush across the world and nip her throat.

"Yes, Mama."

"Right after," her mother repeated. Arwa looked around at her cluttered living room. When they'd first moved in, the cottage—on the cusp of Echo Park, where the junkies met the hipsters selling vegan dog biscuits—had seemed charming, like something out of a Disney movie, with the shedding jacaranda and large windows. Tag had built a small fire pit in the backyard, and they'd drink mojitos there. Now it's overrun with weeds. When he left, he only took his clothes, but sometimes she wishes he took more, the house feeling claustrophobic at times, all that evidence of their old lives.

"I need a week." The timeline was arbitrary but felt right. Teta's body—the very thought of it, a body removed from its master, gave Arwa the chills—would be buried right away. The formal *azza* would last three days, well-wishers pouring in from all over, with food and flowers, her mother and aunts weeping into each other's arms. A week was perfect. She'd miss all of it.

ß

Four days in Beirut and she already feels herself regressing; on the ride from the airport, she'd held her breath while her mother drove through the tunnel. In Los Angeles, winter is a concept, evoked by iced pumpkin lattes and tinseled palm trees. But the air was too sharp outside her mother's car to keep the window down. She's always hated January in this country. Even the Mediterranean looks unappealing, gray as oatmeal. At least she remembered to pack a jacket. It is leather, one of Tag's old biker ones, with patches on the elbows.

"The Alami children came," her mother said as she drove. "And the Ghosseinis, and the Salems. All the way from London."

Arwa said nothing. She decided on the plane over, she will be silent, submitting to her mother and aunts. It is easiest this way. Her mother suggests a hair trim, and Arwa goes, the salon thick with hairspray and cigarette smoke. Everyone still smokes here. Arwa always forgets. The hairdresser offers her a cigarette and *oohs* over her hair.

"You've got curls for days, *chérie*," he says. His eyebrows are manicured to perfection. Her mother and aunts have been coming to him for years, for the identical hairstyle that every woman over fifty in Lebanon boasts, that helmetlike bouffant, highlighted with reddish streaks.

The television in the hair salon is on FashionTV, the sullen, bony models of Arwa's youth stalking the catwalk in feathery lingerie. She used to dream of being one of them, back then. The very thought of Los Angeles would make her salivate. Now her strongest association with LA is the heady scent of diesel, snaking traffic, the click of heels in audition waiting rooms.

Back in her mother's apartment, the television stays on reruns of a popular Turkish soap operas. There is still food leftover from the *azza*, and they all return to the same bowl of *roz bel haleeb* a neighbor had brought over, holding out spoonfuls of the sugary rice. The building is old but in a nice neighborhood, her mother and her two sisters sharing an apartment. Her grandmother had lived in the one below. There is no elevator. Garo, their doorman, is Armenian and pushing sixty; he has been there as long as she can remember. His quarters are on the ground floor, a small room that she has caught glimpses of over the years—stove pot, plaid blanket on a twin-sized mattress.

"May the remainder be in your life," he murmurs to Arwa when she first arrives and she thanks him. He used to give her licorice sticks when she was a child. Her grandmother always liked him.

For the first few days, Arwa avoids looking at her grandmother's door when she climbs the stairs. It is childish and superstitious, but she hurries past up the stairwell, like something might try to catch her.

ß

Her grandmother was spritely and magnetic. She raised three girls on her own, her husband dying before the war even started. Her girls were barely out of middle school when the first bullets rang out. During the war, when the neighborhood heard of soldiers coming their way, her grandmother had gathered every piece of jewelry in the house, making her daughters remove even their cheap bracelets, and neatly arranged them on a silver tray next to her engagement ring and wedding gold. The soldiers went from house to house, ransacking the bedrooms and china cabinets, forcing gold from women's wrists. She was waiting at the door for them. She had the tray in her hands. The neighborhood folklore was there had been a dozen men, rifles hoisted on their shoulders like purses. Her grandmother hadn't flinched, holding the tray out to them. *For your daughters*, she'd said, and they'd left without taking a thing.

ß

Arwa goes to the grave with her mother and aunts. They listen to weather reports on the car radio on the drive there. As they all walk down the path to the cemetery, she can feel them glancing at her. She is hit by déjà vu, a vague memory of years ago, walking along the Corniche as a little girl with them. It may be colder than California, but it's hot for Beirut, it's all anyone can talk about, how it hasn't snowed in the Cedars once this year. Her leather jacket is too heavy.

The cemetery borders south Beirut, with rows of headstones and a backdrop of unadorned trees and shrubbery. Arwa is glad for the winter. She cannot imagine this place in the spring, verdant and in bloom, with cherry blossoms littering the gravestones. It would feel too mocking, all that new life. She feels guilty for her own legs, the easy pitch of her lungs against her ribcage. Her grandmother used to balance books on Arwa's head, *if you want to be a star we need to fix your posture.* And now Arwa is standing on the dirt that buried her.

Her mother kneels near the gravestone, puts her lips against the stone. Her sisters do the same. "*Immi,*" her mother croons. They turn to Arwa, waiting. There is something expected of her, Arwa understands. A performance.

She bows next to them. In high school, she'd played a nun in *The Sound of Music* and they'd knelt just like this, her and the other fake nuns, on wooden pews some kid had built. Arwa places a palm on the gravestone. It is smooth and cool. Who inscribes gravestones? she wonders suddenly, almost violently. Her grandmother's name, the years that went along with her. When Tag came to Beirut with Arwa, that one time after they got married, her grandmother was the nicest one to him. She taught him how to make spinach pies, his slender guitarist fingers alongside Teta's. *She's good people,* he'd said to Arwa. It occurs to her she should probably call him, let him know. Arwa digs her fingers into the dirt, pretends it is cool, swollen dough.

The other women get up, dusting their pants. There is a small bench near the gravestones and they sit, not realizing the sound carries. They whisper about her. Arwa hears them talk about Tag and Los Angeles and how she has wasted her life. Her aunt says that she should be crying and Arwa does the watering trick, the one she learned in college, where she blows air up towards her eyeballs, but it doesn't work, her eyes sting and prickle but don't water.

When they aren't looking, she sucks the dirt from her fingernails.

ß

Afterwards, she goes out alone. Garo the doorman is lugging water bottles when she leaves the building. She is wearing a black dress, a nightgown actually, from the thrift store near her house in LA, but when her mother asked she said it was Dior.

"*Bonsoir*," Garo says. He always has a half-stricken expression on his face, the consequence of too-wide eyes. "Enjoy your evening, Arwa."

"Thank you, Garo." She feels a strange impulse to ask him about grave inscribers, or the recipe for spinach pies, or whether she should call Tag now or wait until she returns to California. Maybe she can ask Tag to meet for a drink, that tiki bar they love, with the Latin music and fish mango tacos. She can envision it clearly—the sexy flicker of the candles against their clasped hands, Tag repeating that her Teta was a class act, then the inevitable drunk walk home, Arwa pretending to twist her ankle. Much of her time is devoted to such fantasies these days; scheming ways to get Tag back.

"The remainder in your life," Garo says again, and Arwa feels crashed back into herself, into the memory of her grandmother's silhouette against the kitchen counter, guilt at the Tag daydream.

"And in yours," Arwa says, nonsensically, the response idiotic, and besides that, Arabic feels awkward in her mouth, a leather jacket in the wrong weather.

Her mother told her to take the car but Arwa walks instead. She'd given some vague response about where she was going, about old friends. A semi-truth, the divvy college bar unchanged from her youth, the same bartender who greets her with a hug and air kiss. Ever since she moved to California, he calls her Monroe. *Don't miss us too much, Monroe. Hey, Monroe, you ever see Brad Pitt out there?*

The bar is filled with university students, impossibly young in polo shirts, drinking B-52s. Arwa orders a whiskey, clean, then another. She doesn't say anything about her grandmother to the bartender who, anyways, loses interest after the first half hour, drifting to a trio of pretty girls in tight sweaters. Arwa waits an hour before she signals for the check and, when he brings it, she leans in.

"Half a gram, if you've got it." She slides the folded bills across the sticky bartop.

A shuffling beneath the bartop, his folded palm in hers. "It's good to have you back, Monroe. Good thing you're not too famous to visit." He winks at her.

"Good thing," she echoes. His smile is too wide to convey the sting. She leaves.

ß

Tag had seen her on television before they ever met. Her biggest break, the one that led her and her friends to reserve a table at the elite Rosehip, ordering oysters and cognac like stars in a rap video. It was a guest-starring role on a popular sitcom about four men living in Manhattan. She was the main lead's love interest, an ill-fated plotline, no repeat appearances, the director made sure to tell her, but still it was a prime-time spot, something for her reel. Later, Tag would confess that he'd seen the episode, months before they met at a friend's birthday. She remembers now, years later, the day of that shoot, how she'd been getting over a cold, blowing her nose in the trailer bathroom, pinching her cheeks for color. The studio was massive and lively as a beehive and the fluorescent light fixtures were too bright. She'd sweat so much the assistants had to keep blotting her neck. She had no idea, walking to her car that evening, after a twelve-hour shoot, the cool air exhilarating against her bare arms, that her life was different now. That someday a man would watch what she'd just done and marry her.

ß

She is drunker than she'd like to be, but it is too early to go back. Her aunts don't sleep until midnight, after the late-night news. They are upset with her, were terse on the drive back from the cemetery. The least she could've done was cry.

The road outside the bar ends at the entrance of the American university, and Arwa waits until the security guard turns, then darts in, trailing a group of students. They are laughing and speaking loudly about some party. One of the girls has an earbud in and the wire dangling, and when Arwa passes her, she catches a refrain from the song, French, pop-y. She remembers when it first came out, dancing to it with Tag at a housewarming party in Los Felix, a bedraggled yard with Christmas lights entwined around strawberry cacti.

The song reminds her of another one, the *je t'aime, je t'aime, comme un fou* one, that her grandmother had inexplicably loved, back when Arwa was in high school. Her grandmother, stick-thin, embroidered duster, twisting her toe like she was putting out a cigarette.

"What time's your flight?" somebody asks the pop-song girl, who grins. She pulls the other bud out of her ear.

"Six a.m. Just enough time to get *wrecked*."

"So lucky, Lisbon sounds epic."

They hustle past Arwa. She has no understanding of Lisbon, has never been. What she envisions comes from movies, airlines ads—candy-colored houses, uneven hills. And this girl, coltish, wearing a furry coat, walking through the paved streets. Arwa is surprised to feel jealous.

There is a large map near the library, but Arwa doesn't stop; even though it's been years, her body moves fluently through the campus, under the oak trees, from one building to the next. It is comforting how little has changed—only cosmetically, renovations, electronic charging stations, but the actual buildings are imposing as ever, the brick shining whitely in the dark. She walks until she reaches the green oval, uncreatively named after its color and shape. Facing it, tall and shadowed, is Fisk Hall. The English department.

Her memories of that time are mostly faded. All-nighters on the quad, huddling in oversized hoodies on the damp grass. Hash browns and cigarettes after a night of drinking. A perpetual autumn, leaves crunching beneath her boots, a dramatic fringed scarf she'd worn for an entire semester because her grandmother said it made her look like Grace Kelly. Her first blowjob behind the Chemistry department, the antiseptic taste of semen in her mouth. She remembered time as something different back then, not just less paltry, but the very smack of time felt more luxurious somehow, a berry waiting for her to bite.

There had been a professor, Haidar or Haider. It became messy, of course, a ripple of gossip through the department, rumors of elopement though in truth they'd barely dated, a few times crammed in the back booth at an Armenian restaurant near the marina, the two of them smashed on arak. The best rumor was that he'd gotten a tattoo of the letter *A* on his bicep. She may have started it herself. Had there even been a tattoo? She can't remember anymore.

Arwa climbs up the stairs to the building. The doors at Fisk Hall are locked, but there is a small ledge that she sits on. She doesn't have a key, nobody in their neighborhood locks their door. She pulls out the baggie and does a bump, messily, on the back of her hand, which she hates, because some always spills, but the coke is decent and she wishes she'd bought more.

Two voices, footsteps. Arwa peeks out over the ledge. A couple of students approach. They are walking across the oval, toward the male dorms. The name, Penrose, blooms in Arwa's mind like a bud.

"Hey!" she calls out. They look startled. She always forgets that teenaged boys are like this, more afraid than fearsome.

"Yeah?" The taller one seems suspicious. He has nice arms.

"I want to ask you a question." She moves toward them, jumps down the last two steps. This is her favorite part—when the drug whispers up and down her spine like a bass beat.

They glance at each other. "Lady," the other boy says, more politely, "we have something to get to."

"Totally, totally." She sounds feverish to her own ears, which is a little unnerving. "Real quick, I promise." She hooks her thumb toward the building behind her. "Do either of you know Professor Haidar? Or maybe it's Hashem?"

The boys look at each other again.

"Is Professor Haidar still here?' Her voice is a little hysterical, and she swallows. "Never mind." She wants to ask if they have any cocaine, then has a vision of the security guard slipping her wrists into cuffs. "My grandmother died," she says instead.

They look at her as though she is speaking another language and for a moment she wonders if she is. "Let's get out of here," the tall boy whispers, loud enough for her to hear. "This lady's weird as fuck."

"Sorry about your grandmother," the other boy, the nicer one, calls over his shoulder as they turn to leave.

"Thanks," she whispers.

"Fucking weird," she can hear the tall boy repeat, their bodies receding into the dark.

ß

There are dozens of bars in Hamra, winking like beautiful women. But Arwa ignores them, walking homeward instead, shedding the university and its memories like a dress. Beirut has grown and shrunk in the last decade, become a facsimile of itself with its kitschy bars and Anglicized locals. If she never had to return, she would be fine. Her grandmother, a stone grave with years on it. That first year in California, the same dream plagued her over and over—turquoise waves rising from the beaches in Tripoli, Saida, Jbail, and crushing the city, flooding the cafés and gas stations, reaching even the skyscraper rooftops. She was always in the exact same spot, on the verandah outside her grandmother's bedroom, her grandmother's bare feet propped up on the railing. When Arwa started to panic, her grandmother would sigh, speak in Arabic, a phrase Arwa could never remember hearing in her waking life. *Everyone removes the thorn from their own hand*, her grandmother would say. After that, it was just silence, emptiness, the two of them watching the water coming for them.

ß

Garo is sitting on a plastic chair near the back entrance when she arrives at the building, a nearly finished cigarette in his hands. He tosses it when he sees her, and rises, the sort of old-fashioned, gentlemanly decorum that reminds her of being a child. She can't remember a time before Garo, though it must have existed; her mother and aunts have wistfully mentioned a handsome doorman from their twenties.

"How is your evening going?" Arwa asks. This, too, from her youth—the feeling of being caught, trying not to slur her words. In this way, Garo knew about her adolescence better than her mother and aunts, the one who'd unlock the gate when she came home after midnight, tactfully looking away as she got into cars with old boyfriends. She never thanked him for it. To do so would have implied negligence on his part; better to pretend the driver was her violin teacher, the late night was for studying.

He smiles shyly. His teeth are awful, browning. Garo is not attractive, but he is tall enough, beloved. "Good, good. The winter has been kind, God is good."

"God is good."

This time, Arwa pushes the doorknob of her grandmother's apartment, but it is locked. This makes her angry. In her entire life, she's never found it locked. She clomps up the stairs to her mother and aunts' apartment, hoping to wake them, but the house is quiet and dark when she enters. On the living room mantle, there is an ugly ceramic swan Arwa had made one of her aunts for a long-forgotten birthday. There, a bundle of keys, marked with little letters. Arwa takes the one with a lowercase *d*, for Delilah, and goes back downstairs.

Her grandmother's apartment is the same as always, save for some packed boxes in the foyer. Someone has brought in the laundry from the balcony clothesline, a sad heap on the couch. They will bring in a cleaner, Arwa suddenly realizes, someone to disinfect the floors and bathroom, and the bleach will drive the scent of flesh and illness away.

She could cry now, if she really pushed it, but instead she walks down the hallway, spotted with photographs of family and trips. They are all from before, when her grandmother still had her sight. The biggest one, Arwa, twelve, thirteen, in a bikini, tan and wild haired, oversized sunglasses on the tip of her nose like Lolita. There is a photograph from the wedding, Tag in a white suit, Arwa's arms mid-dance. It was in Los Angeles, none of the family had come, but her grandmother had still framed the photograph. Nobody had told her grandmother about Tag leaving, Arwa understands. She unhooks the back of the frame and takes the photograph, folds it into her pocket.

In her grandmother's bedroom, a tidy bed. The dusted dresser, pill bottles nowhere in sight. The drawers are mostly empty, except for socks and a camera, one of her grandmother's, from years ago. It is a Pentax K1000, heavy, banged up. She distantly remembers using it herself, a brief crush on photography, her grandmother's fingers over hers as she taught her to adjust the light.

There are ten photographs left. The little red arrow counts numbers down as Arwa tugs back the shutter release. She stands at the window, overlooking the empty street. She knows enough about photography to know there isn't enough light; if someone develops this roll, these will be rectangles of black. She snaps photo after photo until the shutter release won't budge anymore.

ß

The last of the cocaine, a speckle on the armoire. Arwa snorts. She turns off all the lights and lies down on her grandmother's bed. She tries to remember the rest of the lyrics to that French song. She checks her Instagram, but Tag's last photograph is still the Joshua tree with a police streamer around it. The caption reads: *only in cali.*

A murmur from the street below. Arwa goes to the window; it is Garo, speaking on the phone, lowly, though she can make out random words. He is talking about the funeral, the other inhabitants leaving flowers with him for Arwa's family. She wonders who is on the other end. There isn't a wife or children. Just a couple of nieces, black-haired girls she would play with when they visited, for Christmas or Armenian New Year. They always wore matching, clean dresses.

It happens quickly, the coke doing its whisper-dance in her veins, Arwa shutting her grandmother's apartment door behind her, realizing a moment too late, *shit*, that she left the key inside, then the stairs clacking beneath her heels. She wants to catch Garo talking and she does, standing outside his little room, whispering. When he catches sight of her, he gets off the phone hastily.

"Is something wrong upstairs?" he asks. Arwa shakes her head. He studies her face for a moment. "It has been a long day for you, dear," he says gently. "You will feel better tomorrow."

"I want to feel better now."

She knows what she has done before doing it. In that sense, it is already over, the narrow mattress in Garo's room rocking beneath her back, the headboard snagging her hair in its splinters, his hands trembling over her body. His hairy belly skimming hers with each pump, sweaty, slick.

Garo sees it. "Dear." His voice shakes. "You are good woman, the daughter of fine people. Your grandmother—"

She moves towards him. "Uncle—" the word from childhood, the common phrase for any man not her father, the word suddenly filthy in her mouth, "Uncle, don't say another word about my grandmother."

He doesn't.

ß

Afterwards, there is silence. There is an insistent whirr from some appliance, like wings beating against glass. It was quick and ugly, Garo jumping up immediately after to get Arwa a towel, straightening the blanket that has fallen to the floor. What has happened is, irrevocably, her fault, but Arwa knows that Garo will blame himself. He is the sort of man who believes in integrity and sin. The sort of man who will quit a beloved job if he thinks he betrayed his employers. He shuffles around the small room. He repeats the remainder is in her life.

"My husband won't call me," Arwa speaks into the quiet room. She is dressing herself, slowly, buttoning the Cavalli jeans. They were expensive, a splurge after she first booked the commercial a few years ago. The boutique had been like the inside of a candle—fragrant, warm, beige.

"God rest her soul," Garo says shakily. She knows he is talking about Delilah. Her Teta. He doesn't care about Tag or Los Angeles or internet commercials. A woman he loved is dead. Arwa is something unnecessary, collateral. *Everybody removes the thorn from their own hand.* She remembers the dream, the phrase her mind crafted; she asks Garo if he has ever heard it.

A surprised look on his face, reminiscing. He almost smiles. "Ah, yes. Of course. It is an old saying. My aunts used to say it to us, when we'd fight with each other." His face wanes again. "Where did you hear it?"

"Teta used to say it." This must be the truth. If Arwa hadn't invented it, she heard it somewhere, likely from her. A false memory: Arwa, a toddler, wrecking something, her grandmother towering above her, frowning. At some point, there must've been some disaster. At some point, Arwa must've asked for help.

ß

It is clear Garo wants her out of his room and the craving to talk has left her, so she leaves, smoking one of her last three Parliaments on the perch that overlooks the street. There are the same windows she has peered into every day for decades. Her mind is fried with the same memory loops. Every time she thinks of Garo, she thinks of her grandmother, and her hand shakes a little. She smokes the cigarette to the filter, then leaves it, burning, on the ledge. In the morning, there will be a little burn mark on the brick.

She doesn't stop at her grandmother's apartment this time, goes to the one where her family sleeps. She knows the houses like her own body. The women snore in their beds. Arwa tiptoes across the rooms, lifts jewelry boxes from the armoires. She takes their rings out, the necklaces and bracelets. She removes her own, the earrings from Chile, the pendant Tal gave her when she booked the commercial. With her palms cupping the jewelry, she goes back downstairs slowly and knocks on the Garo's door with her sneakered toe. He opens the door and she steps in, drops the jewelry on his small dressing table.

"For your daughters," she says.

ß

Outside she walks until she reaches Hamra street. She has her purse and her credit card and her passport. The rest doesn't matter, the small suitcase in her mother's apartment. Footless leggings, favorite boots, MAC lipstick in the shade Merlot in Paris. They are irrelevant now. She never wants to see them again anyway. There are the distant lights of a taxicab down the street. She holds her arm out. In college, she spent every winter in the theater department, preparing for Blanche DuBois and Shakespeare's Miranda, countless hours spent in the rehearsal room that smelled like chalk and feet. Her favorite part of any play was always the audition. It still is—the moment of possibility, ev-eryone frozen in anticipation, waiting to see what you can do. It reminds her of the split second after a plane lifts from the air and gravity seems like a lie.

That's what this moment is like, as she holds her arm out for the cab, the car slowing down. She is auditioning, for the part of a woman who is letting something end. She wants the role.

When she gets in, she tells the driver, "The airport," in her breathy audition voice.

The last time she saw her grandmother, there were protests near the airport. The parliament had shut down again. Watching the burning tires on the news, her grandmother was somber. She'd said, What is coming is better than what is gone. She said that from time to time. Arwa always forgot the phrasing in Arabic. That was four years ago. Four non-winters in Los Angeles.

Tag had asked her not to call anymore. He told he couldn't keep trying. Arwa tries to imagine a first date, someone new to Los Angeles from Tulsa or Columbus. She'll fall in love with the next man she meets. She feels this so irrefutably it is a decision. It will be what happens next to her. Love is like that, a can kicked down the road.

As they drive through the tunnel, she takes a big gulp of air. She imagines that somewhere, off the coast of a country thousands of miles away, India or Nepal, a tremor hits and the earth begins to move, a tiny seismic shift, puckering the waves bigger and bigger until they reach Beirut. She'll buy a ticket at the airport, somewhere cold and cloudy. To Lisbon, she suddenly decides. She wants to see it snow. Maybe they'll seat her next to that cool girl from the campus. Arwa will tell her about Garo and the soldiers, her grandmother unhooking her daughters' bracelets. By the time the sun rises, she'll already be in the air.

Jennifer Militello
On Time

A moment is makeshift. It is constructed of sticks and child's glue despite the strong wind. Huff and puff and you can blow it over. Watch it dissipate like dandelion seed. It sinks between the cough and the orchard, the bow and the string. The elbow in time is the part that gives. Milk stilled in the glass. Trains arriving late. One fabric rubbing at another. Scrimshaw holding the memory of the whale surfacing and sounding, scribble of bone.

I remember when I first felt the future might influence the past. I was expecting a letter and thinking of the letter's arrival in the box. Wondering whether it would be there when I returned, lying pale on its side like a market fish, sealed gills still, happy news or sad. Suddenly I felt the way I crossed the street or the route I took could alter its news, what was said inside. That time didn't just happen one way, past to present. That cause and effect were not as linear as we might think. That what I did right now was influencing my mother's childhood. That the way the weather behaved tomorrow would influence the dawn of the earth.

Einstein tells us all time happens at once.

When I try to remember my first conscious moment, I grasp the vague dream of a red mitten in snow. I know it isn't my first awareness, but is only the first moment my memory has held.

My life of memory began the night I dreamed of the single red mitten in the snow.

I was four years old. The dream was colorful and tangible and soft. Like touching a chimney full of wind. It was like the small moths that rise up from the uncut grass when one walks through it. Like kerchiefs, like dust, like eyes edged in fright, like the miles before the train comes, or headlights gone dim. Like sunlight coming through a lens to set fire to dried-out leaves

This mitten was the present and the past. I had dropped a single red mitten in the snow that afternoon, while the light was waning, and when I noticed, I pulled on my mother's hand, but it was too late. She was in a hurry, and hadn't seen.

So the mitten was left behind.

Because the clouds filled up and the rain came down. Because the drywall went up and the struts went in. Because the threads let loose and the seams unraveled. Because even houses are filled with wolves.

When I woke from the dream, I felt a serious dread. An understanding that the world in my mind was dead, but that the world itself was very alive. I had made something in my mind; it wasn't memory, and it also was. All the wormholes opened. All the realities and their shadowy fictions clashed. I understood that I could never truly understand what was real.

I understood the past. I understood the self. I understood that the two were separate, and the same. I was dreaming something in a dream that wasn't real. But I could go outside and the reality would be made. The mitten could be there.

The sensation mimicked the one I felt when I went to the house where I'd grown up. The house was there, and was real. There were trees outside. There was a road out front. But inside the sleeve of that house, inside the tunnel of my seeing that house in my mind, there was the other house, still white with blue shutters, still with a pine tree at the corner that was small. Still with two children playing by digging holes and pretending to cook in them pine cones and stones.

Too much lushness: I couldn't make myself drive past. Everything had grown out of control. The oak at the corner cut back from the telephone wires, the neighbors' bushes along their suspension wall. The pine tree my sister had planted as a sapling towered taller than the roof. Its shadow fell along the length of the house. The room at the corner that had been mine I imagined no longer filled with sun.

It was there beneath the skin of what I was actually seeing, this other skin, the neighborhood of the past. This surface neighborhood was a stranger. That deeper ancient neighborhood was in my very blood. The place where I'd turned off the road to walk the path to elementary school, the sign there once sprayed with graffiti, the kind neighbors who knew me, all grown old. The pain of that. The pain of loss.

The sensation that came with those two houses dividing. Again, the red mitten was in my dream, and also outside in the snow.

Maybe it wasn't a dream, but a memory so vague, so far at the beginnings of memory, that it seemed like one.

When I carried my children, I remember reading they could dream in the womb. I remember looking at my daughter during the ultrasound, as she sat curled at the bottom, a long way down, gazing straight up, seemingly at me. I remember the camera traveling my son's spine until it looked like the backbone of a dragon or a fish. I remember holding him as a sleeping newborn in the hospital as he twitched, as his eyes paced the rooms beneath their lids, back and forth, and feeling excluded. He'd known me such a short time. A dream. He was inside himself. I wasn't there, and I doubted he could remember me; I was so new. Then suddenly his lips puckered and his mouth suckled, and I was overjoyed. I was there! He was dreaming of eating. And so dreaming of me.

I was in that moment aware: I was my son's past, his present, his future. I had grown his teeth and eyelashes and fingernails and wrist bones in my body, with the material of my body. Someplace, cells of his still floated in me. He had made me a chimera. His cells were in my body. His cells were in my brain.

When Einstein dreamed of the universe's shape, he dreamed differences added in velocities, at 186,000 miles per second: light speed. The moving beam versus the moving ball. He was dreaming of people aging more slowly on spaceships shaped like whales and traveling at the speed of light. He dreamed of density, hyperbolic curvatures, flatnesses and spheres. He dreamed of an infinity. Sheets of paper and leather saddles, tidied bedspreads and empty shoeboxes. Collapsing. He dreamed existence as the skin of a balloon, spinning teacups and fireworks and tailspins of stars.

Traveling quickly, we age more slowly. Even in cars. Even on trains. We may travel more quickly in space, but any forward accelerated movement means the slowing of age. How is this possible? Don't we age by years? Don't we age by moments strung together in a necklace of our memories and developments and scars? Time is elastic, is relative. And, for us, is largely dictated by memory.

But my brain at times also remembers the future. I know someone will call. And they do. I know I will see someone I haven't seen for years at an event, am *sure* of it, and they are there. I know six deer will appear in the road. The six deer appear.

Déjà vus occur that are so powerful, I know what will be said next. I follow a conversation I already remember. Perhaps an as-yet-unpractical or unawake part of the brain contains a memory of the future. Perhaps our ancestors will see all time at once, and cause and effect will move forward instead of back.

Right before it happened, I dreamed of my grandfather's death. It was the day after my grandmother died. In the dream, my grandfather sat on the passenger side of a gray wagon. It was hitched to a gray horse, in a gray room. The reins draped lax in the driver's seat. I went around to the back of the wagon, where a gray mirror hung on the gray wall. When I looked in the mirror, I saw my dead grandmother's face. Then I got up on the bench beside my grandfather, took the reins in my hands, and drove the wagon off.

A week later, I got the call: my grandfather had been struck by a car while crossing at the crosswalk on 86th Street in Brooklyn, four blocks from their apartment.

Three days after that, I found myself saying goodbye to him as he lay unconscious in a hospital bed. Never before had I seen stubble on his chin. When I wasn't watching him, I watched the East River barges move like the slow bodies of those who have come to witness the last days of those they love.

The moment is a drop about to fall from a leaf, a floor about to be swept, an empty parking lot at dawn, seashore-white. The moment is water from a faucet poured into a cup.

I can't tell you how because there is no how. Or maybe there are too many. An orb weaver builds a web in the corner of my daughter's room, lays eggs there, comes down from the ceiling on a long strand. I examine the web, places the strands intersect, shapes made and contained in the structure. In the scaffolding, strands that aren't there, but also make the web: air, atom, molecule, nucleus, material from an exploded star, black hole pull, the spider's last meal, the creation of webbing in her spinnerets.

I examine the abdomen of the spider, hourglass shape, nautilus shape, cactus shape, iris shatter, galaxy splay. Fragment and fractal. Einstein's universe there. Time there, future and past. A language there, an obelisk of hieroglyphs, spinning words not quite understood, as though they were whispered just below the threshold of the ear's ability to hear.

My daughter dreamed this spider while still in the womb. My daughter dreamed it there in the time before she could remember, until it was real. There in her brain, the contours and movements, the intricacies, angles, and absences, the legs, the hourglass abdomen, the fractals and webs of her synapses firing, the darkness before and after it exists.

COLLABORATIVE AND
CROSS-DISCIPLINARY TEXTS

Laura Christensen (art) and Marjorie Thomsen (poetry)
To Float, To Breathe, To Hear

—after John Cage

Three vintage photographs, acrylic paint, cherry wood,
curly maple veneer, metal leaf, brass. 30 x 15 x 4 inches.

Some mornings are for mulling,
like this one; I contemplate what if
not everyone had to die. I hear
whatever song I sing in my head
because that's what you do
when you float on a lake and your ears
are on the cusp of hearing and hearing
silence. It seems the water and I care
for each other, the way my mother
is a stalk of yellow turning her face
to any temperature of sun and the sun's
guaranteed another day of life because
of her. Focusing my eyes on a cloud
that's not there, I imagine fish beneath me,
never still, never just floating. They're breathing
water and whispering about not seeing
my toes. They wonder about the where-
abouts of my face, my personality. The fish
have met my father and would see
the resemblance. I came here to breathe
this day of summer and to feel
my weightlessness after searching
for flowers pressed between pages
of a book. I found the mahogany-
brown stems and crinkly blossoms
at the end of the story.

Ryan Mihaly
from *B-Flat Clarinet Fingering Chart*

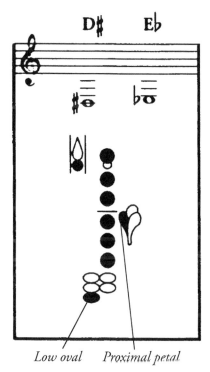

Low oval   Proximal petal

[D♯/E♭] When tilling the soil or harvesting fruit, riding a horse or climbing a tree, when praying, both hands and all ten fingers must be used: so it is with D♯, the deepest pitch and the closest to the earth. The integrity of this pitch relies on the strength of the hands' weakest digits: the right little finger, which, holding the low oval, allows the pitch to sound, and the left little finger, which reinforces what the right does by holding the proximal petal along the clarinet's torso. When sounded, D♯ sends shocks to the upper root canals, granting feral visions; or to the soles of the feet, which feel mud-covered and warm; or to the tailbone, which gives the clarinetist either a sudden bout of vertigo, or the kind of peace only afforded by the eye of a storm.

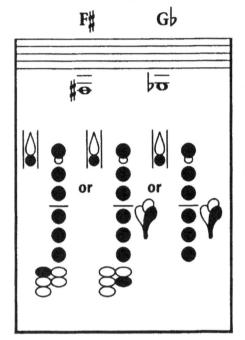

[F♯/G♭] Someone in the room turns your way when you play F♯; they did not expect to hear a cello. They see you playing the clarinet, of course, but they do not see how you are imagining yourself playing it, like a cello, your tongue and breath sending a bow of air sliding through the body of the clarinet. Imitation is the sincerest form of flattery, and in this case there is no other option: the clarinetist who does not imitate the cello makes a dull, hollow sound, like a dying owl—which, in the end, could be the sound you're after. Mimicry is unavoidable and must be cherished, for mimicry is another form of authenticity. A chameleon isn't fake for blending in with a tree.

D

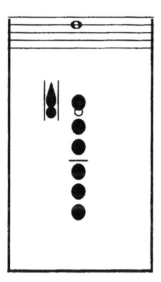

[D] How dark? How dark can you make D? Can you cover it in night? Dress it in black licorice robes? Eliminate any trace of moonlight? Tell the sun not to come back? Each key along the body of the clarinet is a star you must finger, a flame at the end of a wick you must pinch out. Every key an eye you must make blind. Press fists into your closed eyes and follow the patterns that appear. These patterns fill the breath you send down the clarinet with its eyes you hold shut. The patterns dance like snakes inside the pitch, but the pitch is a lake so still it is mistaken for the sky. Practice this until you are synesthetic.

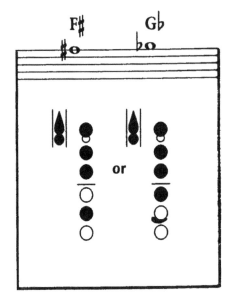

[F♯/G♭] Waiting is a form of absolution, a fasting of action. Time moves around you as you sit there, freeing you from long-forgotten guilt suddenly resurfacing: all the old words and those small, wretched acts flare up once more and disappear for good like a will-o-the-wisp. Then God, that ardent photographer of the soul, appears. He takes a snapshot of your spirit in a state of grace and promises to show it to you the next time you lose track of the truth, that divine virtue that always dissolves into a fog of subjectivity when you consider the myriad reasons behind any action, speechless. The antidote to speechlessness is the consultation of song, such as the bronze hum of F♯ or the low indigo cloud of G♭, and their attendant nostalgias.

F

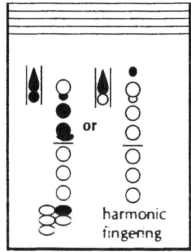

or

harmonic
fingering

[F] Vision: midday, snow falling, winter sun blazing; blue shadows on bricks lovingly arranged, textured by salt and dirt and footprints, barefoot children cartwheeling and leaping over them because of the game; snow melting making reflecting surfaces, children staring into river-mirrors suddenly forming, seeing self in watery splotches, asking "who?," earth rejecting bricks, bricks flying, children cartwheeling in the mud underneath, hopscotching, counting *one two fee fou,* children asking "who?," someone answering "I, who fell from the sky to lay a mirror on the ground for you," snow falling, snow falling.

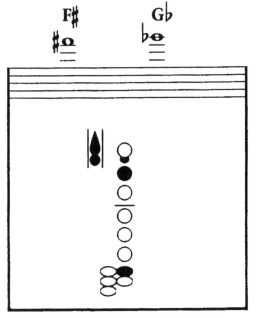

[F#/G♭] Vision: nighttime foaming at the mouth with stars; angels under duress, roaming the erotic waters of adolescence, enchanted by gossip; revelry in the forest, searching for kinship; rumor mill, speculation, threads lining their clarity net, through which hearsay passes and truth is caught, intensified by darkness and the party; fountain of atmospheres, eruption of hills, reminiscence of an origin, reliving a creation myth; stories realized by a commanding breath; a visit to the beach, shell shrapnel at the ankles, primeval ocean heaving away; primeval pink clambering over the horizon like a timid visitor; everyone wading into daylight to wonder.

Kristy Bowen

from *The Summer House*

Soon, the baby is full of bees. Bees in the bathtub, bees in the bassinet. Floating the surface of your coffee each morning without fail, tiny wings sticky with cream. Who can be a good mother amidst all this hum, the summer house thick with hives. The lives you've given up to get there. Every tiny shoe, every tiny spoon slick with honey. Who can be a good mother to child made of wax, even now softening in the sun.

All night the baby won't sleep. Moonlight seeps through the curtains and into the milk. Tell her a story and she goes silken in the crib. Unrolls and tumbles to the floor again and again. All night, we feed her sugar and water and hope for the best. Place her in the dresser drawer for safe-keeping while the outside animals long to be inside animals, their tiny snouts nestling at our knees. The inside animals grow claws and teeth and keep hiding the baby in the pantry, where she cries all night until we rescue her, always, at the last minute.

We hide the baby when the lights go out. When bright light scatters the sky, down we go. Into the ground with our blankets and kettles, the metal of our chair legs scraping the concrete. Play patty cake with the ghosts in our cellar, red rover with the lovers losing their sweetness. How they hover provocatively over the washing machine, the cans of rotting fruit. Everything we saved for later gone bad with every season. The baby busts open a box of stale raisins while we sleep beneath a thousand mattresses piled one atop the other, while outside, the wind takes one house then another.

By 7 o'clock, the ghost is knocking at the window. We fasten the locks and hide the matches, but something still smells like sulfur, the catch of a hundred tiny sticks bursting into flame. When we were children, we'd watch the boats roll in, one by one. Troll the breakwater looking wreckage, splintered bow, busted stern. Turn over in our beds. Eyes shut tight. My mother was made of smoke, every Virginia Slim catching her dress on fire while she waved from the dock mouthing *I love you. Come back.* Sometimes we'd float for days and return starving to the kitchen where she would not recognize us for all the lake grass caught in our hair. The wateriness of our stare. Her ghost moving away from the house, while we cried *I love you. Come back.*

We take the baby to the doctor on Mondays. Place her in a box and poke holes in the top. Sometimes she sighs or coughs and we raise the lid to find her vanished and back in the crib. It's hard to place who she takes after more. Me or the tree I rescued her from. Her father, rowing his boat on the horizon indefinitely. The baby sometimes pops herself right over the side and into the deep, deep water. We fish her out with a giant net and place her back in the box where sings til all the bees gather, a swarming cloud above us.

Jill Magi

A Triptych from *SPEECH*

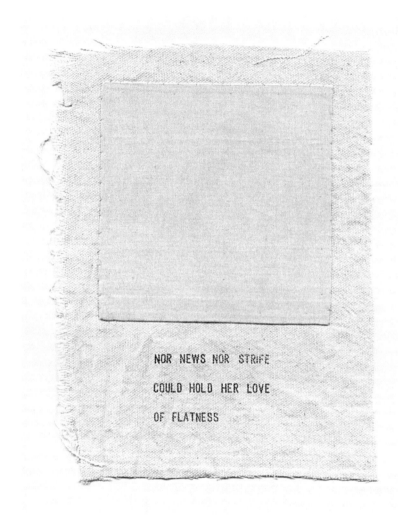

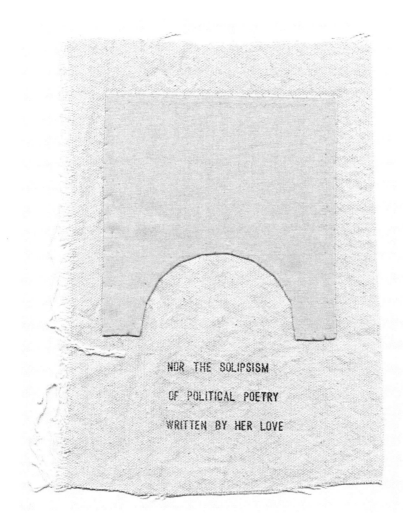

NOR THE SOLIPSISM

OF POLITICAL POETRY

WRITTEN BY HER LOVE

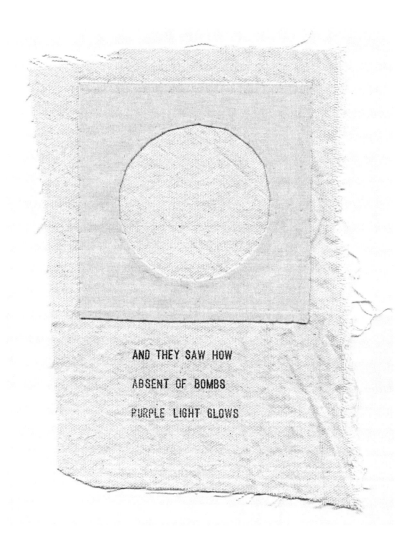

Leslie Nichols

Textual Portraits
Alice (Terrell 1904)

Marie-Eve (Beauvoir 1949)

Kathy (Stanton 1892)

Allison Titus
from *Obliterated Traces*

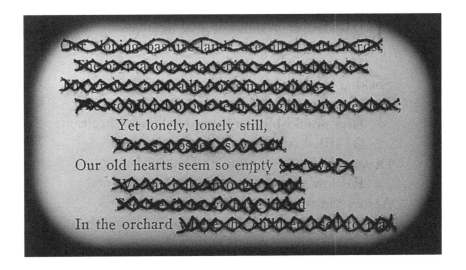

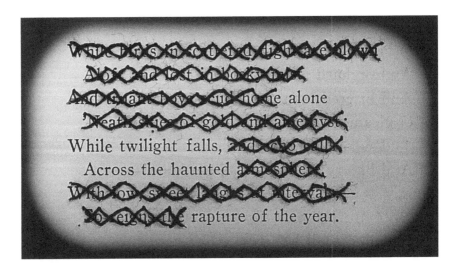

LITERATURE IN TRANSLATION

Aleksey Porvin, translated by Isaac Stackhouse Wheeler

A Few Banal Modes of Liberation and a Stroll Along the Broad-Gauge Tracks

I.

Francesco Petrarca, better known as Petrarch, compares a poet to a bee who makes honey with nectar gathered from many different flowers.

Francisco Sánchez de las Brozas, better known as El Brocense, described the power and originality of the art of poetry in terms of force. The poet is an imitator who defeats the imitable with the power of his erudition, mastering it by force, conquering it. Like a warlord, a poet should not hesitate to make what belongs to another his own.

While Hannah Arendt distinguishes between Dichtung (poetry), Diktum (what can be expressed), and Diktat (an agent acting upon another in manner that must almost be called violent), she assigns poetry the function of breaking the vicious cycle; in her writings, poetry draws a person into the process of conversing with himself.

Capitalism, in weathering its own permanent crisis, has long since begun to lose the economic instruments that enable it to function as an active agent and is thus seeking to buttress itself by manipulating people, building itself into the forms of their collective consciousness.

All four of them are strolling among the flowers and the smoking shell holes.

2.

There's a particular way someone walks when they're crossing a thundering battlefield, and it comes from the desire to get a closer look at the ground; the lower you bend, the better you can see the little cracks in the earth.

The reasons that drove me, a poet best known for lyrical poems that are not written from the perspective of a subject, to turn toward politics four years ago, come from the very constitution of my poetic process. The route to that realization was difficult, however; the cracks in the earth meandered like a snake, or murmured like runnels of emptiness, without becoming written words.

"Subjectless lyric," when founded on the strata of tradition, contains not only the necessary semantic potential for estrangement from one's cultural, national, or other identity, but also the potential to resist violence, in as much as the "I" is always complicit in the violent discourses involved in any form of power, regardless of its discursive regimes or external circumstances.

Poetry, by entering into an open dialogue with power (and thus facing the constant risk of plunging into the abyss of monologue), even when all other points of contact have been deformed, is capable of not only articulating a civic position, but also of mobilizing the individual and collective consciousness against the manipulations inflicted by those in power. Poetry is a crack that opens up in the air, the tectonic fault line where a new space breaks away from the continent of blood-soaked literal language.

The point of reference for political poetry is reality—both external and internal—and the politics of human inner reality, of the "I," is the starting point of a chain reaction of liberation from oppressive contexts. A very old religious song tells us that Christ can trample down death by death (*morte mortem calcavit*). When we've trampled down one crack with another, we can stroll through the trenches and tank traps with our friends.

So what does political poetry actually do? Its apparently binary mode of address (directed at both power and itself) is actually unitary, since the "internal" components inherent in violence which it addresses are also always located inside the speaking "I."

Poetic speech built on the absence of a subject—or that explicitly eliminates its subject before the reader's eyes—is you; your "I" is always getting jammed in the cracks between the flowers and the explosions.

3.

There are a lot of things you can appropriate when you're strolling across a battlefield with someone, but you'd be best served by appropriating new rhythm for your steps and new optics for your gaze.

Politics appropriated a lot of rhetorical devices and tropes from poetry—especially repetition. Repetition became more than an element of the discourse of power; it became the foundation of every wretchedly factual "dispatch from the warzone." Repetition feels ridiculous in contemporary poems. We know that it's dishonest, tainted with violence. Contemporary poetry should be free of any form of violence; we can feel it in our guts that repetition has no place there.

Things are going badly when it comes to metaphor, too, but at least violence has a poorly developed imagination; violence is encapsulated in its own inability to achieve lasting recognition, and its limits soon rise up to confront it.

Culture has given us the metabole the metarealists were so enamored with; the mode of thought reflected in Ivan Zhdanov's line "the unfinished gesture of a tree—whirlwind" is fundamentally unusable in the discourse of power, and so it opens up a road into a domain free of violence, demonstrating a mode of liberation.

They say *viam supervadet vadens*—the path will be overcome by the person who walks it—but the path has lost its rhythm—that makes it weak. He should walk in a way that makes it stronger.

4.

Petersburg, as the bearer of the Empire's spirit, helped Taras Shevchenko to elucidate an unbelievably painful sense of the binary opposition between freedom and unfreedom at its heart. During the reign of Nicholas I, he used that awareness as the foundation of his comedy "The Dream," yet not all of the vast weight of living in an enslaved Ukraine could be melted down and poured out as a text. The degree of courage required for a young poet to do what he did at the time he did it is inconceivable.

Nicholas I, whose person became the embodiment of ascendant

absolutism, began the construction of railroads in Russia. He ordered that the track gauge be expanded to ensure that potential enemies' rolling stock could not reach Moscow and Petersburg unhindered. That broader gauge was a sign of isolation from a Europe fraught with upheavals and revolutions, from Europe with its interminable bubbling of thought. It was the ultimate symbol of that era, more so even than the Cathedral of Christ the Savior, an edifice embodying the Russian spirit and the full might of autocracy.

In 1941, the broad Russian gauge prevented Army Group Center's advance on Moscow from being fully resupplied, which enabled Soviet troops to resist the fascist invasion more effectively.

These facts are crouched in the cracks in the earth, like soldiers in foxholes, ready to defend themselves against being included in poetic thought.

5.

Hugh MacDiarmid initially wrote in Scots, in an effort to spark a Scottish cultural renaissance, but soon enough he began to sue "the language of the conqueror" in order to reach a broader audience. Withdrawals from radicalism, exceptions to the law that conquerors must be hated—this is the emptiness full to bursting from which the subject of poetic speech can be molded, as if from earth.

This earthen man smells like the roots of flowers and grasses, and also like the disintegration of the bullets buried in him over all those centuries.

Political conflicts are always based on a sense of the "otherness" of one's rival. The opponent does not and cannot bear any resemblance to humanity, and any dialogue with him, if it is even possible, will be a dialogue between beings of different species. Edwin Morgan understands that very well; his poems describe political conflicts in nonsense language, which actually proves to be the path to compromise.

The earthen man should smell like the roots of roses and thistles as he observes Burns and Keats drawing inspiration from the same landscapes.

6.

Thinking of poetry as a black-and-white substance that can be either for those in power or against them won't get us anywhere. Making poets' spiritual instruments more primitive is of no use, except perhaps to the world's counter-extremism bureaus. As early as the *Res Gestae Divi Augusti* and other texts dedicated to Augustus, one can see a complex interweaving of values and multifaceted thematic play being achieved in the context of a close association with those in power.

No literary text—and especially a poetic one—can be reduced to a thesis or set of theses. They will never be a substitute for the text. The illusion that such an exchange could ever be possible is an instrument of propaganda.

A poet's membership in a particular political camp is nothing compared to the content of his work, the way it describes their experience of the world and how it is ordered. Thus, the Aeneid need not be viewed exclusively as a panegyric if we consider the other themes woven into the text.

Attention to detail, to particularity—that's what we need in discussions of political poetry, not generalizing theoretical gestures.

7.

Political poetry has always reinforced identities—racial, national, religious, gender. "We're Marxists." "We're liberals." "We're Catholics." These slogans not only root any given human "I" in a field of battle, but also cement it there, like a bunker with a black mouth that will go on yawning decades after the war is over, reeking of homeless men's piss and beckoning to the children who come to the field to play.

The building of reinforced concrete identities goes hand in hand with the anthropocentrism that produces crises in so many domains. An object-oriented ontology, realized through poetry, effaces the subject-object opposition, relieves man of the habitual burden of being the ontological "center of the world" and presents him as an ordinary object among other, equally ordinary objects.

In his writings on politics, Latour notes that victory belongs to those who can translate other people's interests into his own language. He offers Louis Pasteur and his laboratory as an example. Having identified microbes as the cause of disease, Pasteur "translates" the problems of humanity (including those in power) into his own language and offers a solution. His laboratory model begins to spread, giving him an instrument of control, and, more importantly, giving him power over the language used to express various problems. That is the moment when traditional oppositions, such as internal vs. external, begin to lose their effectiveness and ultimately become irrelevant.

Pasteur's terminological apparatus was translated into the language of "simple" people not merely to simplify it, but to ensure a broader distribution of vaccines and promote the laboratory model. Pasteur's goal was not to adapt scientific truth and make it accessible to farmers; he was not motivated by the desire to subordinate himself to the ignorance of the popular consciousness.

When a poet writes about politics, he should avoid plunging into elitism, although a certain amount of it is inevitable. A poet's goal is not to adapt any given truth and make it accessible for the popular consciousness. His goal is to distribute a vaccine that can prevent the disease of violence, but a vaccine has to be distributed everywhere if it's going to be effective. A poet translates other people's interests into his own language, and in this context, "translation" is really an act of construction. At the same time, the poet knows very well that no social group ever has predetermined interests.

8.

Hannah Arendt plucks the blooming blasts, converses with them, and recognizes herself there.

El Brocense rejects any form of violence.

Petrarch just goes on comparing the poet to a bee making honey from nectar gathered from different flowers. The literal flower has long since given way to the flower of a wound, its earthen fragrance driving the words deeper, into the domain of immutable human oneness.

Aleš Šteger, translated by Brian Henry

Thirst

When a black hour takes the color of my blood on a red desk

When books don't open to speak but to whisper

When I become as wicked as

When every door closes and gasps in the darkness

When an orange is not an orange, a shoe not a shoe, and my shirt is put on in the morning by the one who will kill me in the evening

When I drink long gulps of water that fall into me like glass

When I am cut

When I don't believe in now, lose the before and don't see my reflection in shop windows

When someone starts to run after me, but just before he catches me I disappear again

When nothing whispers but everything is screaming because it is mute

When I am dicing an onion and think that the knife is the key with which I can open a wrist so that sand rushes from it

When Michelangelo touches Adam and goes through the world of cracks

When I am the left and right segments, the one that searches and the one that doesn't want to find

When I withdraw a finger and won't say *that's when* anymore, no when, no bones, no one—

You

Andrea Chapela, translated by Kelsi Vanada

Experiment One: Seeing Through

Object of Study: Window

—from Grados de miopía [The Visible Unseen]

1. I grew up in a house made of wood and glass. "Nothing to see outside. The house should look inward," said the architect, and in the center he built a garden.

2. In that house there lived a Physicist, a Mathematician, a Biologist, and a Chemist. These are the roles I give them when I want to talk about my past as if it were a story. Then it's easier to explain that what actually happened is the same thing that happens in all families. The Chemist left, gave up chemistry. But there's a catch: can what's absorbed through osmosis ever be fully left behind? My only answer is the definition I memorized in university: chemistry is the study of changes in matter.

3. The roof of the house is also made of glass. In the morning, the sun comes through its twenty-six panels, nourishes the two ficus trees in the indoor garden—and, at the end of August, hits me in the face as I sit there wasting time. I tell my parents *while I'm in Mexico I'm going to start a book*, but instead of writing, I'm sprawled in an armchair looking up at the roof. I look through it at the sky. I spend so much time looking at it that the object of my study stops being what I see *through*, and becomes what I *see*. The glass.

4. A definition from Horst Scholze in 1933: "Glasses are undercooled solidified melts."

5. I'd be lying if I said that my mother, the Mathematician, and my father, the Physicist, tried to stop me from quitting chemistry. They knew that after four years of the study of matter, and twenty-five years of scientific cohabitation, I'd already absorbed scientific thought and language. I was the only one who didn't know this when I left Mexico for the United States to write. But there's no escape if what you find when you look inside yourself is always science. Little by little, words like *bond, synthesis,*

reaction, decay filtered into my poems. Hybrid words trapped between two worlds.

6. There are other ways to define chemistry. Linus Pauling wrote the first *General Chemistry* in 1940, and he defined it as the science of substances—their structure, their properties, and their reactions that change them into other substances over time.

7. Why build a roof out of glass? A skylight, maybe—but a whole roof? Glass is fragile, breakable, amorphous, cold, translucent, without order, without equilibrium, *untrustworthy*, and—as I discovered with my first boyfriend—it doesn't allow for privacy.

8. Two months in Mexico. A static equilibrium between the United States and Spain. The days dissolve one into the next, one long day, longer than long, with no school and no work—days that remind me of summer as a little girl or weekends as a teenager. I sleep in my childhood bed, surrounded by the dolls I collected and the books that returned home with me. My suitcase is in a perpetually half-packed state, and disorder radiates from it. Piles of books that will stay, notes that will come with me, sweaters, shoes, notebooks, tax forms. My surroundings reflect my circumstances: I'm in between two phases.

9. One day, a few years ago, the roof leaked. All fall, the gutters had filled with leaves, and during that first storm the rainwater trickled in between the glass roof and the stone wall, turning the wall into a waterfall, the floor into a puddle, the interior into an exterior.

10. "A glass is an example, probably the simplest example, of the truly complex."

11. What is glass? Even the most basic sources disagree. The Royal Spanish Academy (RAE): glass is a hard, fragile, and transparent or translucent solid without a crystalline structure. A delicate and breakable thing or a person of delicate temperament, easily irritated or angered. Colloquial Spanish expression meaning "to take the blame": *to pay for broken glass*. Another, Google: glass is a supercooled liquid, a viscous material that flows very slowly, so slowly that it would take hundreds of years to flow at room temperature. One more, Wikipedia:

common glass, composition: silica, lime, and soda melted together at 1,800°C and cooled until they form a disordered structure. A material that doesn't behave like either a solid or a liquid.

12. In his introduction to *General Chemistry*, Pauling writes: "The words that are used in describing nature, which is itself complex, may not be capable of precise definition. In giving a definition for such a word the effort is made to describe the accepted usage." But when I said to the Mathematician *coming, ten more minutes*, I wasn't thinking about how ten minutes is 600 seconds and one second is the duration of 9x109 periods of the radiation corresponding to the transition between two hyperfine levels of the ground state of the cesium 133 atom. In everyday life, a minute is relative—but in science, words aspire to mathematical precision, to a perfection that evades them in their fluidity.

13. In Mexico City, the city of forgotten rivers, everything that flows is piped, stagnates, buried underground. Everything except the rain. The fat, cold, noisy drops revive the seven lakes and forty-five rivers. There used to be a rainy season, but now there's nothing to hold the rain back, so it pounds against the roof all year long. One afternoon at the end of August, the area around my neighborhood floods, the water reaches car roofs, the Biologist is stuck and can't get home. From my bed I listen to the storm, remembering my childhood fantasies. I used to imagine that one day the raindrops and the hail would pierce the roof. The crashing rain and shattered glass would pour in onto the garden. A river would form and flood my room, set my bed adrift. It never occurred to me to swim, so I would steer along the newly created rivers until I ended up far, far away from home, with no way to get back. The return of the water to Mexico City. As I write this, I realize it's not the first time I've described this fantasy.

14. The difference between a solid and a liquid is the difference between the two ways of fitting a set of billiard balls into a box: carefully, one by one, one on top of the other, in neat lines, creating order, a compact packing, a solid; or, letting them fall with only chaos as their guide. When it comes to a box of billiard balls, my sense of order has always been liquid.

15. When I was a teenager, the Mathematician used to ask me to pick up my room every three days. The perfect answer: *but Mom, I can't—all spontaneous processes tend toward entropy, toward chaos.* I made her smile, but it never worked. She always answered that I just had to use more energy. In my house, applying the Second Law of Thermodynamics to my chores wasn't enough to get out of doing them. Now that I'm back, my mother's request returns too, but after more days have gone by, as if distance has changed her standards.

16. The American Society for Testing and Materials defined the simplest method for differentiating a solid from a liquid in 1996. Place the sample in a closed container at 38°C. Take off the lid and turn it over. Observe the material. If it flows a total of 50mm or less in three minutes, it's considered a solid; if not, it's a liquid. All my attempts to test this methodology end in disaster. A puddle of water, a handful of rocks, a dribble of honey. They all end up on the floor.

17. An experiment: stand in front of a window. Touch its surface with a finger. Feel the resistance. Now a second finger. Rest your entire hand against it. Push. Feel its solidity. Understand that a macroscopic view is useless in this case. Imagine instead that it gives way beneath your fingers, liquifies. Would it be cold, wet, viscous? I forget about the experiment and rest my face against the glass.

18. Main characteristics of a solid: resists changes of form or volume, has a defined shape, its particles are closely packed and ordered. Main characteristics of a liquid: has a defined volume regardless of pressure, but takes the form of its container. A cubic milliliter of water is the same in a cup, a bowl, a vase, the palm of my hand, a bathtub. And all those milliliters share the most important characteristic of a liquid: they're fluid—that is, they can flow.

19. And glass? Does it flow?

20. The language of science today is English, but writing in it would make things more complicated for me given this particular subject. In English, "glass" is a broad category, in which everything made of this material is *a glass.* Maybe this expresses its great instability more

accurately than Spanish's many words. Not only is the threat of breaking glass ever-present, but *a glass* can be the thing for holding water *or* wine—then there are eyeglasses for seeing, hourglasses for measuring time, sunglasses, the spyglass that enlarges small things and observes the faraway, the glass used for measuring the weather, and even the glass formed by lightning at the beach. *Glass* is one, *glass* is all of them. In English, even growing up under a ceiling made of glass would be full of connotations.

21. "The deepest and most interesting unsolved problem in solid-state theory is probably the theory of the nature of glass and the glass transition."

22. To flow: atoms can be displaced easily, they're not tied to each other, they're not static. Fluids flow (it's one of their characteristics, not redundancy—scientific language isn't afraid of repetition) because under any force, they transform, give no resistance. The Mathematician used to tell me: *you're like a fluid, you adjust to your containers, you transform, you choose to go around the obstacles in your way.* How easily the scientific becomes metaphorical.

23. Among the types of fluids are the Newtonians and the non-Newtonians. Before I knew who Newton was, I understood these categories. At dinner, the Physicist used to take a jar of crema and shake it as he explained for the nth time (science sneaks in at the slightest provocation) that crema is a non-Newtonian fluid. "If you exercise a force on it, it becomes more liquid, it's easier to serve." In my childhood, even the most everyday thing became the source for scientific explanations.

24. I spend hours watching videos of glassblowing. Years ago, in a lab in Wisconsin, a PhD student showed me how to heat glass test tubes, deforming them to connect beakers to a vacuum pump, creating a many-legged lab insect. This asymmetrical creature held a translucent liquid preserved inside it that slowly changed color, a magnetic stir bar spinning it for hours, a chemical reaction in process. Centrifuge for a day, let rest for a few hours, then break the insect open and extract the new compound.

25. A supercooled liquid is a step between a solid and a liquid. Near the melting point, the molecules are moving, but run the risk of sudden crystallization. A glass is cooled beyond cold—beyond its freezing point—that is, beyond what's solid, until the molecules have lost all possibility of movement, stuck between order and disorder in a metastable state. Christian Bök said it best in his poem "Glass": "Glass represents / a poetic element // exiled / to a borderline // between / states of matter: // breakable water // not yet frozen, // yet unpourable."

26. September finds me working at the dining-room table—not just because it's glass, but because I can spread out all the books and notes I need to write. During a family dinner, sitting at this very table, I can see my sister's long legs, my father's same old moccasins, my mother's compression socks. We used to have a dog that would jump up thinking the food he saw was for him, crashing into the table. They ask what I'm working on and I tell them about glass' aggregation dilemma. *No one knows what it is.* My sister says that in school she learned that cathedral windows are thicker at the bottom, due to gravity, because they're liquids. Later, I investigate. The windows of European cathedrals are made of blown glass framed in lead. At room temperature, the viscosity of glass is 1020 poises and that of lead is 1011 poises. If a European window began to flow, drops of metal would fall first, not glass.

27. Pitch is a supercooled liquid, though other studies describe it as a breakable solid—in the end, it's more or less the same thing. In 1930, a piece of pitch was placed in a glass funnel in Queensland. Since then, nine drops have fallen, the last one on April 17, 2014. It's estimated that the viscosity of pitch is 2.3×10^{11} times that of water. It can drip. Unlike the glass funnel that holds it, it flows.

28. It's two in the morning. The page is called The Tenth Watch, the tenth watch for the tenth drop. As the video loads, a message appears: *Hi! Only 14 or so years to go.* A camera steadily observes the sample of pitch: its glass funnel, the black drop suspended. Everything under a glass bell jar. Each time I log on, I'm one of seventeen viewers. Who else in the world is watching? Will I be alone, the only human being alongside the computers supervising the drop? For a few moments, my

imagination gets the best of me, and I think it moves, the drop widens, maybe it's almost there, *it's going to fall, so close* . . . But nothing happens.

29. Where does the myth of the stained glass in Gothic cathedrals come from? Someone observed that a few pieces of glass were thinner near the top, as if gravity were slowly making the material flow, thickening the base. It's false proof, still taught in schools. The difference in thickness is a characteristic of blown glass, a flaw in the process. To disprove the concept, a theoretical experiment was proposed: suspend a plate of glass one meter high and one centimeter thick in a room at room temperature. The question: how much time would it take for the glass to flow so that the base widened by 10 angstroms? The answer: the age of the universe.

30. The myth that glass is a liquid is produced by analogy—but it's not a solid, either. So, what is it? Which matters more: how much time a glass takes to flow, or the image of the windows melting, the drops falling, all the glass in the world transformed into water? Is the mystery of the nature of glass strong enough to hold all my worries, all the words I'm putting together? Is the necessity of describing something unknown, something language can't reach, enough? Glass is a destabilizer.

31. Imagine you're a melted material, boiled at more than 1,800°C till white-hot. Imagine you begin to cool slowly, so slowly that each of your atoms stops moving. You get heavy, you coalesce. On a phase diagram, you're moving toward solid, toward crystallization. Or not. Maybe you have the nature of glass, and you can feel your molecules keep moving beyond the melting point, as you drop along the slope. Imagine the disorder inside you, growing along with your viscosity, growing as the temperature lowers to 20°C. You are almost a solid, but only barely.

32. I was in my second year at university when I studied phase diagrams for the first time in Kinetics and Equilibrium class. The basic example is the diagram for water. Two axes, pressure and temperature; a line curving out from the origin to branch into two. To the left, the first line indicates a solid, the space between the two branches is liquid, and below that, vapor. The lines represent all the points of sublimation, melting, and evaporation, where water is, at the same time, liquid and

solid, or liquid and gaseous. But there is just one point at which water is a solid, a liquid, and a gas at the same time. This point is found at 273.16K and 4.65mmHg.

33. The type depends on its composition. Glass with boron in it is used in labs because it resists heat and doesn't crystallize; it doesn't break easily. The lenses of my glasses contain lead—greenish glass, or "forest glass," produced in Cologne until the 15th century, had that color due to its iron content. But 90% of glass is just silicon, oxygen, calcium, and sodium. The composition affects the glass transition, the moment in the phase diagram at which the slope changes, and instead of crystalizing, disorder begins: a glass is formed. Systems at those points are very fragile, a change in temperature or pressure can alter the result. A liquid, instead of a solid. An experiment from university: cool milk slowly, little by little, using cold water, ice, and salt. At -5°C, the milk is still liquid, but one tap of a fingertip and crystallization begins. In one second, it's a solid, unrecognizable.

34. Phase diagrams are graphical representations of the boundaries between the different states of matter of a system. As a liquid freezes toward becoming a typical solid, it experiences a phase change; the molecules line up, one on top of the other, in a simple pattern. They form a crystal. When a glass cools, the liquid becomes more and more viscous until it solidifies: the molecules move slower and slower until they stop. They're trapped in a strange state between liquid and solid. Is it possible that one theory could explain all the kinds of glass? In the end, glasses are defined not by one common characteristic, but by the lack of one: order.

35. Another experiment: I'm in my Kinetics and Equilibrium lab, looking at a creature made of a glass beaker and rubber hose. The transparent liquid resting in its belly is cyclohexane, a hexagonal molecule that looks like a honeycomb. The boiling flask, suspended by a clamp, is connected to a vacuum pump and a thermometer. As the pressure is lowered, the temperature goes down, too. We're looking for a point at 45mmHg and 6°C. Lower, lower, lower—the cyclohexane bubbles, but it's not boiling like water. The bubbles slow little by little, the liquid

gets more viscous, the surface solidifies, and the gas turns into ice with each bubble that reaches the surface. The system comes to life. Inside the flask, a solid sinks, a liquid bubbles, and a layer of gas solidifies and forms droplets. At the triple point, cyclohexane turns opaque and is— at the same time—all three states of matter.

36. After my Spanish visa appointment, all I can do is wait. To distract myself, I talk with old friends, tell them all the interesting facts I've learned about glass. I become monothematic, full of *did-you-knows*. I ask a friend: *did you know that cotton candy is a glass?* and he answers that glass breaks because the driving force crystallizes the edges. To test this, I buy a drinking glass because my mother would get mad if I started breaking the glassware: our current cohabitation, since my return, feels too fragile to experiment with. When I tell her what I plan to do, she says that for the sake of art it wouldn't have bothered her that I'd broken a glass, and she encourages me to break it inside a plastic bag, or two, for safety's sake. I pause multiple times before dropping it. It's strange breaking something on purpose, with a purpose. The first time the impact sounds opaque, flat—the glass bounces, but doesn't break. The second time, with more force—again a muffled sound. The third, the bag above my head, much more force, *it has to work this time—* there: the piercing sound, crystalline, of something breaking. When I pick up the bag, I notice it's warm.

37. In the book *Líquidos exóticos* [Exotic Liquids], the authors speak of the eventual crystallization of glass. "It's estimated that some glasses, like the leaded glass in Gothic cathedrals, will take thousands of years to crystallize. When this happens, the glass will be transformed into a crystalline solid and will break, like car windshields, for no apparent reason." My nighttime terrors could become reality. The roof of my childhood could break in a second, for no reason, just because over thousands of years, each panel will crystallize, and the weight of order will shatter them.

38. No state is more metastable than waiting.

39. I open the bag outside, in the garden, and take out the fragments one by one—gingerly, so I don't cut myself. My fingers are covered in

a glassy dust. I observe the edges carefully. They aren't translucent, you can't see through them—it's as though someone had polished them, you can see waves, cracks. What was I hoping for? How did I imagine a crystal would look? Crystals are solids, but these edges are the first thing that makes me think maybe glass *is* a liquid. Later, I look on the internet to see if what my friend told me is true. I learn that glass, in its disorder, has microcracks, and these invisible cracks make it fragile despite its durability. How glass breaks depends on chance, on the impact, on the force, all the microcracks of the cooling process. Not a single page talks about the crystallization of the edges, but does it matter? I observe a fragment of glass, now shapeless, useless, more liquid than when it was whole. Science needs precise, testable explanations, but do I need them? Does this writing exercise based on the reappropriation and transformation of my own language need them? Do I need to find some truth? Or are the edges of this debris enough for me: wavy, fluid, splitting the light to form a tiny rainbow in each crack.

40. On September 18, my visa is denied. The next day, everything breaks.

41. This is what breaks: molars, the voice, peace, childhood friendships, plant stems, language, the mind, ancient vessels, my dreams of working in research, ionic bonds, necks, hips, clavicles, bellybuttons, the whole body, emotions, sounds, my grandmother's wine glasses, summer romances, independent clauses, health, good moods, hair, social fabrics, pinky toes.

42. When the floor loses its solidity and ripples, I'm in bed reading. In one second, all action is reaction, is in the imperative: *jump out of bed, cross the indoor garden, get out of the house, look for your sister, call her, keep breathing, wait.* Dogs bark, birds chirp, and we humans keep silence. The glass roof creaks, shudders, vibrates with each undulation. *It's going to break.* A half-formed thought. But when the earthquake passes, we only find that the quartz geode has tumbled off the shelf and shattered on the floor. The glass roof, on the other hand, didn't break.

43. How to write about the cracks, between the cracks, when even language is in ruins?

44. Normal life shatters, too. I stop writing, lose the thread of my project and all thoughts of glass, language, or my place in my childhood home. I stare at the TV with my father, the rest of the rooms in darkness and silence. An infuriating succession: buildings collapsing in clouds of dust and uproar—cries and banging from beneath the debris—pairs of dogs—young people in human chains passing empty buckets that return full of stones—pets abandoned and found—tables, backpacks, homework, dolls, frying pans, the signs of many lives—dishes full of food—empty metro cars running for free—people helping and waiting, people searching for a place to help or wait—messages asking for flashlights, helmets, medicine, water, and comfort—the fragmented images are superimposed during our vigil, as if the power of the gaze—televised, collective—could restore order.

45. Not everything that breaks crystallizes.

46.

47. In October, I get my visa. After I buy my plane ticket, the days speed up. I start packing. I put photos, letters, and postcards into a metal box. Images and words of my family and friends that will travel with me. I pause on a postcard from last summer. It has on one side, "I hope you'll visit Madrid," and on the other, a picture of el Palacio de Cristal. An epiphany: *that's where this book is headed, toward Madrid and el Palacio de Cristal.* That's the ending: the writer changes countries and finds her written efforts made monument. Both architectural and narrative growth—from a glass roof to a whole palace. I start to feel relieved: I can think of my departure as a destination.

48. My approaching journey makes me take up writing again. I read *Glass (Object Lessons)* by John Garrison. I appreciate his attempt to track glass through the art of the past and the imaginations of the future, but I only write down one quote: "Even when it's transparent and trying its best to be invisible, it's still affecting how we experience what is beyond it." He's talking about glass, but this idea could apply to all of language—or scientific language, to be precise. How to write about science from the outside? Stop seeing through language, using it as a tool, pretending exactitude is possible in words? What happens to scientific

words when they're observed? And if we stretch the metaphor, it could be said that words become unstable and change aggregation states.

49. When I get to Madrid, I plan my visit to el Palacio de Cristal carefully. I go alone, walking through el Retiro on a day when I already feel far away, when novelty begins to give way to routine. The first time, I don't go in. I sit down to take notes on the other side of the pond. There's a long line around el Palacio to see the exposition inside. Doris Salcedo, the Colombian sculptor, called her intervention in the space *Palimpsesto*—a memorial made of water, formed by invisible, fluid words. In this case it is a funeral oration, a poetics of pain and a way of mourning the people who have lost their lives trying to cross the Mediterranean. Salcedo says in an interview: "The future is built on the ruins of the past, and art helps clarify this call to attention." That afternoon, when I get back for dinner, I find out that Doris Salcedo was in la Residencia de Estudiantes talking with my fellow residents when I was still in Mexico.

50. Over the course of the next few weeks, I return again and again to el Palacio de Cristal in search of the ending.

51. Doris Salcedo defines herself as a "maker of objects." She was the first woman invited to take part in the Unilever series, in which an artist was invited to intervene in the Turbine Room of the Tate Modern in London. For her intervention, Salcedo cracked the floor of the room. Of the work, the director of the Tate said: "There is a crack, there is a line, and eventually there will be a scar. It will remain as a memory of the work and also as a memorial to the issues Doris touches on." Salcedo wanted to represent borders—migrants' experiences of crossing them, as well as their destinies upon reaching the other side. For Salcedo, the crack is negative space; because of everything that fits inside it and is "too many things," as Borges says in *Other Inquisitions* of the crack that appears in the Roman Forum in Hawthorne's *The Marble Faun*. "It is the crack of which the Latin historians speak and also the mouth of the hell *with shadowy monsters and atrocious faces* and it is also the fundamental horror of human life and it is also Time, which devours statues and armies, and it is also Eternity, which locks away the ages."

52. I leave el Palacio de Cristal without answers. I feel as though my curiosity must have stayed behind in Mexico, even though here, far away, I identify more than ever with glass and its metastability. Maybe I should have explained it before. It's the property, due to slow transformations, exhibited by a system with various states of equilibrium, when it stays in a barely stable state for a considerable amount of time. Writing this definition, I wonder: where is the equilibrium when you're no longer part of your childhood bed, or your girlhood—or part of the rooms in the countries you choose as resting points?

53. Metastability is always temporary—with the force of external disturbances, these systems evolve toward a more stable state.

54. In 2016, at the University of Sheffield, during the conference of the Society of Glass Technology, Edgar Dutra Zanotto gave a keynote speech entitled "Glass: Myths and Marvels," during which he proposed a new definition: "Glass is a non-equilibrium, non-crystalline state of matter that appears solid on a short time scale but relaxes toward the liquid state. Their ultimate fate, in the limit of infinite time, is to crystallize." It's the most recent definition published to date. Scientists circle around the idea of glass, refining the definition word by word, as if they were progressing millimeter by millimeter. That's what science does. It presupposes that there is an absolute truth we approach with each repeatable experiment and proven hypothesis. The main idea is the truth of being able to explain what's around us and understand it completely. When I studied chemistry, I developed the bad habit of searching for certainty and precision in words—but that's the same error as believing that the fog I can see in winter when I breathe out is an ideal gas. I thought they were solid, trustworthy, but the exercise of writing taught me that they mold to whatever container you put them in. They *flow*.

55. Glass, because of its metastability, doesn't belong to any one state of matter. It's a material without a family. Its orphanhood comes from the limitations of language, the rigidity of taxonomy. Definitions in scientific language *can't* be fluid. Faced with the mystery of glass, we have to accept the fragility of language, its lack of precision. But doing so opens the door to a way of talking about the most elusive experiences,

sensations, and feelings—which can only be understood through metaphor, though many times we fail in our attempt to capture them in language. In failing to define glass, in having to make comparisons and create new categories, I discover that the orphanhood of glass is, in its turn, the primary failure and the orphanhood of writing.

56. On the day I arrived in Madrid, everyone told me it was the first cold day since the end of summer. In the morning, as I cross el Retiro, the chilly air feels crystalline, and under my feet I hear the crunch of leaves. I no longer need a map to find el Palacio de Cristal. I enter it and amble through, more occupied with searching for my own reflection in the windows than looking at the names on the floor. Unlike my house, el Palacio was built to look out: the pond, the blue sky, all the trees in the park. In Mexico, I always looked toward the outside—but now, in Madrid, I'm looking inside. *You're always so contrary.* As I look at the glass, I think how one day everything around me will crystallize, will shatter, and in doing so will find equilibrium. Will I, too? It's hard to determine the final state of the system from this perspective. Between two states there's a transition, which sometimes reaches equilibrium, and sometimes metastability—it all depends on the circumstances. Only with the passage of time, by looking back, can you tell which of the two it was.

57. Some days it comforts me to remember that Lavoisier's law applies to all of nature.

Miren Agur Meabe, translated by Amaia Gabantxo

The Price of My Pearl

My left eye is made of glass. They gave it to me so that my sick eye wouldn't infect the healthy one, to avoid what they call sympathetic ophthalmia. When they told me that they had to remove my eye I was terrified: it's not an easy exercise to put aside something you've always had and to imagine your face with a fake eye on it, like a scream.

I couldn't erase two childhood images from my mind: the first one, of the gardener in the park and, the other, of an uncle from my father's side, because the glass eyes of those two men were exactly like targets, fixed, unmovable, dead. However, they explained to me that how the eye was lost (if by accident or by illness) and how neat the scar was after the extraction had an effect on the overall state and look of the eye socket.

Shotgun pellets took the gardener's eye out in a hunting accident; in my uncle's case it was a firecracker and a childhood friend's trick that did it. "Look in the hole in that wall," his friend said, "there is a coin there, but I can't get at it . . . You try." My uncle brought his eye close to the wall.

I lost mine to glaucoma. My eye became a twisted red marble. That deformity weighed heavily on my teenage years. Every now and then whispered words would reach me. "Such a beautiful girl . . . it's a great pity." Because of this, irony of ironies, I've always been much more despondent about the contours of my waist.

I kept my deteriorating eye until I finished my studies and started work in a Basque school. When I heard the nickname some students used for me I was very hurt, but what can you expect from cruel students?

Early on I had a doubt, an important one since I'm very emotional: whether it would be possible to cry without an eye. I cry easily. Tears are necessary to me, to prove to myself that I am a good person. At the same time, I also like that they provide transcendence to the events I experience. I find them a reliable measure.

The first time I wore my fake eye felt like walking out in the streets naked. But the shame, however, didn't last.

After weighing my existing preconceptions against the final result, I am pretty sure that I have been lucky with my pearl because, modern prostheses, being individualized, look rather natural—unlike the old ones.

Be that as it may, when I get in the sack with a man for the first few times I am careful with the eye. Since I can't control the pressure in my eyelids at all (I don't like it, but my left eye is always half-open, even when I'm asleep), when I fuck I consciously try to control the eye and close it. Those who aren't used to it might find it disconcerting that my two eyes don't behave like identical twins all the time.

Helena Granström, translated by Kira Josefsson

from *The Possibility of Love*

I had just stepped out of the tub when the first letter arrived—I say letter, but of course it was an email. Wrapped in a towel, with the water dripping from the ends of my hair onto the floor, I leaned closer to the computer and, having dried moisture from the track pad with the towel, I moved the cursor with my right hand.

The email had the disquieting subject line "On love" and my initial re-action was that it had to have been sent by the wife of The Dad, a man who I at that point had been seeing on the sly for close to a year. The Dad was an unusual specimen in the category of unfaithful men, insofar as he was evidently not ashamed or apologetic about his extramarital affairs, even though he obviously had no intention of telling his wife about them. When we met, he had recently been obliged to end a long-term relationship with another lover—"a soul mate, I'd call her, we were such a good match that not seeing her would have been to squander the gift of life"—why, I never learned. I couldn't be sure, but I had the sense it was something more than being found out. The wife, also the mother of their two young twin boys, had come across a text message he'd sent to the lover-soul mate; nothing dirty, he claimed (something I doubted), but intimate enough that she could tell something was wrong. He told me the story while kneeling on the rock-hard parquet floor where we'd just made love—or, I should say, where he'd just fucked me in the ass until he came, surprisingly quietly, and then he gave my already rosy butt cheeks a couple of hard, final slaps before pulling out and straightening his back. I remained on all fours in front of him; he lightly caressed my lower back with his left hand before walking to the bathroom, his sex cupped in his right hand. I could hear the water flushing and the sound of toilet paper pulled from the roll. It wasn't long before he was back, now dressed in the loose-fitting white T-shirt he'd worn when he showed up, having created the illusion of going to the gym. I noted that he'd also wetted his hair and pulled it back—clearly, he was cunning—before he pulled me up to a sitting position and hooked one of his long, slender arms around me in a not exactly tender gesture.

Once I had plucked up my courage after a moment's hesitation and clicked on the brightly marked line in my inbox, it turned out to be something altogether different. The email had been written by a woman, Amelie Spetz-Rosén, who by all indications was not the wife of The Dad, and the body of the message contained nothing but a short greeting: "I would be very grateful if you read the letter and got back to me. Best, Amelie Spetz-Rosén." My sense of discomfort intact, I clicked the link and listened to the hard drive whir as it launched the word processor and opened the document, titled "multiverse.doc."

I read:

Hello,

I heard your radio essay about love and possessiveness on P1 the other day. You described true love as something that demands you let go instead of cling to someone. I have also read your philosophical essays in the newspaper, for example the one about Max Tegmark's book *Our Mathematical Universe*, in which he writes that our universe is only one of many, and that the world is perpetually branching out in something like infinite possibilities as per Hugh Everett's many-worlds theory, which Tegmark appears to subscribe to. I have also read physicist Brian Greene in his book on the topic, *The Hidden Reality*, and it seems he thinks this is the only reasonable inference to be made from quantum physics.

This makes me incredibly troubled and anxious. Take the unconditional love you describe in your essay—how can such a love mean anything if its opposite is just as real as it is? Or how can it mean anything that I care for my child if I know there is another, equally real, universe where I abuse the child? I have an infant child and reading that description makes it feel as though everything we experience is absolutely void of meaning, and I hope you can help me by responding with your beliefs about this. Do you find the multi-world theory promoted by, among others, Max Tegmark, convincing? How do you make sense of it all?

Would be very grateful if you'd answer me.

Best, Amelie S-R

By now I was feeling cold. I closed my laptop and walked across the floor to get away from the window so I could remove the towel and wrap it around my hair outside of the view of my neighbors. The neighbors below were playing something with a heavy bass; I could make out a repetitive melody grinding over equally monotonous beats. Around this time of day either The Dad or his beautiful, dark-haired wife would usually pass by below my window, pushing their similarly dark-haired, big-eyed boys in a double stroller. As I had been quick to discover, though he never mentioned it himself, the boys' kindergarten was located on the same block as my apartment building, and the doors that every morning swallowed countless children only to spit them out again in the afternoon absorbed also his two sons; it happened that I heard crying or excited voices through the window when they walked by.

The Dad and his family lived nearby, too, just a few blocks away, and this was what enabled our relationship; he could take the dog—a large, wolf-like German Shepherd that often surveilled our coitus from a corner of the room, save for when it burst forth with ungovernable excitement and started to lick its master's hard-working thigh muscles, at which point he would command it back to its spot—and come straight to my place, just as he could head to the gym and stay for an hour before returning from my apartment, his hair slicked back after a simulated shower and sweating as evidence of a workout he hadn't done. Weight lifting, with those skinny arms?

Of course, I thought as I bent over and rubbed my hair with the towel, I could just not write back to Amelie Spetz-Rosén; probably the best solution. Or I could send her some vague reply about the incompleteness of quantum mechanics, explaining that it's a theoretical model and we would probably be best off not interpreting its consequences so literally; that, moreover, the many-worlds interpretation is just one possible view and not necessarily the correct one. But it didn't help, because for some reason it had now fallen upon me to ensure the world would remain whole.

I imagined Amelie Spetz-Rosén, sitting somewhere, agonizing over the lost meaning of life and love. If I was the one who had caused this rift in the universe, then I had to be the one healing it. Heal it, how could I heal it?

I looked around the room, observing the desk, the chair, the bookshelf, the reading chair; I looked at them as though I imagined each would confirm its own unique existence. But instead they did the opposite: the harder I focused on them the more negotiable they seemed, the more open to interpretation; as my gaze bore deeper into them they also appeared to bore into me, such that finally the pieces of furniture could not be distinguished from my understanding of them.

The desk: from my position on the floor I watched myself sit down at it, apparently deep in thought. I saw myself sink down into the reading chair, where I initiated a conversation with Amelie Spetz-Rosén, who was now seated on the floor before me, looking up with a rapt expression. I could see myself staring into the eyes of people I encountered and I saw them turn away. I took my focus from them, trained it again on the shiny surface of the desk, shifted it even closer to the tabletop, closer and closer until the wood dissolved and its solidity transformed into an indistinct haze. Inside the world there was an unlimited quantity of words, and seen up close they would all fall apart, transmuted into nothingness. Reality was not whole and I would never be able to heal it.

And what exactly was her question about anyway? Did it concern the many-worlds interpretation, or did it have to do with love? And if it was about love, would that not make it even more difficult for me to respond?

If two weeks prior I had been seated in a radio studio, speaking with a soulful voice about the possibility of a love beyond possession; if I had insisted, with the microphone as my disinterested mute witness, that such a love was possible, this idea was as theoretical as any multi-worlds interpretation—no, more so, because I didn't even have any observations to support its theoretical existence. What kind of great and unconditional love had I imagined anyhow; unselfish, all-encompassing, what love had I been talking about? It was definitely not my own.

It was an incantation, it was nothing but a prayer; the one could not be in conflict with the other because one of them did not exist. It is only the belief in such a love that makes it possible, I had intoned into the microphone, but could I not just as well have intoned the same about an infinite multiverse? Because when it came down to it, what did I know about either of them, what did I know of their existence? I knew nothing of it.

Maybe that's what I should write her. Briefly, now at once to get it over with. Still naked I walked up to the computer and opened the screen to read over her letter anew. It really did contain a tangible anxiety, an anxiety of existential character, and if I'd learned anything from my several years as a professional writer, it's that these are precisely the messages you should refrain from answering, these are the exact correspondents you should under no circumstances engage, since their hunger is insatiable. You write them, and they reply immediately, to which you respond, to which they reply immediately, and you see that their hunger is in fact about something else, about some form of human connection you will never be able to give them, and now it's gone so far that when you retire you'll only confirm them in all their despair and loneliness. They have opened up, they have revealed themselves before a stranger who had the potential to understand them, and even this stranger turns away.

Amelie Spetz-Rosén: I could imagine her sitting on the couch reading my texts, which inspired her to feverishly start searching the internet. "Tegmark parallel universes," "multiverse reality," "Everett 1957 relative states"; I imagined how her more or less newborn child began to cry in the bedroom and how she left it crying as she went deeper and deeper down a representation of the world as dissolved, splintered, in shards; entirely deterministic but also, from the point of view of the individual subject, determined by chance, because how can the individual know which of all possible universes she happens to exist in, which of them she will exist in one second from now; is she the perpetrator or the victim; how can she mean anything by the word "I"? I imagined that now she attached all her despair to this image, all her loneliness and desolation and fear, the crying infant and the infant who in a different universe is held, not by her, not in this one, and I quickly closed my computer.

Michael Ende, translated by Elisabeth Kinsey

The Jester's Fairy Tale

Act I

Setting

Construction site on the outskirts of a big city. A winter evening. The sky still reflects light, but during this first act, little by little, it will become fully engulfed in evening. A looming, pallid, full moon rises over the vapor silhouette of a smokestack amidst factories. A light, yet pervasive cold wind blows.

In the foreground lies a stark building site, flattened and waiting for excavation. At its edges, skid loaders and dump trucks of every variety at the ready. Rising behind, vast halls and compounds of the Chemical Works.

In the middle of these industrial plains huddle three squalid, almost tremulous, formerly colorful circus trailers. All the windows, roofs, and floors are shabbily patched together, their colors peeling from wind and weather are washed out and faded. The hitches to the circus trailers remain horseless. They gather themselves into a small M-shaped corral to bolster against the wind.

Out of the naked earth, in this equation of sorts, burns a small flame, nourished by paper cartons and flammable garbage. Warming themselves around it are the last members of the circus troupe. They all seem neglected and starving. They wear ordinary, tattered winter clothes. That they are artists, one can only tell by a few strange markers.

BUX, the ventriloquist, sits near the fire on an old suitcase. He is a small, frail man around sixty with white hair and a white, thin, handlebar mustache. He conducts himself like an English lord. He wears a black jacket that at one time was high-end, though now, is threadbare and worn. On his knee sits OTTOKAR, the puppet, who wears a bellhop costume with an unusual expression on his face. Both of them busy themselves, either whispering in each other's ears or turning to one another in speech. BUX has completely forgotten that OTTOKAR is only another part of himself. For him, the puppet is a living being.

Near him, JUSSUF the magician, an indefinable age, speaks in a curious accent. He wears a knuckle-length military security jacket. Around his neck, a long, colorful woolen scarf hangs and on his head is a battered top hat. When he speaks, he points to his overbite and rolls his eyes. From time to time, his fingers, of their own volition, make a cigarette appear and disappear, riff a tattered deck of cards into a bridge, and pull an egg out of a colleague's nose. But no one's paying him much attention. He seems to do this all automatically.

On the other side of the fire, PIPPO crouches, the red-faced, forty-something acrobat and juggler. He wears baggy corduroys, a thick naval coat with a turtleneck, and on his bald head sits a tiny, knit stocking cap. His voice is hoarse, his nose runs, and he is unshaved. During the conversation, every now and then, he gathers a few small stones, juggles with them or balances a stick. But then he settles down and either plunges his hands in his pockets or warms them over the fire.

Near him, squatting on her heels, the tightrope walker, LOLA, warms her hands. She is girlish and dainty but her face reveals an aged haggardness. Her black hair is parted and tucked into a ballerina's bun. She is bundled in a plethora of different tattered blankets. When she adjusts the blankets, one can see the layers of pink wool and thick ballerina tights. Around her neck is flung a moth-eaten pink feather boa.

Left: Outside of the trailer corral, WILMA, the knife thrower markswoman, jerks herself away and leans opposite the troupe. She peers expectantly over at the chemical plant. She's wearing riding breeches with tall boots, a gun belt, and a shabby fur coat. She has ginger hair and her face is marked heavily with too much rouge.

On the other side of the trailer corral, off right in the foreground, squats **ELI**, a young girl around ten or twelve who digs channels with her fingers to link one puddle to another. She is very dirty. All the clothes she wears are buttoned incorrectly and hang strangely on her small, emaciated body. They are all fit for nothing and left out of the troupe fund.

By the way the child moves and speaks, one can tell she is behind in growth.

After long silence, Pippo, the acrobat, throws his head up at the sky, as if awakening, and says lightly:

Pippo: It's already dark.

Lola: And cold. (Pippo throws an arm around Lola to warm her.)

Wilma (comes closer to troupe to warm herself): We don't need to wait for him anymore.

Jussuf: No. He is certainly not coming.

Bux: I would have never thought of him to leave us like this. At least not this time.

The Puppet: I, for one, think that guy over there looks like him.

Bux: You hold your mouth, Ottokar!

Eli: Jojo's coming. Eli knows for sure. Jojo is kind.

Wilma: Yes . . . yes, Jojo is kind! How many performances have we given without him because he was suddenly lost! The poor dog, he's always consoling himself at a Schnapps bar that only has an entrance, no exit, says he.

The Puppet: It can't happen today.

Wilma: Why not?

The Puppet: We don't have a performance today, he he he!

Bux: This is not a time to joke, Ottokar! After that joke, no one will be in the mood.

Pippo: Maybe he didn't get very far with them?

Lola (ironic): Yeah. Sometimes he's actually reasonable.

Jussuf: That he hasn't come back could mean that he hasn't given up, that he still has hope.

Pippo: And I bet you a sack of gold that he's left us high and dry.

The Puppet: Bux! Did you hear? Bux? Pippo bet a sack of gold! (He screeches for effect.)

Bux: Shut your face or you'll end up in the box!

The Puppet (sing-song and brash):

Cain spoke to Abel
Shut your face!
Abel was stuck
with a fork
after the chase.
Never in the box, Bux!
My face is stone cold.

Lola: But, listen—what if they are holding him? (She crosses herself.)

Pippo: Like, locked up? Why?

Lola: Maybe we're overstepping some local law? I mean, because we're basically loitering. Perhaps they'll come and get us all together tonight?

Wilma: Well, for my sake, at least if they lock us up, it will be warmer.

Eli: Eli is kind. Eli hasn't done anything. We are all kind?

The Puppet: Exactly, Eli. You don't need to be afraid. Lola's only joking. No one is going to do us harm.

Wilma: We should send someone there. Who can seriously speak to those people?

Jussuf: Jojo can speak for all of us, for sure.

Wilma: Yeah, he can speak to little children and make them laugh. But that doesn't help us in this situation.

Pippo: Well, we all voted for him. You, too, Wilma.

The Puppet: Me, too!

Wilma: I know him. He did something wrong. These people are always afraid of being made fun of.

Eli: Wilma shouldn't be afraid. Eli isn't afraid.

Lola: What can he do now? The reason is the same and you all know it. Whether they chase us away tomorrow or in two days, this is the end of the line . . . everyone off the train! Since the Believers have taken away the last three donkeys, what can Jojo get from the factory people? They're increasing the construction so they can push us out. Do we pull the trailers out? And where to? We have nothing more to give . . . whatever's not nailed down has already been taken. For the last two months, it was already clear to me when we hocked the tent and the costumes to buy horses. When a circus has to sell their tent . . . our reign is over, the show at its end.

Wilma: It started a lot earlier than that. Don't fool yourselves. You know exactly what I mean. Three years, to the day, is when we hit this bad-luck streak. I was against it from the get-go but no one would listen. We used to be twelve, but then we added one more and became thirteen. Thirteen! You all knew what that meant. First, Nick got sick. Then, Carlo got into an accident and in one year we lost Leo and his entire family. From then on everything went to shit. We shouldn't have brought this kid with us, or at least campaigned to help her out. We could have been seventeen. But thirteen!

Pippo: Campaign with whom? When?

Lola: We couldn't very well have left her in the gutters, Wilma. Eli was deathly ill. She would have died.

Jussuf: Besides, kids like her bring luck, Wilma.

Wilma: Luck? Alright. Then show us.

Pippo: Our bad luck is not Eli's fault.

Wilma: Fault? Who spoke of faults? The count was even . . . the count, do you understand?

Lola: Be quiet. She can hear us.

Wilma: Pshaw. She can't understand.

Eli (goes up to Wilma and pats her.): Wilma is kind. Eli is also kind? All of us are kind? (She goes to everyone and strokes them tenderly.)

The Puppet: Actually, with me we are fourteen!

Bux: Unfortunately, you don't count, Ottokar.

(Break)

The Puppet: Could we try another, bigger circus that maybe needs us?

Lola: All of us together?

Pippo: All of us or none. We promised. We need to stick together. Or does anyone think differently now?

Jussuf: We've already asked the five biggest ones. They all sent us away.

Pippo: There's one more.

Wilma: No, Pippo—don't even go there. We're simply not good enough. None of us. Nowadays, we'd have to draw a huge crowd, otherwise we can't compete. Audiences aren't like they used to be.

Bux: Not even the children. They're happy to watch a circus on TV. Even in the villages. For all of us it used to be better. We were useful members of society.

The Puppet: Me too? Tell me, Bux, does this hurt?

Bux: A little.

The Puppet: Then I'd rather run away. (They struggle.)

Bux: Quiet down, my small one. Without me, you can't run away.

Wilma: Have you all heard that Leo's in a movie now? As a stunt double, exploding and jumping off tall buildings into cushions. He makes pretty good money, they say.

Pippo: Yeah, he left us high and dry.

Wilma: Sooner or later we'll all have to ready ourselves.

Eli: Jojo's coming! Look, Jojo's here! (She runs up to him and throws her arms around him.) Jojo! Jojo! Eli wait so long!

(Jojo, a man around fifty, wears a shabby winter coat and in a baggy pocket, a bottle sticks out. On his head, a pointy clown hat sits askew, which he takes off ceremoniously and bows to his colleagues, as if they are applauding him uproariously. He wears an accordion strapped across his back.)

Pippo: Well, tell us something, Jojo!

Lola: Did they tell you anything?

Jojo (situates his hat): Yes.

Wilma: What then? Yes or no?

Jojo (lightly): No.

Pippo: Jojo, don't joke!

Bux: What did you do, Jojo?

The Puppet: Why did it take you so long, Jojo?

Jojo: Because (he thinks hard), because (he hits his forehead). Well, before I knew, for sure . . . but I lost it somewhere. (He looks around him.)

Wilma: What did I say? He did nothing!

Pippo: So, everything was for nothing? Tell us, Jojo!

Jojo: (Defends himself with his hands held up and looks around the ground.)

Bux: It's what we anticipated, Ottokar.

The Puppet: It's all very reasonable, Bux.

Jussuf: Such teeth! They have such teeth! They worry me.

Lola: What are you talking about, Jussuf? Who do you mean?

Jussuf: The monsters. The dragons. The sorcerers. Them, over there . . . there and there.

Lola: Oh, the tractors. That's just a front loader and a dump truck.

Jussuf: They wait. They are waiting there. For us.

Pippo: Nonsense, Jussuf. Look at them together. What could they do to us? We live in a civilized city. We're not going away. We'll stay together. Then they can't do anything to us. Do you think the front loader will plow us under?

Jojo: Stop! Now I have it! Do you know what I did? Total suffering!

Wilma: Who is suffering, Jojo? You hurt someone?

Jojo (with big gestures): Everyone.

Pippo: That's great! What else did you do?

Jojo: I personally spoke to all of the higher-up generals.

Pippo (stunned): You did?

Jojo (proudly nodding): I did.

Pippo: With the general director of the plant there?

Jojo: Certainly. And personally. From person to person, you know? Him there and me there. Or actually, opposite of that. Him across there, and me here. And do you know what they all told me . . . the highest personal general directors? They told me that they were very sorry, very, very sorry . . . personally.

Pippo: And what are they very, personally sorry for?

Jojo: That everything is already determined, and they can't change any of it at this point. Here, where we're standing, the Chemical Works will be building a new factory wing, that they urgently need to begin work. Tomorrow morning, early, they begin. Here—everything will be scraped. Also, our trailers, if they are still here. But, naturally we have time before tomorrow morning to put them somewhere else.

Pippo: And where would that be?

Jojo (he points here and there and finally lets his arms sink): See now, Pippo, that's exactly what I asked.

Pippo: And what did the general director say to you?

Jojo: Your short memory has failed you, too, Pippo?—That they're very sorry.

Pippo (sits down): Then we're done! Out and over!

The Puppet: You, Jojo. Listen a minute, Jojo. Did they truly tell you nothing else?

Jojo: Wait. Yes. Let me remember, a second. What was it? Oh, right. They wanted us to campaign for them.

Pippo: *What* do they want us to do?

Jojo: Campaign for them.

Pippo: All of us together?

Jojo: All of us together.

Wilma: And this is the first time you're telling us this?

Pippo: Wait a minute. Wait a minute. What . . . are they hiring us as?

Jojo (sees a paper in his bag): As an advertisement circus. Here is the contract. We need only to sign it. We'll get new trailers, motorized, naturally. And new costumes. And everything absolutely new. Even new numbers. The advertisement office will think for us. Naturally, also a new name . . . the circus will be the same name as the plant.

Wilma: And the pay?

Jojo: Not bad.

Wilma: Children—Will wonders never cease!

Jussuf: And what do we have to do for them?

Jojo: We pull our trailers through the area and advertise for the Chemical Works. Throughout the small villages and everywhere. And we'll make ads for TV, too.

Pippo: This is our saving grace. (He cries.)

Lola (takes Pippo's arm gently): We're still a big troupe.

Pippo: Has anyone an objection?

Jojo (points a finger): I do, please.

Wilma: Of course! Him! What is there then to think about?

Pippo: So say something, Jojo.

Jojo: The rulers have a small condition. We must part ways with Eli.

Jussuf: With Eli? Whatever for?

Jojo: They say it doesn't make a good impression with her around. We are supposed to trust their chemical products to advertise. We should show how harmless and useful their products are, they say. Such a child could give false opinions, they say. And they don't want that.

Lola: And what's to become of Eli?

Jojo: Oh, we don't need to worry ourselves about that, they say. The firm provides an institute for such children. It's modern and state of the art. Fabulous physicians, fabulous nursing staff. Top-of-the-line science. They want to admit her there.

Wilma (after a pause): Alright. Then everything's in order. She'll have more development there than with us. Perhaps they could even help her. What do you say, Eli? Would you not like to go to a super nice home where you can get healthier and even learn?

Eli (holds Jojo's hand anxiously): Eli is kind. You are all kind, right?

Jojo: You all know that I'm dumb. Too dumb for this. We must all decide together. Until tomorrow morning, we have time. But something else has happened to me. Perhaps it is very dumb. Do you know how it was three years ago? When we pulled up into a spot that was so funny. The people were all on the run. In the streets everywhere they toted hens and dogs and cats. And then it started to rain and the grass turned yellow. Later, in the news it said that it was a poison gas cloud. It's at that time Nick got sick and has remained so to this day. And also, there we found Eli, creeping in the street. That's all, what happened to me.

Pippo: Yes, that was a catastrophe. Whoever's fault in a facility, only a kilometer away from us. Why do you bring it up?

Jojo: That facility belongs to the same company here. And they make the same product. And for that we have to publicize for them, and part ways with Eli. (The whole troupe appears helpless.)

Wilma (restless): Children. Now I also need to say something. With how it is, we don't have much choice. We must take what's offered us. If we don't, we won't change the world. Besides, we aren't ultimately responsible for what they are doing.

Jojo (staring at Wilma for a long time): No? I'm too dumb to know. You all must decide what we should do.

(A long pause.)

The Puppet: Don't all speak at once!

(Jojo takes his accordion and begins to play a melody. He pulls through an old Luxemburg song.)

Eli: Jojo? Jojo is kind. Jojo tells Eli something.

Jojo: A story? I don't have anything to tell today. You know that I'm dumb, my child. You know that's so.

Eli (laughs): No. It's not true. Jojo tells Eli a fairy tale, yes?

Jojo (strips off accordion): A fairy tale? And about whom shall it be?

Eli: About us. (Points to each individual.) About Eli and Jojo and all of us.

Jojo (pulls the bottle out of his pocket, drinks a sip, looks around the circle pensively, treads closer tentatively, takes another sip and sets down the bottle.): Let's see, how does it go . . . (He begins again to play lightly on the accordion. While he speaks it begins to darken quickly. The scene disappears. One only hears Jojo's voice.) Well, listen now, Eli. Once upon a time there lived a beautiful, small princess named Eli, who wore silks and velvets, who lived high above the world in a castle made of colorful glass. She had everything that one could dream of. She ate only the finest meals, and drank only the sweetest wine. She slept on silk pillows and sat on ivory thrones. She had everything—but she was all alone. Then everything around her, her attendants and maidens, her dogs and cats and birds, yes, even her flowers . . . all were mere reflections, mirror images . . . (The music goes on, until the next image appears.)

The First Reflection

Slowly from the dark emerges the castle of colored glass high above the world. A big hall. Morning sun breaks glistening in a thousand sparks of color, in translucent walls and columns. Princess Eli rests in a grand, heavenly bed. The feeble child from the prelude has now become a wonderful young woman between sixteen and twenty. Into her chamber, maidens bring her a beautiful dress. They open the heavenly bed's curtains and wake the princess. Eli rises and is anointed by the maidens with all sorts of precious perfumes, after which she is dressed, combed, and adorned with jewels. Lastly, they place her sparkling crown on her head.

Eli: A new dress! A new day!
Ready for something new to play.
Servants, all, dumb,
what should we begin?
My life is all play,
fun everlasting days.
Time's lapse, time still.
Oh, if you were mirror images, all—
You would not shout.
Also, pets and sprouts.
All mirror images, abound.

I dreamed I was far away
In a foreign place.
In a bad and dark place
were beings like me,
they spoke, sang and serenaded me.
Their human answer was

so comforting and pleasing!

Oh, to me please converse.
Once, like those of the earth.
I want to listen to them all
and to sleep, never fall.

And for you to be nearby
one must to earth fall,
must one die,
to be equal?

How tired I am—no, oh, no!
Stuck in a castle of glass—yet colorful!
Forever a queen child,
rich for all time
I can never die.
(A remote, nearing, multivoiced, glassy sound is heard.)

Eli: My magic mirror nears, my Kalophain!

Kalophain (a distant and dark voice of a woman): Turn away, my child.
Be wise. My gaze could be deathly.

Eli (turned around): Come now and rest from your journey,
You're fine. On your journey, away day and night,
did you bring with you, a thousand new mirror pictures, a thousand
new games, delights?

Kalophain (very close): I only come if you shut your eyes, so you don't
reflect in me or die.

Eli (covers eyes with hands): She says day in and day out,
Don't look into her,
I follow her advice with a pout,
to remain eternal, and alone.

(The magic mirror hovers like a sliver of moon that descends down. A
silver female figure wears the sliver and expands into his frame, com-
prised of ornaments.)

Kalophain: Obedience, my little mistress, you,
bring me the pictures I've collected.

Eli (to herself): How different her voice sounds to me,
as if she rang out of my dreams.

Kalophain: Does princess Eli order me to begin?

Eli: No! Wait a minute! Answer first and tell me: When you see people
while hovering high above their world and their lives, what makes them
so different from me?

What do they have that I cannot have?

Kalophain: No, little mistress, don't think of that!

Eli: Yes, I will! You must give me an answer!

Kalophain (begins to jingle and sing enchantingly): Let yourself be
satisfied with the stifling pleasure of looking at the pictures.
Fateless, floating high above life in eternal dream!
The pictures, they silence, so still your own, for all time.
With you as playmate, let love go, and feel no pain.

Eli (as in a trance—sweet anesthesia): True, I do not understand the
meaning, it sounds so sweet I fade away, in your gentle shimmer.

Kalophain: In my tender magic, the questions—only you forget them.
(Aside.) And so I never lose you and you stay with me forever.

Eli (waking): What did I want then? I never know . . . What did you
say, dear Kalophain?

Kalophain: You were satisfied with my answers. (The frame of the mirror begins to glow.) Come forth, come forth, you delightful glowing
figures! Now emerge from the silvery-lit round—Your pictures, that my
magic has gathered, now free once more, full of life and colorful!

(Out of the depths of the mirror come fantastic figures of all sorts: animals, mythical creatures, men in outlandish costumes. They emerge
from the mirror frame and fill the room. The people from the circus
are underneath, now, though, in their restored and glorious circus

costumes. The mirror pictures begin to dance a labyrinthine "round" dance around the room, that bewilders all.)

Kalophain (hovering): Flying away over land and sea,
high over cities and fields until
I move motionless, my compass eyes,
looking and gathering with glassy feel,
what I can catch in my sight,
beautifully strange and wonderful
I bring to you now to play and revel,
for my little mistress, for you all things joyful.

(The dance of the mirror pictures becomes wilder and wilder. Lastly, Jojo's picture emerges as Prince Johan. The clown from the circus appears now as a handsome young man in a princely cloak. He immediately disappears into the vortex of the dancers.)

Eli: Everyone still! Give me not this beautiful face, shame,
I will see you again.
Stop the wild dance! O lovely eyes shine.
Now comply!
Now the dance is at an end!
(The dance breaks up, the mirror pictures freeze.)

Kalophain: What is this, my little mistress?
Just like the others, this was a picture,
sit back and enjoy, let it go on. Is it not fun? Come, sit here!

Eli (finds the prince picture and stands in front of it): How is it so strange to me? I can't understand it.
This visage here, it calls to me,
a deep, dark sense wakes.
O Kalophain, O mirror of mine, never before
have you given me pictures like these.
Where did you find them? And who is he?
The one who left this image, beautifully?

Kalophain: I know it not. And if I'd known what it does to you,
I wouldn't have brought it.

Eli: I seek him! Ask, what's his name. Bring him to me!
Will you, it will go on.

Kalophain: Me? Bring him? Mistress, you know:
I cannot. I am a ghost
and can only pictures bring.

Eli: You will not?

Kalophain: Tame your will!
Forget your wish! He can't live up to you.

Eli: Forget? What makes me dizzy, fades from a dark future, as my life
secret, deepest life? Forgetting him? How could I do it? And if I can't
give him a sign, I will become mortal. (The mirror nears her.)

Kalophain: Come back, come back! You bring yourself danger! What
are you doing? Stop! Stop!

Eli: You magic mirror, bright and clear,
my Kalophain, hear my will!
Whatever threatens me,
your command I must fulfill.
Take my picture and bring
it with you over land and sea.
Perhaps he doesn't know where I am.
Perhaps he wanders about.
Perhaps he looks around and sees
my image in you.
Perhaps he follows your laugh
and finds me that way.

(She steps resolutely in front of the mirror and sees her reflection.)

Kalophain: Too late! Oh, too late! With your threat,
now you've forced your needs on me.

Eli: How suddenly I become so peculiar? I feel completely
transformed.

Kalophain: You saw your image! You, who had eternal life—
And me . . .

Eli: What holds me and burns inside? O Kalophain,
I have one heart! But it seems like only half!
I miss the other half
How poor and miserable it makes me.

Kalophain: It is the longing that torments you, but greater suffering
now awaits you!

Eli: Do not extend them. Do not leave them unsatisfied. Arise yourself.
Rush, fly into the distance. Surely, he will see the image which lacks me.

Kalophain: I will do it. Yes, I will do it gladly.

(Eli's image remains in the magic mirror while the other rises and floats
away.)

Eli: All mirror pictures away! Go to the garden!

(Eli forces the image of the prince, who also wants to disappear, to re-
main with a gesture.)

Only this one will remain with me through day and night. I will wait,
wait, wait . . .

Charles Baudelaire, translated by Lola Haskins

The Journey

—*for Maxime du Camp*

I

When we were children, in love with maps
and stamps, the universe seemed enough.
Ah! how clear and large the lamp-lit world
that in memory's eyes was small.

One morning we set out, our minds aflame,
our hearts rancorous and bitter,
to follow the rhythm of the waves
that rock our infinities on finite seas.

Some, happily escaping their infamous country;
others, the horrors of the crib, and a few,
astrologers, death by drowning in a woman's
eyes, some Circe of dangerous perfumes.

So as not to turn into beasts, they drink—
space and light and fiery skies—
as the stinging cold and bronzing suns
erase, slowly, the kisses from their skins.

But the true voyagers are the ones who leave
for its own sake; their hearts light as balloons,
these never force their fates, and, without
knowing why, say always: *Allons y*!

The desires of these are like clouds,
and they dream, the way a conscript dreams
of guns, of sensualities, vast and shifting,
that no man has ever named.

II
We mimic—horrible!—tops and bowled balls
in their spins and bounds; as curiosity
torments us in our sleep and rolls us like
a mugger, or a cruel angel flogging suns.

It's an odd luck whose goal keeps moving,
which, being nowhere, could be anywhere!
In which man, who never tires of hope,
courts his rest by running around like a fool!

Our soul is a caravel in search of Ikaria;
a resounding voice from the bridge: *Open your Eyes!*
A voice from the crow's nest, ardent, crazy:
Love . . . Glory . . . Happiness! Hell! We're aground.

Every small island the watchman reports

seems Destiny's promised El Dorado;

but Imagination, setting up her orgy

finds only a reef in the light of day.

Oh, pathetic lover of chimeric countries!

Must he be put in irons or thrown into the sea,

this drunken sailor, inventor of Americas,

whose illusions only turn the pit more bitter?

Like an old hobo, sloshing through the mud,

who sniffs the air and dreams a glowing paradise;

whose eye, enchanted, sees marshy Capua

anywhere a candle illuminates a hut.

III

Astonishing travelers! What noble histories

we read in your eyes, as deep as the sea!

Show us the case of your rich memories,

those wonderful jewels, made of air and stars.

We're yearning to travel without steam or sail!

To illumine the ennui of our prisons,

Show us, as if stretched across canvas,

your recollections in their horizons' frames.

Tell us, *What have you seen?*

IV

We have seen stars

and waves, we have also seen sand;

and, despite shocks and unforeseen disasters,

we were often bored, as we are here.

The glory of sunlight on a violet sea,

the glory of cities in the setting sun,

lit a restless impulse in our hearts

to dive into the alluringly reflected sky.

The richest cities, the grandest landscapes,

will never have the mysterious allure

that chance makes from clouds.

And always, desire renders us uneasy!

—Yet enjoyment fortifies desire.

Desire, old tree whom pleasure fertilizes,

however hard and thick your swollen bark,

your branches will still reach for light.

Will you grow forever, great tree more vital

than cypress? No matter; we have carefully

chosen some sketches for your album, voracious

brothers, who find beauty in all from afar!

We have kowtowed to fraudulent idols;

to thrones studded with glittering gems;

to palaces awash in fantastic pomp

that would be for you bankers a ruined dream;

to costumes that are rapture for the eyes;

to women who paint their teeth and fingernails,

to knowing jugglers, caressing snakes.

V

And then? And then?

VI

What children!

Not forgetting the main thing,

We've seen, everywhere, without effort,

up and down the fatal ladder,

the dull spectacle of immortal sin.

Woman, low servant, proud and stupid,

self-adoring without humor or disgust;

Man, grasping tyrant, bawdy, hard and greedy,

slaves to slavery, rivulets in the sewer;

The hangman who loves his work, the sobbing martyr,

the fête that flavors and perfumes the blood,

the poison of the power that saps a despot's strength,

the amorous users of the brutalizing whip.

So many religions similar to our own,

climbing toward sainthood and heaven,

the way the sybarite wallowing in her feather-bed

takes pleasure from horsehair and nails.

Babbling Mankind, drunk on his own genius,

as stupid now as he was jaded before,

cries out in fierce agony to God,

Oh my likeness, my master, be damned!

Meanwhile, the less dim, bold lovers of insanity,

flee the milling herd hemmed in by fate

to take their ease in clouds of opium!

—So reads the eternal dispatch from the world!

VII

It's the bitter savant, who goes traveling!

The world, so monotonous and small today,

yesterday, tomorrow, forever, forced to see itself:

an oasis of horror in a desert of ennui.

Must he leave? Stay? Stay if you can;

leave if you must. The short, and otherwise,

crouch to fool the vigilant, always fatal enemy.

Time! Alas! Some flee him without stopping,

like apostles or wandering Jews,

for whom no wagon or ship will suffice

to escape the infamous net; others know

how to kill him without leaving their cribs.

And when, finally, his foot's on our necks,

we can still hope, shout *Onward!*

and, as we once set out for China, our eyes wide,

our hair blowing in the wind,

we embark on the darkening sea

with the joyful hearts of the young.

Do you hear those charming funereal voices

singing *Here, come here if you'd try*

the fragrant lotus! And here we offer
miracle fruits for your hungry hearts;
come here, drink in the strange sweetness
of this afternoon that never ends.

From his familiar accent, we recognize the spectre,

our Pylades, who is stretching out his arms;

To refresh your heart, swim toward your Electra!

says the one whose knees we kissed long ago.

VIII

O Death, old captain! Raise the anchor.

This country is boring us, Death! Let's prepare!

Though the sea and sky are black as ink,

you know our hearts are light.

Pour us your poisons that they may comfort us.

We are worthy now, for fire is burning in our brains,

to plunge into the abyss, be it heaven or hell,

to the bottom of the unknown, to find something *new*.

Zhu Zhu, translated by Dong Li
The Invisible Man

—an elegy for Zhang Zao

I

An extended winter,

snow was still falling in March, no leaves were

on the branches and yet migrant birds returned in time,

completing their great expedition; in Tübingen,

your place of departure, you laid down your wings,

tangled into shrouds, and flew no more.

For a long time you had been an invisible man,

poetry did the flying for you, casting shadows among us,

their traces followed, their lines recited; before

tank treads crushed the carnival age to pieces,

before I staggered to write the first line, you departed.

An isolated nest by the edge of the Black Forest,

a black dot wriggling on the aerial map, anonymous flotsam;

there you experienced the first shocks on the journey,

like a hot, red iron you fell into the Neckar river in winter . . .

after the sizzling dispersed in the ripples, not only were there delusional fumes with life-denying claws, but also riled youth

and ears everywhere, swelled with blood at the sight of beauty—

strings not tuned by friendship or echoes of home,

plucking is a gesture to beckon ghosts,

seething like Orpheus from the netherworld, unsure

whether true love followed close behind. There,

alms of freedom could not be cashed in for bread,

outside the probation door, a lonesome K and his rolls of castles.

Ah, the surveyor doubled over in boredom; often quiet snow

blanketed night as you drank to yourself in the window pane,

body desirous of inebriation like a slowly sagging scale,

tired of weighing every word,

letting them flutter and then lie buried on the horizon

of white papers spit from Mr. Lichtenstein's typewriter.

II

I first saw you in Shanghai. In a cramped elevator

your pudgy physique was more corpulent than ever,

not a sign of the handsome youth of hearsay.

Then at a bar, you showed off a card trick,

as if it would redeem your miraculous image—

I was taken aback by your boyishness, your bloated sweetness, yet you were tough at your core; I was taken aback

by your snoring, loud as a dump truck

waking up the streets, like the "bad rhymes" you mentioned,

shifting strenuously in the two airs that you breathed—

rather than saying German is ice, Chinese the ember, why not

say the present is ice, the past is ember, sizzling inside of you.

China is changing! We are all in the throes of migration.

Seeing remembrance as regression, nostalgia as a terminal disease,

we scuttle like lizards, afraid of lagging behind,

but everything we pass cracks into an abyss . . .

you folded your wings under the static eaves of Europe, dreaming

of timeless grief, missing the current epic of displacement.

You returned, like a watchman patrolling the wrong latitude,

like Diogenes of Sinope daydreaming with a lantern in hand,

searching tirelessly . . . there were no longer fragrant discourses

in the air, the likes of Zhong Ziqi were going deaf,

laughter like fireworks set off on the bleak outskirts many years ago;

only you spread out the map of the last age, stubbornly,

until a dagger's flash made you your own assassin.

Heart in pieces, you returned to a new invisibility,

and were reduced to a teacher's ruler, to a barroom table,

to your homemade prison of words; preferring to lose voice,

behind the clamor, your strings were snapped, no more lingering

in rhetoric's political arena, on a rapper's stage.

Tonight, I pull your slim volume from the shelf.

After closing the book, I see a comet with its tail trailing behind it.

Down below, the cages of two continents open up—

just as poets are myths after death,

birds among apes, kings of no land;

perhaps you never truly landed on earth.

Note: In a Chinese legend, Zhong Ziqi is a woodcutter who truly understands the music of the Chinese zither player Yu Boya. After Ziqi's death, Boya smashes his zither and plays no more. This legend exemplifies the Chinese ideal of friendship.

VISUAL ART

Jeremy Dennis
Luycia Natalie Daughter Santa Fe

The Sacredness of Hills series is based upon recurring desecrations of indigenous burial grounds surrounding my tribal community in Southampton, NY, which largely bases its economy on real estate and development.

On Monday, August 13, 2018, skeleton remains were found during residential development on Hawthorne Road in the Shinnecock Hills. The developers and homeowners contacted the Southampton Town and Suffolk County police department, who quickly disturbed the ground further for evidence of recent criminal activity.

Scarlett Santa Fe

Rachel Eliza Griffiths
CM Burroughs

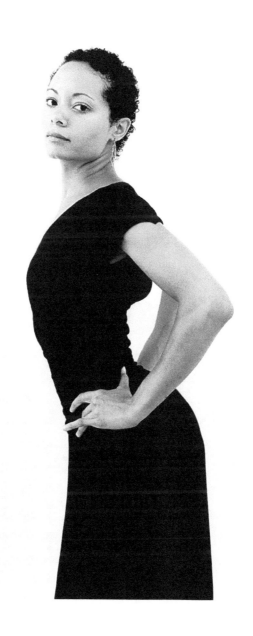

Lucille Clifton

Nandi Comer

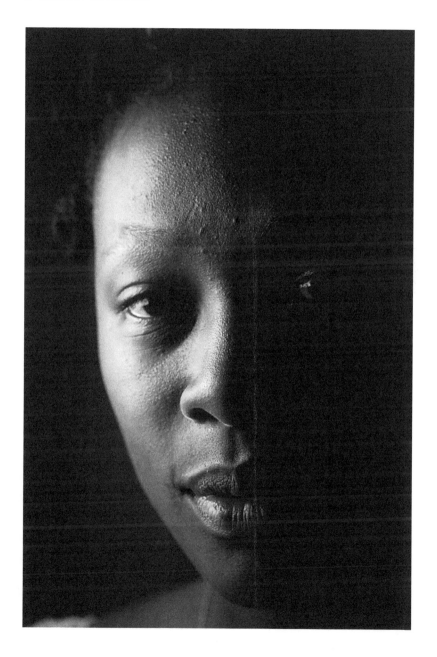

Marvin K. White and L. Lamar Wilson

Other Black Collective
(Angel Nafis and Morgan Parker)

Ross Gay

Portrait of the Ancestors Looking through the Veil as I Look Back

Two Elizas, 2009

Ellen Wiener
Mason & Miner

These objects are altered books using mixed materials. They are homages to the work writers do as excavators and architects of the imagination. Some respond to the legible text, the contents of the volume, or to the author's biography. I am not a sculptor or a writer and I make these as side dishes to my usual work, which I tend to take over-seriously. They reflect the pleasure and wonder I feel when offered the world of a fresh book.

Mason & Miner. 2017. 14.5 x 16.5 x 4 inches.

Mason & Miner, detail.

Thread Ladder

Thread Ladder. 2018. 11 x 8 x 3 inches.

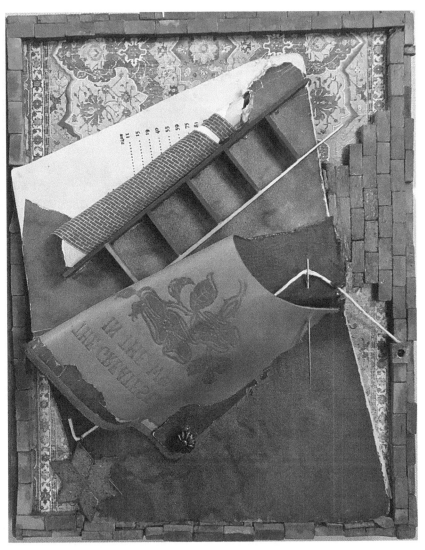

Thread Ladder, detail.

Chestnut

Chestnut. 2018. 14 x 14.5 x 7 inches.

Peale & Reveal

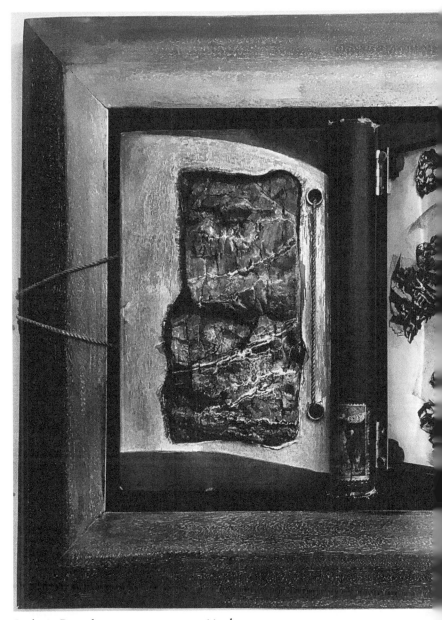

Peale & Reveal. 2020. 14.5 x 17.5 x 6 inches.

Passerine

Passerine. 2017. 12 x 14 x 3 inches.

Passerine, detail.

Mrs. B.

Mrs. B. 2018. 9.5 x 9.5 x 2 inches.

Diane Samuels

ALL PHOTOS: THOMAS LITTLE

Scheherazade

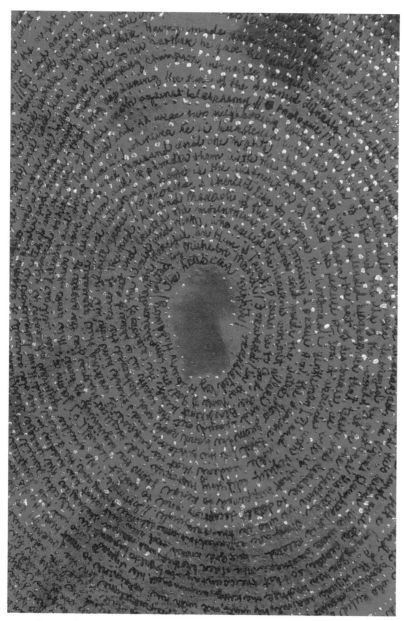

Detail, *Scheherazade,* The Arabian Nights, tr. by Husain Haddawy,
Forward and Prologue.

First Lines

Detail, *First Lines* with magnifier.

Moby-Dick, or the Whale, Herman Melville

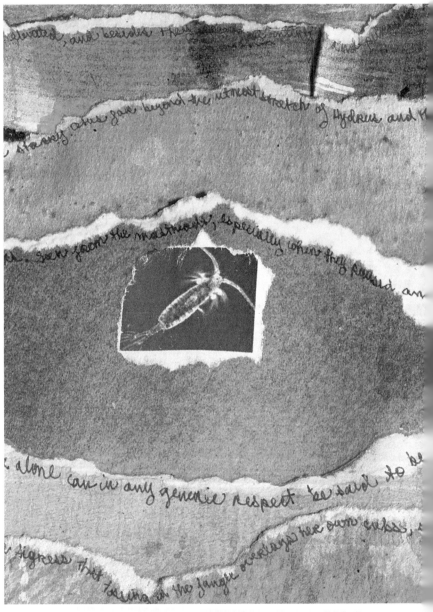

Detail, Chapter LVIII, *Moby-Dick, or The Whale,* Herman Melville.

Hand off... you cannot exting... them

...ch of with a frigate's anchors for my bridle —

tionary for a while, their vast black forms look

aative analogy to him.] But though, to

...ashes even the mightiest whales against the rocks, and

First Lines

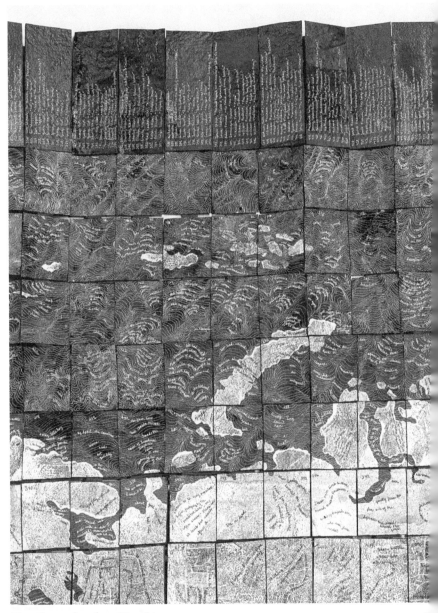

Detail, top border, *First Lines*.

First Lines

Detail, *First Lines,* Persian Gulf and Strait of Hormuth.

Scheherazade

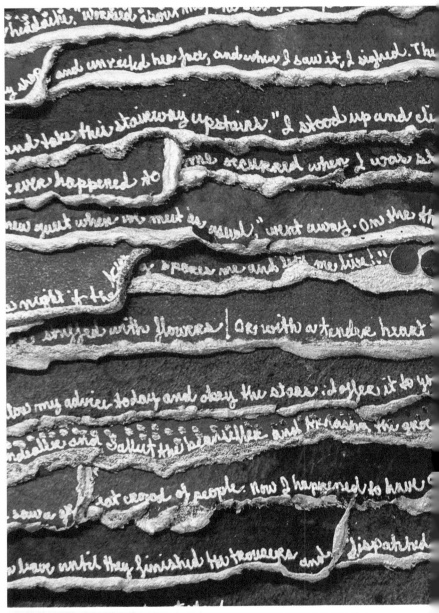

Detail, *Scheherazade,* The One Hundred and Thirty-Eighth Night.

...ed me, "Do you have any fabrics?" I replied, "my lad...

...t of the chest, and hardly had she closed the lid an...

...cine in Damascus. One day a mamluk...

...prepared a banquet. / [But morning overtook...

...E ONE HUNDRED AND THIRTY-EIGHTH NIGHT Lm...

...g unseen! / O let the watchman come, she has...

...charge, for it is nothing of reducing my affection...

...he darkest river, and Steward the porter and...

...of money hidden in my sleeve for such a day; so...

...v. Then he went home, confused, and unable to buy...

...from her maids, as if...

Scheherazade

Detail, *Scheherazade*, The First Night.

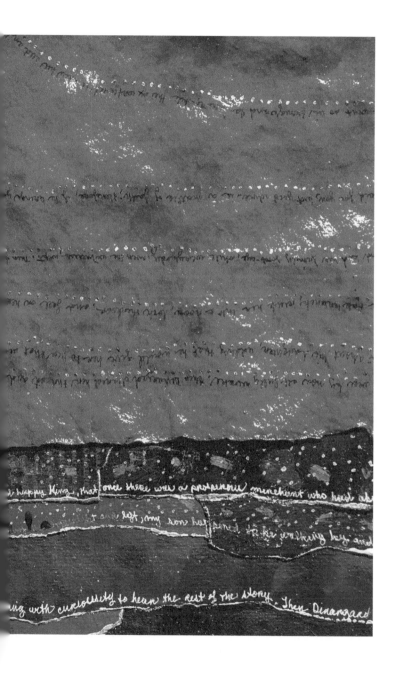

Elana Herzog

Here and Now

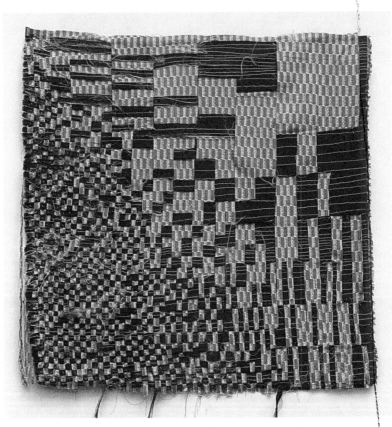

Here and Now, 2020. Mixed textiles, thread. 31 x 31 inches,
plus hanging elements.

CONTRIBUTOR NOTES

POETRY

Kara Candito is the author of *Spectator* (University of Utah Press, 2014), winner of the Agha Shahid Ali Poetry Prize, and *Taste of Cherry* (University of Nebraska Press, 2009), winner of the Prairie Schooner Book Prize in Poetry.

Julie Carr is the author of six books of poetry, including *100 Notes on Violence*, *Rag*, and *Think Tank*, and the prose works *Surface Tension: Ruptural Time and the Poetics of Desire in Late Victorian Poetry*, *Objects from a Borrowed Confession*, *Someone Shot My Book*, and *Mud, Blood, and Ghosts: Populism, Eugenics, and Spiritualism in the American West*, forthcoming from University of Nebraska Press. Carr's co-translation of Leslie Kaplan's *Excess—The Factory* was published in 2018, as was a mixed-genre work, *Real Life: An Installation*. Carr is a professor at the University of Colorado in Boulder. With Tim Roberts she is the co-founder of Counterpath Press, Counterpath Gallery, and Counterpath Community Garden in Denver. The line, "I was just learning how to see" is from Brandon Shimoda, *The Grave on the Wall*.

Jennifer S. Cheng's work includes poetry, lyric essay, and image-text forms exploring immigrant home-building, shadow poetics, and the feminine monstrous. Her book *Moon: Letters, Maps, Poems* was selected by Bhanu Kapil for the Tarpaulin Sky Award and named a "Best Book of 2018" by *Publishers Weekly*. She is also the author of *House A*, selected by Claudia Rankine for the Omnidawn Poetry Prize, and *Invocation: An Essay*, an image-text chapbook published by New Michigan Press. She is a 2019 National Endowment for the Arts Literature Fellow and has received awards and fellowships from Brown University, the University of Iowa, the US Fulbright program, Kundiman, Bread Loaf, and the Academy of American Poets. Having grown up in Texas and Hong Kong, she lives in San Francisco. www.jenniferscheng.com.

Caroline Crew is the author of the essay collection *Other Girls to Burn* (University of Georgia Press, 2021), winner of the AWP Prize for Nonfiction, as well as the poetry collection *Pink Museum* (Big Lucks). She holds a PhD from Georgia State University, as well as an MA from the University of Oxford. Currently, she is based in Pittsburgh. You can find her at caroline-crew.com.

Gillian Cummings is the author of *The Owl Was a Baker's Daughter*, selected by John Yau as the winner of the 2018 Colorado Prize for Poetry (Center for Literary Publishing at Colorado State University, 2018), and *My Dim Aviary*, winner of the 2015 Hudson Prize (Black Lawrence Press, 2016). Her recent poems have appeared or are forthcoming in *Big Other*, *Colorado Review*, *Laurel Review*, *The Night Heron Barks*, *Schlag Magazine*, and *Tupelo Quarterly*. She lives in Westchester County, New York.

Asa Drake is a Filipina American writer and public services librarian in Central Florida. She is the recipient of fellowships from Tin House and Idyllwild Arts and is a 2020 92Y Discovery Poetry Contest winner. Her poems can be found in *Copper Nickel*, the *Paris Review Daily*, *Southern Humanities Review*, and elsewhere.

Sally Rosen Kindred is the author of three books of poems: *No Eden*, *Book of Asters*, and *Where the Wolf*, winner of the 2020 Diode Editions Book Prize. Her poems have appeared in journals including *Gettysburg Review*, *Alaska Quarterly Review*, and *Kenyon Review Online*.

Vera Kroms was born in a displaced persons camp in Germany to Latvian parents who soon emigrated to the Boston area. There, Vera followed the family's scientific bent and earned a BS and an MA in mathematics, followed by years of working as a computer programmer in financial and educational institutions. She'd begun writing poetry after college, studying with local poets. Eventually she met Lucie Brock-Broido and became a regular member of Lucie's summer workshops. She has published two collections of verse, *The Pears of Budapest* (Red Mountain Press) and *Necessary Harm* (Finishing Line Press).

Julia B. Levine's awards for her work include the Northern California Book Award in Poetry for *Small Disasters Seen in Sunlight* (LSU press, 2014), and first prizes in the 2019 *Bellevue Literary Review*, 2019 Public Poetry Awards, and the 2018 *Tiferet* Poetry Prize. Her fifth collection, *Ordinary Psalms*, was published in spring 2021 from LSU press. She lives and works in Davis, California.

Brianna Noll is the author of *The Era of Discontent* (Elixir Press, 2021) and *The Price of Scarlet* (University Press of Kentucky, 2017), which was named one of the top poetry books of 2017 by the *Chicago Review of Books*. She is poetry editor of *The Account*, which she helped found, and her poems and translations have appeared widely in journals, including *Kenyon Review Online, Georgia Review, Prairie Schooner, Crazyhorse*, and *Waxwing*.

Jeffrey Pethybridge is the author of *Striven, The Bright Treatise* (Noemi Press, 2013). His work appears widely in journals such as *Best American Experimental Writing, Chicago Review, Volt,* the *Iowa Review, LIT, New American Writing*, and others. He teaches in the Jack Kerouac School of Disembodied Poetics at Naropa University, where he is the director of the Summer Writing Program. He lives in Denver with the poet Carolina Ebeid and their son Patrick; together they edit *Visible Binary*. He's currently at work on a documentary project centered on the recently released torture memos entitled "Force Drift, an Essay in the Epic." He grew up in Virginia.

Raena Shirali is the author of two collections of poetry. Her first book, *Gilt* (YesYes Books, 2017), won the 2018 Milt Kessler Poetry Book Award, and her second, *summonings* (Black Lawrence Press, 2022), won the 2021 Hudson Prize. Winner of a Pushcart Prize and a former Philip Roth Resident at Bucknell University, Shirali is also the recipient of prizes and honors from VIDA, *Gulf Coast, Boston Review,* and *Cosmonauts Avenue*. Formerly a co-editor in chief of *Muzzle Magazine*, Shirali now serves as faculty advisor for *Folio*—a literary magazine dedicated to publishing works by undergraduate students at the national level. She holds an MFA in Poetry from the Ohio State University and is an assistant professor of English at Holy Family University. The Indian American poet was raised in Charleston, South Carolina, and now lives in Philadelphia.

Yerra Sugarman is the author of three poetry collections: *Aunt Bird* (Four Way Books, 2022), *Bag of Broken Glass*, and *Forms of Gone* (both published by Sheep Meadow Press). She has received an NEA Fellowship in Poetry, among other honors. Her poems have appeared in such journals as *Ploughshares, Colorado Review, The Nation, AGNI, Bat*

City Review, and *Prairie Schooner*. She holds a PhD in Creative Writing and Literature from the University of Houston.

Cole Swensen is the author of seventeen books of poetry, most of them focused on the visual arts and on land-use issues, often centering on their intersection in the treatment and depiction of public spaces. A former Guggenheim Fellow, recipient of the Iowa Poetry Prize and the San Francisco State University Poetry Center Book Award, and finalist for the National Book Award, she organized and executed the 2020 twelve-week Zoom reading series *Ecopoetics: Poetics for the More Than Human World*, viewable on the Chax Press YouTube site. Her most recent book, *Art in Time*, a series of twenty poem-essays on innovations in landscape art, was published by Nightboat in 2021.

G. C. Waldrep's most recent books are *The Earliest Witnesses* (Tupelo/Carcanet, 2021) and *feast gently* (Tupelo, 2018), winner of the William Carlos Williams Award from the Poetry Society of America. Newer work has appeared in *APR*, *Poetry*, *Paris Review*, *New England Review*, *Yale Review*, *Iowa Review*, *Colorado Review*, *New American Writing*, and *Conjunctions*. Waldrep lives in Lewisburg, Pennsylvania, where he teaches at Bucknell University.

JinJin Xu is a poet and filmmaker from Shanghai. Her hybrid work has appeared in *The Common* and The Immigrant Artist Biennial, and was awarded the George Bogin Memorial Prize from the Poetry Society of America. After traveling for a year writing poetry with dislocated women all over the world as a Thomas J. Watson Fellow, she received her MFA from New York University, where she was a Lillian Vernon Fellow and taught hybrid poetry workshops. Her debut, *There Is Still Singing in the Afterlife,* won the inaugural Own Voices Chapbook Prize, selected by Aria Aber. She is currently Features Director of *LIFE Magazine*, China.

LITERARY CRITICISM

Mary-Kim Arnold is the author of *Litany for the Long Moment* (Essay Press, 2018) and *The Fish & The Dove* (Noemi Press, 2020). Other writing has appeared in *Conjunctions*, *Hyperallergic*, Poem-a-Day, *Georgia Review*, *Denver Quarterly*, and *The Rumpus*, among others. She teaches in the Nonfiction Writing Program at Brown University and in the low-residency Newport MFA.

Rachel Blau DuPlessis is a poet, literary critic, essayist, editor, and in the past decade and a half, a collagist. She is known for her work on gender and poetics in modernist and contemporary poetries and her interests in the long poem. She lives in Philadelphia and taught at Temple University.

Danielle Dutton is the author of several books, most recently the novel *Margaret the First*. She is founder and editor of the feminist press Dorothy, a publishing project. Born and raised in Central California, she lives in St. Louis with her husband and son.

Amy E. Elkins is assistant professor of English at Macalester College. She researches twentieth- and twenty-first-century literature and feminism, as well as contemporary art, craft, and critical making. She is currently finishing her first monograph, *Crafting Modernity: Remaking Feminist Time from Literary Modernism to the Multimedia Present*. In addition to her scholarly publications, Elkins lectures on creative pedagogy and writes a series of author interviews that explore the intersection of visual culture and women's writing for *Los Angeles Review of Books*.

Camille Guthrie is the author of three books of poetry, including *Articulated Lair: Poems for Louise Bourgeois* (Subpress, 2013). Her new book, *Diamonds*, was published by BOA Editions in 2021. She is the director of undergraduate writing initiatives at Bennington College.

Lucy Ives is the author of two novels, *Impossible Views of the World* (2017) and *Loudermilk: Or, The Real Poet; Or, The Origin of the World* (2019), and the short story collection *Cosmogony* (Soft Skull, 2021). Her essays and stories have appeared in *Art in America*, *Artforum*, *The Baffler*, *The Believer*, the *Chronicle of Higher Education*, *frieze*, *Granta*, *Lapham's Quarterly*, and *Vogue*, among other publications. In 2020 Siglio Press published *The Saddest Thing Is That I Have Had to Use Words: A Madeline Gins Reader*, a selection of Gins's poetry and prose, edited and with an introduction by Ives.

Karla Kelsey is the author of *Of Sphere*, a book of experimental essays, and four books of poetry, most recently *Blood Feather* (Tupelo Press, 2020). She co-edits SplitLevel Texts with Aaron McCollough and is on the faculty of the Writers Institute at Susquehanna University.

Ashley Lamb is an artist and educator who currently resides in Chicago. She is a co-founder of the feminist collective Joan Desert, named in honor of Eileen Gray's Parisian storefront, Jean Désert. She is passionate about the intersections of craft and social change.

Poupeh Missaghi is a writer, a translator both into and out of Persian, *Asymptote*'s Iran editor-at-large, and an educator. She holds a PhD in English and creative writing from the University of Denver, an MA in creative writing from Johns Hopkins University, and an MA in translation studies. She is currently a visiting assistant professor at the Department of Writing at the Pratt Institute, Brooklyn. Her debut novel, *trans(re)lating house one*, was published by Coffee House Press in February 2020.

Lisa Pearson is the founder and publisher of Siglio, an independent press dedicated to publishing uncommon books that live in the rich and varied space between art and literature. She is the editor or co-editor of several books, including by Nancy Spero, Dorothy Iannone, Mirtha Dermisache, Joe Brainard, and Robert Seydel as well as *It Is Almost That: A Collection of Image+Text Work by Women Artists & Writers*.

Chet'la Sebree is the director of the Stadler Center for Poetry & Literary Arts and an assistant professor of English at Bucknell University. She is the author of the poetry collection *Mistress* and the hybrid project *Field Study* (Macmillan, 2021).

PROSE

Hala Alyan is a Palestinian American writer and clinical psychologist whose work has appeared in the *New Yorker*, the *New York Times*, *Guernica*, and elsewhere. Her poetry collections have won the Arab American Book Award and the Crab Orchard Series. Her second novel,

The Arsonist's City, was published by Houghton Mifflin Harcourt in March 2021.

Kate Bolton Bonnici grew up in Alabama and holds degrees from Harvard University; New York University School of Law; University of California–Riverside; and University of California–Los Angeles. Her poetry collection, *Night Burial,* won the 2020 Colorado Prize for Poetry (Center for Literary Publishing, Colorado State University). Her work has appeared or is forthcoming in *Georgia Review, CounterText, Foundry, Arts & Letters, Southern Humanities Review, Image,* and elsewhere. She teaches at Pepperdine University.

Darien Hsu Gee is the author of five novels published by Penguin Random House that have been translated into eleven languages. In 2021, her collection of micro essays, *Allegiance,* received the Bronze IPPY award in the Essays category. She also received a 2019 Poetry Society of America Chapbook Fellowship award for *Other Small Histories* and the 2015 Hawai'i Book Publishers' Ka Palapala Po'okela Award of Excellence for *Writing the Hawai'i Memoir.* Gee is the recipient of a Sustainable Arts Foundation grant and a Vermont Studio Center fellowship.

Lesley Jenike's poems and essays have appeared in *Poetry, Kenyon Review, Southern Review, West Branch, Shenandoah, Bennington Review, Waxwing,* and many other journals. Her most recent collection is *Punctum:,* a chapbook of poems published by Kent State University Press in 2017. She is a professor of Writing, Literature, and Philosophy at the Columbus College of Art and Design in Columbus, Ohio, and served as a regular blogger for *Ploughshares* in 2019 and 2020.

Jennifer Militello is the author, most recently, of *The Pact* (Tupelo Press, 2021) and *Knock Wood,* winner of the Dzanc Nonfiction Prize. Her work has appeared in *American Poetry Review, Best American Poetry,* the *Nation,* the *New Republic, Poetry,* and *Tin House.* She teaches in the MFA program at New England College.

Christina Milletti's novel *Choke Box: a Fem-Noir* won the Juniper Prize for Fiction (2019) from the University of Massachusetts Press. Her fiction, articles, and reviews have appeared in many journals and anthologies, such as *Best New American Voices*, *Iowa Review*, the *Master's Review*, *Denver Quarterly*, *Cincinnati Review*, *Studies in the Novel*, *Zeta*, *Brooklyn Rail*, *American Letters & Commentary*, *Experimental Fiction*, and the *Buffalo News* (among other places). She is an associate professor of English at the University at Buffalo, where she is the executive director of the Humanities Institute and co-curates the Exhibit X Fiction Series.

Brandon Shimoda is the author of several books, most recently *The Grave on the Wall* (City Lights, 2019), which received the PEN Open Book Award, and *The Desert* (The Song Cave, 2018). His forthcoming book on the afterlife of Japanese American incarceration received a Creative Nonfiction grant from the Whiting Foundation, and will also be published by City Lights. He lives in Tucson, Arizona.

Michelle Phương Hồ is a poet based in New Haven, CT. Her work has appeared in *Apogee*, *Black Warrior Review*, and *wildness* and has been recognized with the 2020 Frontier Poetry Industry Prize. Born to Vietnamese refugees, she wrote with the Asian American writing collective, Jook Songs, while a student at Yale University. She is currently an MFA candidate in poetry at New York University.

Sara Veglahn is the author of the novels *The Ladies* (2017), winner of the Noemi Press Book Award for Fiction, and *The Mayflies* (Dzanc, 2014). Her writing and reviews have appeared or are forthcoming in *Conjunctions*, *Fence*, *Caketrain*, *Octopus*, *Full Stop*, and elsewhere. She lives and writes in Denver.

COLLABORATIVE AND CROSS-DISCIPLINARY TEXTS

A writer and artist, **Kristy Bowen** is the author of numerous artist book, chapbook, and zine projects, as well as several full-length collections, including the recent *Sex & Violence* (Black Lawrence Press, 2020). She lives in Chicago, where she runs dancing girl press & studio.

Laura Christensen is a visual artist who paints on recovered vintage portraits. Also a woodworker, she constructs miniature cabinets to cradle the altered photographs. Christensen's artwork has been featured in galleries and museums, including Kidspace at MASS MoCA, Tweed Museum of Art, Bennington Museum, Simmons College, and The Hyde Collection. Awards include MASS MoCA's "Assets for Artists" Professional Development Grant and two Artists' Resource Trust (A.R.T.) Grants, a fund of the Berkshire Taconic Community Foundation. Christensen's book project *THEN AGAIN* features her artworks along with poetic and narrative responses to her art written by several top-notch authors. Please visit her website at https://laurachristensen.wordpress.com/.

Based in the United Arab Emirates and Vermont, USA, **Jill Magi** works in text, image, and textiles. The author of six books of poetry and numerous handmade books housed in the University at Buffalo Poetry Collection, Magi ran Sona Books for ten years, publishing chapbooks of experimental works that she described as "risky, quiet, and community based." Her most recent book, *SPEECH* (Nightboat, 2019), is set in a city of middles: something like the Middle East and something like the Midwest, and the fictional wanderer who navigates these places resides in a female body of middle age. Magi has had residencies with the Lower Manhattan Cultural Council and the Brooklyn Textile Arts Center, and has taught for more than twenty years at research universities, liberal arts colleges, in MFA and BFA programs, and in community-based adult literacy programs. Jill has had solo exhibitions of visual work at the NYU Abu Dhabi Project Space Gallery, Tashkeel, and Grey Noise, and is a co-founder of JARA Collective. Visit her website at https://jillmagi.net/.

Ryan Mihaly is a writer and musician from New England. His chapbook *B-Flat Clarinet Fingering Chart* was published by New Michigan Press in 2022. His poems, translations, and interviews have appeared in the *Massachusetts Review, Fence, Asymptote,* and elsewhere. He works for a nonprofit music school in western Massachusetts.

Leslie Nichols uses a variety of found and original text to create visual imagery. Her works created on manual typewriters are featured in *Typewriter Art: A Modern Anthology* and *The Art of Typewriting.* An NEA Studio Residency Grant from Women's Studio Workshop supported experiments in letterpress printing. Her work has been recognized with additional grants from the Elizabeth Greenshields Foundation, the American Association of University Women, and the Kentucky Foundation for Women. Selected collections that feature her work include Yale University, the Library of Congress, and the Sackner Archive of Concrete and Visual Poetry. Her studio is in Bowling Green, Kentucky, where she teaches at Southcentral Kentucky Community and Technical College. For more information, visit www.leslienichol-sart.com.

Marjorie Thomsen loves teaching others how to play with words and live more poetically in the world. She is the author of *Pretty Things Please* (Turning Point, 2016). Two poems from this collection were read on The Writer's Almanac. One of Marjorie's poems about hiking in a dress and high heels was made into a short animated film. She has been nominated three times for a Pushcart Prize and Best of the Net and is the recipient of poetry awards from the University of Iowa School of Social Work, *Poetica Magazine*, and others. Publications include *Pangyrus, Rattle, SWWIM,* and *Tupelo Quarterly*. Marjorie has been a poet in residence in schools throughout New England. She is a psychotherapist and instructor at Boston University's School of Social Work. She lives in Cambridge, Massachusetts, with her family.

Allison Titus is the author of the poetry collections *The True Book of Animal Homes* and *Sum of Every Lost Ship*, several chapbooks, and a novel. A recipient of a fellowship from the National Endowment for the Arts, she works at an ad agency and teaches in the low-residency MFA program at New England College.

LITERATURE IN TRANSLATION

Andrea Chapela (Mexico City, 1990) has a degree in chemistry from the National Autonomous University of Mexico and an MFA in Spanish Creative Writing from the University of Iowa. She is the author of the tetralogy *Vâudïz*, the collection of essays *Grados de miopía*, for which she won the José Luis Martínez National Prize in Mexico for essays by young writers, and of the fiction books *Un año de servicio a la habitación* and *Ansibles, perfiladores y otras máquinas de ingenio*.

Michael Andreas Helmuth Ende (12 November 1929–28 August 1995) was a German writer of fantasy and children's fiction. He is best known for his epic fantasy *The Neverending Story*; other famous works include *Momo* and *Jim Knop fund Lukas der Lokomotivführer* (Jim Button and Luke the Engine Driver). His works have been translated into more than 40 languages, sold more than 35 million copies, and been adapted as motion pictures, stage plays, operas, and audio books. Ende is one of the most popular and famous German authors of the 20th century, mostly due to the enormous success of his children's fiction. He was not strictly a children's writer, however, as he wrote books for adults too. Ende's writing could be described as a surreal mixture of reality and fantasy.

Amaia Gabantxo is a multidisciplinary artist, a writer, singer, and literary translator specializing in Basque literature. A pioneer in the field, she is the most prolific translator of Basque literature to date. She is a Wingate Scholar, and has received an OMI Writers Translation Lab award, a Mellon Fellowship for Arts and Scholarship, and artist-in-residence awards at the Cervantes Institute in Chicago, the Marine CLEAR Lab in Newfoundland, and Invertigo and Cwmni Tebot in Wales. Forthcoming literary translations include *Old Dogs, Old Bones* by Unai Elorriaga for Archipelago Books in NY, *Burning Bones* by Miren Agur Meabe for Parthian Books in the UK, and *Kantauri: An Anthology of Basque Female Poets,* which she is editing and translating for Parthian. Her most recent hybrid literary pieces can be found in the *Massachusetts Review* and *The New Engagement,* and her soundscape *Transhumantzia,* created with Basque songs, nature sounds, and underwater recordings gathered during her free-diving expeditions, can be listened to in Soundcloud.

Author **Helena Granström** (b. 1983) has a background in physics and mathematics. Her writing ranges from subjects like childhood and pregnancy to technology and the history of quantum mechanics. She is a regular contributor to the major Swedish newspapers *Expressen* and *Svenska Dagbladet,* as well to National Public Radio.

Lola Haskins' work has appeared in the *Atlantic, London Review of Books, Southern Review, Georgia Review, Prairie Schooner,* and elsewhere.

She has published thirteen books of poetry, most recently *Asylum: Improvisations on John Clare* (University of Pittsburgh Press, 2019). Past awards include the Iowa Poetry Prize, two NEAs, four Florida arts fellowships, two Florida Book Awards, the Florida's Eden prize for environmental writing, and the Emily Dickinson prize from Poetry Society of America. She serves as honorary chancellor of the Florida State Poets Association. Visit her at lolahaskins.com.

Brian Henry is the author of eleven books of poetry, most recently *Permanent State* (Threadsuns Press, 2020). He has translated Tomaž Šalamun's *Woods and Chalices*, Aleš Debeljak's *Smugglers*, and Aleš Šteger's *Above the Sky Beneath the Earth* and *The Book of Things*, which won the Best Translated Book Award. His work has received numerous honors, including two NEA fellowships, the Alice Fay di Castagnola Award, a Howard Foundation fellowship, and a Slovenian Academy of Arts and Sciences grant.

Kira Josefsson is a writer, editor, and translator working between English and Swedish. The winner of a PEN/Heim grant, her translations include Johanna Hedman's *The Trio*, Hanna Johansson's *Antiquity,* and Quynh Tran's *Shade and Breeze*. Based in New York City, she writes about contemporary US events for the Swedish press and serves on the editorial board of *Glänta,* a journal of arts and politics.

Elisabeth Kinsey has two creative writing degrees and is ABD in her PhD at Denver University in literary studies. She translated this work under the guidance of Laird Hunt. She lives in Denver and is published in *Emergency, Apogee, Wazee Journal, The Coil,* and more.

Dong Li is a multilingual writer and translates from Chinese, English, and German. He is the recipient of a PEN/Heim Translation Grant and fellowships from Alexander von Humboldt Foundation, Akademie Schloss Solitude, Ledig House Translation Lab, Henry Luce Foundation/ Vermont Studio Center, Yaddo, and elsewhere. His full-length translation of the Chinese poet Zhu Zhu, *The Wild Great Wall*, was published by Phoneme Media in 2018.

Miren Agur Meabe writes poetry, fiction, and books for children and young adults. During her career, she has received the Critics' Prize twice for her poetry collections, and the Euskadi Prize for YA literature on three occasions. Her novel *Kristalezko begi bat* (A Glass Eye, Parthian 2018) and the short story collection *Hezurren erratura* (Burning Bones, Parthian 2022) have been warmly received by readers and critics alike. *A Glass Eye* has been translated into several languages and received multiple awards. In 2020, she published her fifth poetry collection, *Nola gorde errautsa kolkoan* (Holding Ashes Close to the Heart)—which forms a triptych with *A Glass Eye* and *Burning Bones*. It won the 2021 Spanish National Poetry Award, a first for a collection written in Basque. She is a member of the Basque Academy of Letters.

Aleksey Porvin is a Russian poet born in 1982. English translations of his poems can be found in *World Literature Today, Cyphers, St. Petersburg Review, Ryga Journal*, SUSS, *Words Without Borders, Fogged Clarity, The Straddler, The Dirty Goat, Action Yes, Barnwood International Poetry Magazine, Otis Nebula, New Madrid, The Cafe Review*, and *The New Formalist*, among others. Porvin is the author of three collections of poems in Russian—*Darkness is White* (Argo-Risk Press, Moscow, 2009), *Poems* (New Literature Observer Press, Moscow, 2011), and *The sun of the ship's detailed rib* (INAPRESS, St. Petersburg, 2013). His first book of poems translated into English, *Live By Fire*, was published by Cold Hub Press in 2011. Poems by Porvin have recently been short-listed by the Andrey Bely Prize (2011, 2014). He won the Russian Debut Prize in 2012.

Aleš Šteger has published eight books of poetry, three novels, and two books of essays in Slovenian. Four of his books have been published in English: *The Book of Things*, which won the 2011 Best Translated Book Award for Poetry; the collection of lyric essays *Berlin*; the novel *Absolution*; and the poetry book *Above the Sky Beneath the Earth*.

Kelsi Vanada is a poet and translator from Spanish. Her translations include *The Visible Unseen* (Restless Books, 2022), *Into Muteness* (Veliz Books, 2020), and *The Eligible Age* (Song Bridge Press, 2018), and she is the author of the poetry chapbook *Rare Earth* (Finishing Line Press, 2020). Vanada is the program manager of the American Literary Translators Association (ALTA) in Tucson, Arizona.

Isaac Stackhouse Wheeler is a poet and translator, best known for his work on English renderings of novels by the great contemporary Ukrainian author Serhiy Zhadan, published by Deep Vellum and Yale University Press and positively reviewed by journals including the *Los Angeles Review of Books*, the *New Yorker*, and the *Times Literary Supplement*. His work has appeared in numerous journals, including *Little Star*, *Trafika Europe*, and *Two Lines*. Wheeler is also an editor at *Two Chairs*, an online poetry magazine.

Zhu Zhu was born in Yangzhou, Peoples' Republic of China. He is the author of numerous books of poetry, essays, and art criticism. He is the recipient of the Henry Luce Foundation Chinese Poetry Fellowship at the Vermont Studio Center and the Chinese Contemporary Art Award for Critics. He was also a guest at the Rotterdam and Val-de-Marne International Poetry Festivals.

VISUAL ART

Jeremy Dennis (b. 1990) is a contemporary fine art photographer and a tribal member of the Shinnecock Indian Nation in Southampton, New York. In his work, he explores indigenous identity, culture, and assimilation. Dennis received the Creative Bursar Award from Getty Images in 2018 to continue his series, *Stories*. He was one of ten recipients of a 2016 Dreamstarter Grant from the national nonprofit organization Running Strong for American Indian Youth. His group and solo exhibitions include: *Stories—Dreams, Myths, and Experiences*, for the Parrish Art Museum's Road Show (2018); *Stories, From Where We Came*, the Department of Art Gallery, Stony Brook University (2018); *Trees Also Speak*, Amelie A. Wallace Gallery, State University of New York, College at Old Westbury (2018); *Nothing Happened Here*, Flecker Gallery at Suffolk County Community College, Selden, New York (2018); *Pauppukkeewis*, Zoller Gallery, State College, Pennsylvania (2016); and *Dreams*, Tabler Gallery, Stony Brook, New York (2012). He has been awarded numerous residencies, among them: Yaddo (2019), Byrdcliffe Artist Colony (2017), North Mountain Residency, Shanghai, West Virginia (2018), MDOC Storytellers' Institute, Saratoga Springs,

New York (2018), Watermill Center, Watermill, New York (2017), and the Vermont Studio Center hosted by the Harpo Foundation (2016). Dennis holds an MFA from Pennsylvania State University and a BA in Studio Art from Stony Brook University. He currently lives and works in Southampton, New York, on the Shinnecock Indian Reservation. https://www.jeremynative.com/.

Rachel Eliza Griffiths is a multimedia artist, poet, and novelist. Her recent collection of poetry and photography, *Seeing the Body*, was published by W. W. Norton in June 2020. Her forthcoming debut novel, *Promise*, will be published by Random House.

Elana Herzog lives and works in New York City. Her work can be described as a form of domestic archaeology engaging architecture and other, more intimate forms of material culture. Much of her recent work focuses on the global migration of culture and technology as seen through the lens of textiles. Herzog was profiled in *Sculpture* magazine, Summer 2020 issue. She is a recipient of a 2017 Guggenheim Fellowship. Herzog has had solo and two-person shows at the Sharjah Art Museum, United Arab Emirates; Western Exhibitions, Chicago; Cathouse Proper, The Boiler (Pierogi), and Smack Mellon, Brooklyn; the Daum Museum, Missouri; the Aldrich Museum, Connecticut; the Herbert F. Johnson Museum, Cornell University, Ithaca, New York; and Diverseworks, Houston, Texas. Her work has been exhibited internationally in the Republic of Georgia, Norway, Sweden, Iceland, Canada, Chile, and the Netherlands, and she has participated in group shows at the Brooklyn Museum, the Museum of Arts and Design, and the 8th Floor in New York City; the Tang Museum and the Everson Museum, New York State; the Weatherspoon Museum, Greensboro, North Carolina; and the Kohler Museum, Sheboygan, Wisconsin. Herzog has been awarded residencies at Yaddo, MacDowell, Fountainhead, Joan Mitchell Center, Josef and Anni Albers Foundation, and the Marie Walsh Sharpe Space Program; LMCC Workspace, Dieu Donne Paper; Wave Hill; Back Apartment Residency, Russia; Søndre Green Farm, Norway; and Gertrude Contemporary, Australia. She has received a Foundation for Contemporary Art Emergency Grant; Anonymous Was a Woman Award; Louis Comfort Tiffany Award; NYFA Fellowships 2007/1999;

Lillian Elliot Award; Lambent Fund Fellowship; and the Joan Mitchell Award. Herzog holds a BA from Bennington College and an MFA from the New York State College of Ceramics at Alfred University.

Diane Samuels is a visual artist with both studio and public art practices. In both she uses other peoples' words as her literal and figurative raw material. A recipient of a Rockefeller Bellagio Residency in Italy and an American Academy in Jerusalem Fellowship, her exhibitions include the San José Institute of Contemporary Art, Andy Warhol Museum, the Carnegie Museum of Art, the Mattress Factory Museum, National Library of Technology (Prague, Czech Republic), the Leo Baeck Institute, the Center for Book Arts, the Aldrich Contemporary Art Museum, the Contemporary Arts Center of Cincinnati, the Municipal Museum of Art (Gyor, Hungary), Jerusalem Biennale, the Synagogue Center (Trnava, Slovakia), the Bernheimer Realschule (Buttenhausen, Germany), and the Czech Museum of Fine Arts. Her permanent site-specific artworks include *Luminous Manuscript* (Center for Jewish History New York), *Lines of Sight* (Brown University), and The Alphabet Garden, a memorial garden in Grafeneck, Germany, site "A" of the so-called euthanasia experiments in 1940. She holds both bachelor's and master's degrees in fine arts from Carnegie Mellon University and a diploma from the Institute in Arts Administration at Harvard University, and has received honorary doctorates from Seton Hill University and Chatham University. She is the co-founder (along with her husband Henry Reese) of City of Asylum, based in Pittsburgh, which provides sanctuary to writers in exile. Samuels is represented by Pavel Zoubok Fine Art, New York. dianesamuels.net.

Ellen Wiener is a painter and printmaker whose primary subject matter revolves around literary themes and the expansive qualities of reading. Her intimate page-sized paintings and illuminated alphabet made for a contemporary book of hours have been exhibited widely at libraries, universities, and galleries. She has spoken on the medieval sources in her work at the International Medieval Congress by invitation from the Society for Hildegard von Bingen Studies, and the Institute for Medieval Studies at the University of New Mexico. Her research has involved studies at the Morgan Library, the Rare Book School of the University of Virginia, the New School for Social Research in New York, the Christian Index at Princeton University, the American Antiquarian Society, the New York Botanical Gardens, and the Royal Botanic Gardens at Kew, London, UK. Recent work has been seen at the Staatsbibliothek-Berlin, PS1 Moma, the Parrish Museum, the National Academy, the Iowa Center for the Book, the Heckscher Museum, the Islip Museum, the Stony Brook Museum, Vanderbilt University, the Minnesota Center for Book Arts, the Center for Book Arts NYC, and the Central Booking Gallery. Reviews can be found in *Art in America*, *Art Forum*, the *Village Voice*, the *New York Times*, the *Washington Post*, and the *Philadelphia Inquirer*, among others. Honors include the William Randolph Hearst Fellowship for Creative Artists and Writers from the American Antiquarian Society, the Andrew Carnegie Prize from National Academy, New York, residency grants from the MacDowell Colony, the Virginia Center for the Creative Arts, the Ragdale Foundation, and Holy Cross Monastery, and stipends from the New York Foundation for the Arts. ellenwiener.com / *IG@ ellenwienerart*.

EDITOR

Kristina Marie Darling is the author of thirty-six books, which include *Stylistic Innovation, Conscious Experience, and the Self in Modernist Women's Poetry* (Rowman & Littlefield, 2021); *Daylight Has Already Come: Selected Poems 2014–2020* (Black Lawrence Press, 2022); *Silence in Contemporary Poetry*, which will be published in hardcover by Clemson University Press in the United States and Liverpool University Press in the United Kingdom; *Silent Refusal: Essays on Contemporary Feminist Writing*, newly available from Black Ocean; *Angel of the North*, forthcoming from Salmon Poetry; and *X Marks the Dress: A Registry* (co-written with Carol Guess), which was just launched by Persea Books in the United States. Penguin Random House Canada has also published a Canadian edition. An expert consultant with the US Fulbright Commission, Darling's work has also been recognized with three residencies at Yaddo, where she has held the Martha Walsh Pulver Residency for a Poet and the Howard Moss Residency in Poetry; seven residencies at the American Academy in Rome, where she has also served as an ambassador for recruitment; grants from the Elizabeth George Foundation and Harvard University's Kittredge Fund; a Fundación Valparaíso fellowship to live and work in Spain; a Hawthornden Castle Fellowship, funded by the Heinz Foundation; an artist-in-residence position at Cité Internationale des Arts in Paris; two grants from the Whiting Foundation; a Faber Residency in the Arts, Sciences, and Humanities, which she received on two separate occasions; an artist-in-residence position with the Andorran Ministry of Culture; an artist-in-residence position at the Florence School of Fine Arts; an appointment at Scuola Internazionale de Grafica in Venice; and the Dan Liberthson Prize from the Academy of American Poets, which she received on three separate occasions; among many other awards and honors. Darling serves as editor in chief of Tupelo Press and *Tupelo Quarterly*. Beginning in the fall of 2022, she will also serve as publisher-in-residence at the American University in Rome. Born and raised in the American Midwest, she currently divides her time between the United States and Europe.